ART AS AN INTERFACE OF LAW AND JUSTICE

This book looks at the way in which the 'call for justice' is portrayed through art and presents a wide range of texts from film to theatre to essays and novels to interrogate the law.

'Calls for justice' may have their positive connotations, but throughout history most have caused annoyance. Art is very well suited to deal with such annoyance, or to provoke it. This study shows how art operates as an interface, here, between two spheres: the larger realm of justice and the more specific system of law. This interface has a double potential. It can make law and justice affirm or productively disturb one another.

Approaching issues of injustice that are felt globally, eight chapters focus on original works of art not dealt with before, including Milo Rau's *The Congo Tribunal*, Elfriede Jelinek's *Ulrike Maria Stuart*, Valeria Luiselli's *Tell Me How It Ends* and Nicolas Winding Refn's *Only God Forgives*. They demonstrate how through art's interface, impasses are addressed, new laws are made imaginable, the span of systems of laws is explored, and the differences in what people consider to be just are brought to light.

The book considers the improvement of law and justice to be a global struggle and, whilst the issues dealt with are culture-specific, it argues that the logics introduced are applicable everywhere.

Art as an Interface of Law and Justice

Affirmation, Disturbance, Disruption

Frans-Willem Korsten

• HART •

OXFORD • LONDON • NEW YORK • NEW DELHI • SYDNEY

HART PUBLISHING
Bloomsbury Publishing Plc
Kemp House, Chawley Park, Cumnor Hill, Oxford, OX2 9PH, UK
1385 Broadway, New York, NY 10018, USA
29 Earlsfort Terrace, Dublin 2, Ireland

HART PUBLISHING, the Hart/Stag logo, BLOOMSBURY and the Diana logo are trademarks of Bloomsbury Publishing Plc

First published in Great Britain 2021

A catalogue record for this book is available from the British Library.

Library of Congress Cataloging-in-Publication data

Names: Korsten, Frans-Willem, author.

Title: Art as an interface of law and justice : affirmation, disturbance, disruption / Frans-Willem Korsten.

Description: Oxford, UK ; New York, NY : Hart Publishing, an imprint of Bloomsbury Publishing, 2021. | Includes bibliographical references and index.

Identifiers: LCCN 2020049893 (print) | LCCN 2020049894 (ebook) | ISBN 9781509944347 (hardback) | ISBN 9781509944385 (paperback) | ISBN 9781509944354 (Epub) | ISBN 9781509944361 (pdf)

Subjects: LCSH: Law and art. | Justice.

Classification: LCC K3778 .K67 2020 (print) | LCC K3778 (ebook) | DDC 344/.097—dc23

LC record available at https://lccn.loc.gov/2020049893

LC ebook record available at https://lccn.loc.gov/2020049894

ISBN: HB: 978-1-50994-434-7
ePDF: 978-1-50994-436-1
ePub: 978-1-50994-435-4

Typeset by Compuscript Ltd, Shannon

ACKNOWLEDGEMENTS

This book was written in the year 2019/20 but prepared in the previous four years. Two of the chapters found a first exploration in Dutch, and parts of these can still be found in chapter two and seven. The first one was published in a *Liber amicorum* in the honour and remembrance of legal scholar and politician Willem Witteveen: 'Theatraliteit en de wording van rechtspraak: Milo Rau's Congo-tribunaal en twee vormen van *jurisgenesis*' in Carinne Elion-Valter, Bart van Klink, and Sanne Taekema (ed), *Wegen der Vrijheid. Liber amicorum voor Willem Witteveen* (Den Haag, Boomjuridisch, 2019). The second was 'Obstinaat recht: het chiasme van politiek en recht in relatie tot empathie en geweld – George Eliot's *Daniel Deronda*' in a volume edited by Claudia Bouteligier and Timo Slootweg, *Het empathisch supplement in recht en literatuur* (Oud Turnhout, Gompel & Svacina, 2018). One part of an article in English was reused in chapter five: '*Öffentlichkeit* and Law's Behind-the-Scenes: Theatrical and Dramatic Appearance in European and US American Criminal Law' (2017) 18 *German Law Journal* 172. The rest of the chapters were mostly developed as separate lectures at conferences or as lectures in seminars or courses. None of them found a final version before writing this book. In all cases the original arguments were much changed when turning them into the building blocks of a study that I wanted to be systematic.

I was much helped by the Leiden University Centre for the Arts in Society that managed to somewhat lighten my teaching load but also provided me with the intellectual climate in which I could develop my thoughts. Meanwhile my chair by special appointment in Literature and Society moved from the Erasmus School of History, Culture and Communication to the Erasmus School of Philosophy. This was a welcome development, with promising new colleagues and yet another inspiring environment; I was much helped here by Robin van den Akker, Giel van Strien and Hub Zwart. Some of my thoughts were developed in the context of the Critically Committed Pedagogies seminar that I ran with Renee Turner for the Master of Education in Arts at the Piet Zwart Institute, which we organised on a yearly basis with great pleasure in the years 2014–2020.

I was happy to talk about, or discuss ideas with colleagues, students and friends such as Nuno Atalaia, Maaike Bleeker, Thomas Bragdon, Bram Ieven, Andries Hiskes, Nike van Helden, Pepita Hesselbert, Maria Hlavajova, Thalia Hoffman, Çağlar Köseoğlu, Sybille Lammes, Inger Leemans, Ted Laros, Marielle Matthee, Liesbeth Minnaard, Shailoh Philips, Sara Polak, Edward Clydesdale Thomson, Richard Weisberg, Sjoerd Westbroek, Astrid Weyenberg, and Kitty Zijlmans. Text- or chapterwise I had more in-depth conversations with, or comments from Claudia Bouteligier, Maghiel van Crevel, Hans Demeyer, Esther Edelmann,

Jeanne Gaakeer, Peter Goodrich, Greta Olson, Sonja Schilling, Timo Slootweg, Sanne Taekema, Nanne Timmer, Anne-Berthe van der Velde, Berrie Vugts, Lorna Wijna, and Tessa de Zeeuw. Three colleagues helped me in the final phase with great skill, intelligence and commitment: Yasco Horsman, Merel Oudshoorn and, especially, Miriam Retter.

In terms of polishing my style and correcting my English, I am grateful to Berber Bossebroek but most of all to Sophie Mak-Schram (who did a bit more than just look at the language). Any remaining mistakes are mine. I thank my dear friend Katarina Zdjelar for giving the permission to use one of her works for the cover.

Perhaps it is worth mentioning that none of my family members or friends suffered due to my writing this book. I was able to concentrate on my work, though, thanks to their joyous existence. In the process I was often accompanied by the spirit of Eugène Mesman, whose mind is devastated by Alzheimer's but whose complex spirit is unforgettable. The book is dedicated to him.

CONTENTS

LIST OF FIGURES

1

Art as the Interface of Law and Justice

From Annoyance to an Ethics of Affirmation

'You don't have to live next to me
Just give me my equality'
Nina Simone, 'Mississippi Goddam'[1]

I. Law – Justice and Art as Interface

'The call for justice' is a phrase that has a nice feel to it, or an almost inescapable positive connotation. Yet historically and practically speaking, almost all calls for justice have been experienced by many as annoying, at first. The reasons are simple. Calls for justice imply the change of an existing order, they imply accusations, they demand the uncovering of what had been disguised, they seek that people and other legal subjects or persons, are held accountable – they will not let bygones be bygones. In a sense, these calls connote a principle, stubborn, relentless 'no'. The annoyance concerns all parties, moreover, from those who do not want to be bothered with things that happened in the past to those seeking justice by returning to that past. It may even be the case that people who seek justice feel annoyed with themselves. Yet, their ultimate goal is to find a confirmation that things can be put in order, be restored, that the pain that has been inflicted and the damage that has been done may at least be acknowledged, perhaps compensated, or sufficiently repaired. Eventually, those who seek justice seek a 'yes'.

Should the call for justice be answered, this answer will have to come from a system of law. In this context, it is unfortunate that the terms of justice and law are often used interchangeably if not confused. Still, in origin, they are distinct. Justice, in this study, concerns what people consider or feel to be just or unjust.[2] Law concerns the vast array of officially acknowledged competences, rights, obligations and prohibitions that people are supposed to live by. The relation between the two has preoccupied many, from ordinary citizens to prominent philosophers

[1] Nina Simone, 'Mississippi Goddam', *Nina Simone in Concert*, Philips Records, 1964.

[2] The complexities of this seemingly simple definition will be worked out in the chapters that follow. For now I am following Paul Ricoeur in his basic definition at the start of *Reflections on the Just*, trans David Pellauer (Chicago, Chicago University Press, 2007).

and legal scholars. Some, especially in the last century, have argued that there is no intrinsic relation. The law is a practical instrument that keeps an existing order intact, whilst the issue of whether laws are just is purely a matter of subjective assessments and interests. To them, law is an *ordo ordinans*: an order that keeps something else in order. Its justness is only a legal concern in so far as laws are based on the proper ground and applied justly.[3] Many more have argued that any legal system that claims to safeguard justice should answer to standards of fairness, equity and justness formulated both from within and outside of the system of law. Here, the question is how law should answer to principles of morals or ethics.[4] Instead of separating the two or trying to frame one in terms of the other, this study considers the relation between law and justice as the meeting of two spheres. It is a meeting that takes place time and again, in our case, through the interface of art.

Art is an umbrella term here. In the interdisciplinary field in which this study inscribes itself, Law and Literature is the commonly known combination. Yet the field has expanded considerably in the last decades in addressing much more than just literary works. In our case we will consider a performance (chapter two), a couple of theatre plays (chapter three), a few novels (chapters four, six and seven), an essay (chapter four) and two poems, but also an etching and maps (chapter five), contemporary works of art that concern themselves with turning suburban grass turf into 'edible estates' (chapter six) and a movie (chapter eight). A couple of times the work of the independent London-based research group Forensic Architecture will be of relevance. The group gathers architects, artists, coders and scholars of all sorts, including legal ones, to work together against powers that want to obscure a truth. To this order, the group moves both inside and outside of the art world and when operating inside it, they make a form of art that perhaps readers would not immediately recognise as such. For instance, one case they investigated was the murder of Halit Yozgat in Kassel, Germany, in 2006.[5] On the basis of its research, the group made a video entitled *77sqm 9:26min*.[6] The video was

[3] The paradigmatic figures, here, are Hans Kelsen, with *Reine Rechtslehre*, originally published in Germany in 1934 but rewritten and published in English three decades later, as *Pure Theory of Law* (Berkeley, University of California Press, 1967), and Herbert LA Hart, with *The Concept of Law* (Oxford, Clarendon Press, 1961). To Carl Schmitt, equally a rather influential name in the last decades, legal order rests on a sovereign decision, not on some ethical norm, see *Political Theology: Four Chapters on the Concept of Sovereignty* (Chicago, University of Chicago Press, 2005) 10. The Stanford Encyclopedia of Philosophy, usually not fond of qualifying terms, defined this contention as 'blunt'; plato.stanford.edu/entries/schmitt.

[4] Too many scholars could be mentioned in a history that spans more than 2,000 years, ranging from figures such as Aristotle, Marsilius of Padua, Aquinas, Immanuel Kant and Mary Wollstonecraft, to in more recent times Hannah Arendt, John Rawls and yet others. Lon L Fuller is a key figure, with *The Morality of Law* (1964; repr, New Haven, Yale University, 1969). More recently one can think of Amartya Sen, *The Idea of Justice* (Cambridge MA, Belknapp Press, 2009), Martha Nussbaum, *Poetic Justice:* The Literary Imagination and Public Life (Boston, Beacon Press, 1995) or Achille Mbembe, *Out of the Dark Night* (New York, Columbia University Press, 2019).

[5] See Forensic Architecture: forensic-architecture.org/investigation/the-murder-of-halit-yozgat.

[6] See www.youtube.com/watch?v=3yy2neYI_XU.

exhibited differently in several exhibitions, such as the Institute for Contemporary Arts in London, or at BAK, Utrecht, in October 2018. In both cases, the digital model representing the ground plan of the space in which the murder took place, and that is presented in the video, was projected on the floor, on a 1:1 scale.[7] The photograph below gives an impression of what this looked like at BAK:

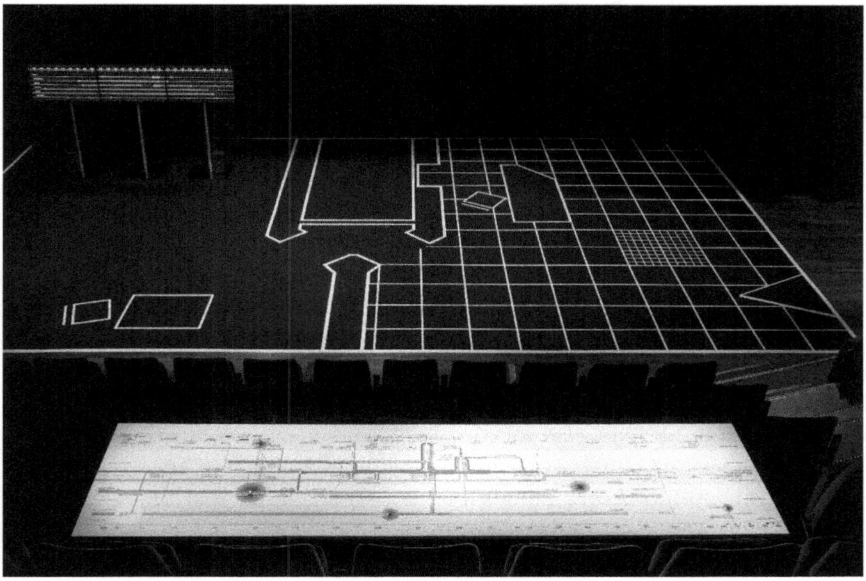

Figure 1.1 Forensic Architecture, 77sqm_9:26min (2017)
Installation with three-channel video, 25:54 min, reenactment video, 15:14 min, carpet with floor plan, and diagram, installation view Forensic Justice *at BAK, 'basis voor actuele kunst', Utrecht, 2018–19, photograph: Tom Janssen*

Perhaps one of the first questions a reader might have is: How should I read this? Well, one should read it, in part, as a report on the investigation into Halit Yozgat's murder. In the next chapter we will explore in more depth why the reflection on art's mediality is of relevance. Truth does not simply show itself, in either a system of law or in a realm of justice. The question of how truth is shown by specific media is thus of relevance. The media used by Forensic Architecture, here, invite the viewer not to enjoy a smart solution, but to start searching together, if only to check things, and to do so performatively. We see the floor plan of the internet café owned by Yozgat. This is not something to only be looked at; anyone can walk in it. It is an icon of the ability to check things or connect to them, and this checking and

[7] For an impression, see BAK: www.bakonline.org/nl/program-item/forensic-justice/propositions-7-evidentiary-methods/propositions-7-4-reenact.

connecting relies on the audience's ability to follow the process of research. This process is represented here in the foreground on the white tableau. It is purposefully placed in the space of the audience, as one can see from the shadows of the chairs. The tableau places the investigation into the wider context of the NSU Complex (on which more in chapter three). It may be clear that this is another kind of art than, for instance, the often mentioned fourteenth-century fresco in the Palazzo Publico in the fair city of Siena, entitled *Good and Bad Government*, by Ambrogio Lorenzetti. In the case of Forensic Architecture, research was involved, for instance into the acoustics of the space, in an attempt to find out whether someone could or could not have heard gun shots. The case itself was connected to a much larger investigation into an underground political-criminal network called NSU, and its possible connections to secret services. All in all, this is not so much a form of art that is to be enjoyed or judged or only interpreted; rather, this is a form of art that instigates public participation. As a consequence, to many, works like this are admirable, while to many others they are annoying.

As this example shows, the meeting of the spheres of law and justice – in their connoting different kinds of power and following different kinds of logics – is either provoked or made palpable, sensible, imaginable and hopefully productive through art. Again, most of these qualifications, just like 'a call for justice', have a nice feel to them. Still, the very meeting itself is often, or even mostly, also annoying. Forensic Architecture's work may annoy because it is also art. And the now canonical nineteenth-century English author George Eliot was annoying in her own times (as were most of the realist painters people now highly valued, by the way). One of the reasons that art can be annoying in its connecting law and justice is that any call for justice is always, in a sense, out of date: it ought to have already been answered. Or, the call for justice addresses bygones that should have already been corrected. Through art's interface unresolved issues of justice are made into something of the present and the future. That is, they are made to persist. It is this persistence that connotes justice's claim towards universality, despite its subjective origins. Yet although the appeal to universality is needed because most unresolved injustices cannot be solved by the parties directly concerned, art's interface is not intrinsically a universal one. Rather, art offers a meeting space, filled with frictions, of alternative possibilities.

Both the annoying force implied by art's interface of alternative possibilities and justice's appeal to universality can be traced when a disturbing case goes unresolved. One such a paradigmatic case is the shooting down of Malaysia Airlines flight MH17 on 17 July 2014, in the eastern part of Ukraine. As far as current evidence suggests, high-ranking Russian military officers and Ukrainian separatists were the culprits of this crime. The loss of lives, most of them Dutch, had traumatic effects on those involved both directly and indirectly. It had traumatic effects for a nation.[8] Up until now, the only work of art operative with regard to this

[8] People still mourn the loss of a scholar and politician who was a pillar in Dutch and international law-and-literature circles: Willem Witteveen (for some of his studies, see ch 2).

case (and by implication the only interface) is a memorial site that was opened in July 2017. This memorial site consists of 298 trees planted in the shape of a crossed ribbon, one tree for each of the victims. The ribbon is surrounded by sunflowers that act as an index to the fields blossoming during the month of July in the Ukraine. At the heart of these two rings there is an amphitheatre with the names of the victims.[9] The obvious aim of this site is to keep those who have passed away alive, in and through memory. Yet, the site is also a work of art that embodies a call for justice, in the double sense this term connotes in English: law and justice.

As for the call to law, in 2017 the countries gathered in the Joint Investigation Team (The Netherlands, Belgium, Australia, Malaysia and Ukraine) decided that the case was to be dealt with by a Dutch court, according to Dutch law. In one sense, then, the memorial site from 2017 called forth the legal handling of the case that started on 9 March 2020.[10] Still, even if the culprits ever appear in court, the issue remains whether law is able to do full justice, when law is considered as that which satisfies a general sense of justice. First of all, in the realm of justice there are many parties involved with different interests; it is as much a realm of consensus as of dissensus.[11] This is where the appeal to universality quickly reveals its limitations. The question is, moreover, whether demands for justice can ever be answered fully by means of law. In relation to this, the memorial is much more than simply a matter of collective memory or an appeal to law. It is also a site that embodies the impossibility of ever closing this case. It embodies an ongoing call for justice that exceeds the limits of law.

The MH17 case also illustrates how the meeting of the spheres of law and justice is related to two distinct forms of power. By studying the confrontation between the two forms of power at stake in the cases that follow, I will use a distinction made by the Jewish-Dutch philosopher Benedict de Spinoza: *potestas* and *potentia*.[12] Power, or *potestas*, connotes the organisation of societies by means of the rule of power, or the rule of law. *Potentia* refers to the empowering abilities of beings and things to exist and realise themselves on the basis of their desires, including their desires for justice.[13] The two relate to one another first of all in terms of their inverse

[9] The monument in Park Vijfhuizen, located in between the national airfield Schiphol and the city of Haarlem, was based on an idea by Arold Jansen and designed by landscape architect Robbert de Koning, with the amphitheatre being designed by Ronald A Westerhuis; see Monument MH17 www.monumentmh17.nl/english.

[10] More info about the Dutch handling of the case can be found on the Swiss Justiceinfo website, functioning under the umbrella of the Fondation Hirondelle: www.justiceinfo.net/en/tribunals/national-tribunals/43990-mh17-why-the-dutch-ruled-out-war-crimes-charges.html.

[11] Dissensus in the field of the humanities and law was central to a volume with a slightly misleading title: Logan Atkinson and Diana Majury (eds), *Law, Mystery, and the Humanities: Collected Essays* (Toronto, University of Toronto Press, 2008).

[12] Not coincidentally, Spinoza was also the author of one of the most important studies on ethics as a kind of logic, the *Ethica*, a work finished in 1675 but only published after Spinoza's death in 1678.

[13] The translation of especially *potentia* has been the subject of many studies, see Antonio Negri, *The Savage Anomaly: Power of Spinoza's Metaphysics and Politics* (Minnesota, University of Minnesota Press, 1991); *Subversive Spinoza: (Un)Contemporary Variations* (Manchester, Manchester University Press, 2004); or Gilles Deleuze in the documentary *Abécédaire*, under 'J for Joy'; on this,

directionality: *potestas* exerts itself in a top-down manner, and *potentia* acts from the bottom up. Furthermore, there is a difference in scale. The space of the potential will be more forceful, in the end, than the domain of sheer power. The space of the potential is always excessive; it exceeds anything. Analogously, when Hannah Arendt posited *natality* at the heart of politics, as something that all human beings embody, this connoted the potential of a new beginning. Consequently, as political philosopher Charles Barbour noted, for Arendt 'action is never localised in a single sphere or realm, but enigmatically conditions and threatens every such a realm'.[14] Action is political action, then, that can threaten an existing order, and as such illustrates that law and politics are distinct, as are justice and the political. Yet, in the end, law and justice cannot be considered without politics or the political, precisely because the latter exist due to binding regulations. Moreover, politics and the political are at the source of the proclamation and maintenance of law (see chapter seven).

The case of MH17 relates to distinct political powers at work in their accordance or confrontation with the realm of the potential. There are political powers, even distinct politicians, who aim to escape or pervert the rule of law. There are those who aim to maintain it, wanting to consider the case within this specific rule of law, and not another one.[15] Then there is the potential of all sorts of actors seeking justice. The two are not unrelated but confront one another and influence each other. For instance, on 14 February 2020, an enquiry found that the Russian populace considered it reasonable that Russia would pay compensation for this crime. However, only 10 per cent of the populace thought that Russia was directly involved in the crime itself. Still, in previous research, only two per cent thought the same.[16] One question, therefore, is whether ruling powers will be able to continue manipulating their populaces in times to come. Instruments of manipulation in the hands of ruling powers have grown considerably of late. Yet they

see Gilles Deleuze (with Claire Parnet), *Gilles Deleuze from A to Z*, trans Charles J Stivale (Cambridge MA, MIT Press, 2011), DVD. In order to mark *potentia* as distinct from power, it will be defined here in terms of 'the potential'. Note that my use of the terms differs principally from studies in which the two terms are considered to be two aspects of power, as when Martin Loughlin distinguishes 'the *ability* to govern and the *right* to govern. This distinction relates to two different concepts of power: the former is *potentia*, the actual ability to control things, whilst the latter is *potestas*, the exercise of rightful authority.' Martin Loughlin, 'The Erosion of Sovereignty' (2016) 2 *Netherlands Journal of Legal Philosophy* 57, available at doi.org/10.5553/NJLP/.000048.

[14] Charles Barbour, 'Between Politics and Law: Hannah Arendt and the Subject of Rights' in Marco Goldoni and Christopher McCorkindale (eds), *Hannah Arendt and the Law* (Oxford, Hart Publishing, 2012). Arendt's idea of natality, developed early in her career, was based on her reading of Augustine.

[15] The Russian Government suggested to the Dutch Government in October 2019 that the case should be considered by Russia and according to Russian law, or perhaps more to the point: Russian legal procedures. In February 2020 the Dutch Minister of Justice replied that this 'was not an option'.

[16] The enquiry was commissioned by Leiden University and research bureau Raam-op-Rusland and executed by the Russian Levada Centre; see 'Russische publieke opinie: Nederland heeft goed imago, eventueel bereid tot smartegeld voor nabestaanden MH17' 14 February 2020, available at raamoprusland.nl/actueel/1525-russische-publieke-opinie-nederland-heeft-goed-imago-eventueel-bereid-tot-smartengeld-voor-nabestaanden-mh17.

can never fully control the potential embodied in all those living, nationally and internationally. Even if Russian governments will continue their policies of misinformation, this will not influence all those concerned; it might even strengthen their resolve to continue fighting for justice.

In the MH17 case, so far, the memorial is the only instance of art's interface, possibly because the case is still too recent. There is no doubt, however, that the case will come to propel many more works of art that want to be an interface for a more in-depth and detailed meeting of the system of law and the realm of justice. The meeting of both will, time and again, be related to different parties involved and to the two forms of power distinguished above. In fact, innumerable, persistent, diverse, complex, local, regional and global battles for or against law and justice relate to this distinction between power and the potential. Consequently, the force of art as an interface is explored time and again, by organisations such as Forensic Architecture, when it aims to create an interface by means of which unresolved cases can be brought to light.[17]

The term 'interface' is a nineteenth-century invention indicating 'a plane surface regarded as the common boundary of two bodies'. The term became more commonly known when media ecologist Marshall McLuhan applied it to mark a place of interaction between two systems.[18] From there onwards it started to travel to, and through, the social sciences and consequently the term 'social interface' was defined.[19] One should understand 'interface' first and foremost as a technical term, then, as a surface on which the system of law and the realm of justice meet. Yet that meeting is socially charged. It is also much more than only a socially charged meeting space. Alexander Galloway, in *The Interface Effect*, referring to French philosopher François Dagognet, contended that the interface:

> [C]onsists essentially of an area of choice. It both separates and mixes the two worlds that meet together there, that run into it. It becomes a fertile nexus. … The interface for Dagognet is a special place with its own autonomy, its own ability to generate new results and consequences. It is an 'area of choice'; between the Muse and the poet, between the divine and the mortal, between the edge and the center.[20]

In the meeting of the system of law and the realm of justice, punctuated choices are pivotal. With art as an interface, the point is that this interface has its own autonomy, and not only makes choices possible, but also provokes them. It is important to note, moreover, that the interface is less a thing than an effect: 'always a process or a translation'.[21] In their meeting through art, system of law and realm of justice are and remain different and in need of a translation that effectively connects the two.

[17] On this see Forensic Architecture: forensic-architecture.org. Also see chs 4 and 8.

[18] Marshall and Eric McLuhan, *Laws of Media: The New Science* (Toronto, Toronto University Press, 1988) 102.

[19] Norman Long, *Development Sociology: Actor Perspectives* (London, Routledge, 2001).

[20] Alexander Galloway, *The Interface Effect* (Cambridge, Polity Press, 2012) 32. Dagognet's phrase can be found in François Dagognet, *Faces, Surfaces, Interfaces* (Paris, Librairie Philosophique J Vrin, 1982) 49.

[21] Galloway, *The Interface Effect* (2012) 34.

And when art's interface disconnects the two, or is not able to connect the two because one of the two is missing, this poses a problem of translation or transformation (on which more in the following two chapters).[22]

II. System, Realm and Two Kinds of Logic: Affirmation and Disturbance

The specifiers 'system' and 'realm' connote different spans, scopes and nature. Following Spinoza's logic, or that of Gilles Deleuze after him, I locate justice in a pre-constitutional realm. With the pre-constitutional I mean something other than legal scholar Peter Goodrich, who says: 'The Law of culture precedes and dictates the temporal law'.[23] Feelings of justice are as much determined by cultures, and as such they follow some sort of constitution. Yet they also exceed the limits of culture. Desire, as Deleuze noted, exists from the moment of birth of any being (or entity), and is not dependent on some sort of prohibiting law and its consequent lack.[24] So within a system of law and a realm of justice, different kinds of practices and logic are dominant. Any specific system of law, whether a national system or the more open system of international law, demands that one acts systematically and according to a logic of reason. This does not imply that such a system is completely autonomous, or that it is a closed and internally fully consistent sphere. As legal scholar Sionaidh Douglas-Scott convincingly argued, any system of law is in practice far from consistent, or rather messy, because it is responsive to many different force fields.[25] One dominant force field is culture, as Douglas-Scott wants it. Still, law may also work against culture, which proves its relative independence as a system. Moreover, even if all sorts of feelings and affects are operative in systems of law (as we will see in chapter three), they are to be held in check.

The search for justice suggests a realm, in the sense of a sphere of activity, as a matter of practice. 'Realm' etymologically refers to a domain that is somehow ruled. The term 'realm' suggests, consequently, that justice is not simply a space that is open on all sides. On the contrary, it suggests an extent, a space or a sphere

[22] My argument is different, here, from literary and legal scholar James Boyd White, who argued in *Justice as Translation* that (constitutional) legal decisions rhetorically produce an ethical and political constituency. I do not underestimate the rhetorical force residing in constitutional verdicts but do not think that legal decisions can produce an ethical or political constituency; see James Boyd White, *Justice as Translation: An Essay in Cultural and Legal Criticism* (Chicago, University of Chicago Press, 1990).

[23] Peter Goodrich, 'How Strange the Change from Major to Minor' (2017) 21 *Law Text Culture* 30, 35.

[24] Deleuze developed his thoughts on desire in different studies, but two prominent ones are *The Logic of Sense*, trans Mark Lester and Charles Stivale (ed), *Constantin V Boundas* (New York, Columbia University Press, 1993) and, together with Félix Guattari, *Anti-Oedipus: Capitalism and* Schizophrenia, trans Brian Massumi (Minneapolis, University of Minnesota Press, 1983). Also see Daniel W Smith, 'Deleuze and the Question of Desire: Toward an Immanent Theory of Ethics' (2007) 2 *Parrhesia* 66.

[25] Sionaidh Douglas-Scott, *Law after Modernity* (Oxford, Hart Publishing, 2013).

within which something is protected. It is a sphere, though, with its own particular force fields and guidelines that differ from the formal, systematic rules in the system of law. These are guidelines that are specific to communities, to different beings, different genders, different religions, and so forth, and as a consequence they connote forms of logic that can either confront, temporarily fuse with or deviate from the systemic rules of law, thus opening up new possibilities of justice. In this realm, all sorts of affects and emotions play a role that need not be reasonable at all. These are not to be taken as a given, and they need some form of organisation, or a practice, if they want to be operative as forces of justice. Yet the realm of justice as such is propelled by desires and fears, feelings of understandable revenge and unresolvable pain, of longing and hope.

In light of the turbulence of affects with regard to what feels just or what ought to be strived for in terms of justice, this study will contend that in the realm of justice the logic of dreams holds a dominant position, whereas in any system of law the logic of reason is dominant. Dreams connote people's desire for the possible and the impossible. Dreams connote people's imagined resolutions, or embody the fear of the return of an event. Additionally, if dreams tend to be perceived as comforting, it is worth noting that, in the context of the realm of justice, dreams can also be nightmares. I will emphasise this a few times: what people in all their difference feel to be just implies that feelings of justice are never universal or generally shared. The dream of justice to one can be the nightmare of another; just as unrealised or perverted forms of justice can be a nightmare.

Clearly, the logics of reason and dream do not coincide. Dreams do not follow the demands of reason, and reason cannot follow a dream logic. This is why they need translation. Yet, both affirm and propel one another because they are intrinsically related and follow a comparable logic: the first works by means of an argumentative structure, the second by means of association. As such, both can make sense to one another. The biblical story of Joseph in *Genesis* 37–50 is one famous example of the both disturbing and affirmative relation between the two. Joseph is asked to explain powerful dreams that puzzle or disturb the Pharaoh. The latter has had a dream during which seven fat cows came out of the water, only to be eaten by seven thin ones. Then he had had a dream in which seven lavish corn heads were eaten by dry and scorched ones. These dreams made sense in themselves. They seemed to suggest that a prosperous order could easily be destroyed. Following the logic of dreams, they expressed anxieties and desires about life and death, which is why they were puzzling or intriguing. They were brought to meet the sphere of reason through the skills of Joseph, as a result of which a reasonable and just policy could be derived from them. Joseph predicted that after seven years of abundant harvests and rains, seven years of drought were to follow. A policy of storage and distribution was put in place. This policy, and the norms on which it was based, no longer belonged to the domain of dreams, but to that of reason (and more on this in chapter eight).

Law has to respond to the logic of reason and by implication to the conceivable and reasonable. What feels just may be the subject of desire and of the imaginable, even though it may be impossible to realise this justness through measures in practice. The logic of reason and dream can meet on and are able to talk to one another through an interface. The paradigmatic story of Joseph shows how art's interface is both an aesthetic and dialectical one, with 'dialectical' understood in an (Aristotelian) argumentative sense. Dialectically speaking, the two affect one another in some sort of argumentative dialogue that can only exist by means of translation, affirmation and disturbance. Whilst in terms of an argument they can be perceived to arrive at a solution, in terms of aesthetics the provocative and propelling force they exchange with one another will never reach a final conclusion, though, because they affect one another by remaining distinct. For instance, in the case of MH17, should the culprits be caught and brought to court where they would be dealt with by law, this would probably disturb feelings of justice in Russia. Meanwhile, the strong feelings of injustice connected to this case also disturb the system of law, propelling it to find the adequate speed, tools and rules to address the case as soon and adequately as possible. Art's interface may bring into motion the processes and relationship between law and justice, but it can also create an impasse, as a result of which things remain inconclusive. The longer it takes to bring the case to a conclusion, the more works of art we will see that articulate this impasse, or that address the affirmative disturbance between the two. And even if a temporary solution is achieved, this will probably spur on the production of yet other works of art because the realm of justice prescribes that a case can never fully be closed, due to the plurality of parties involved.[26]

The verb 'affirm' hails from Latin *affirmare*, which means: to make steady, to strengthen, to confirm, or to corroborate. It may also indicate, more specifically, legal confirmation. If the two logics affirm one another, this implies that they can strengthen one another in their being legal *and* just. Laws that respond to demands of justice are stronger; justice that is supported by law gains in strength. This does not mean that the two only have a single stabilising or strengthening function. Affirmation implies disturbance because change may be required in order for either law or justice to become stronger. The verb 'disturb' indicates that things are put 'out of a settled state or regular order'. For instance, if legally protected private property has become an almost naturalised phenomenon in contemporary Western society, any attempt to question private property in light of a desire for social justice will disturb the legal system. Or take the case of the Dakota Access Pipeline (DAPL), in which the Meskwaki, the Standing Rock Sioux and Cheyenne River Sioux peoples opposed the parties that wanted to build an oil pipeline and had the legal right to do so. The latter's legal right disturbed those who desired to keep the reservation free from such a pipeline. Supported less by legal guarantees

[26] The pluralities of law and justice that are implied in the role of affect in relation to both were charted by Greta Olson, 'The Turn to Passion: Has Law and Literature become Law and Affect?' (2016) 28 *Law and Literature* 335. The dangers of such plurality were charted by Douglas-Scott, *Law after Modernity* (2013).

and led by feelings of justice, they felt such a pipeline was fundamentally unjust within the frameworks of their relationship to the land. They were provoked to either accept the new situation or fight against it in the name of justice, which would become a battle for new legislation.[27]

A powerful example of the simultaneously affirming and disturbing relation between the two logics is the book *Job*, from the Jewish *Tanakh* and the Christian *Old Testament*. The characters involved are God, the Devil and Job, together with the latter's wife, family and some friends. The book starts with the Devil arguing that Job only believes because he has everything he could want. He then tempts God to enter into a wager. What would happen if they would dispossess Job, take away his children, his cattle, his goods? God gives his consent and, due to the work of the Devil, Job loses everything he had. Yet, he still believes. The Devil then wants to scale up the wager. God again agrees. The Devil may now target Job's body, but he may not take his life. The entire book consists of this torturous play, resulting in the deliberations of Job and his friends about God's justice.

A secular reading could consider the wager of the Devil and God as a sick practical joke. However, the stakes of their wager are serious. The issue is not only to whose law Job will answer, but also whether his ethical core, or his being just, in the end is a matter of quid pro quo. As for God the issue is, as many have noted, whether things are just because they are felt to be just or because they find their origin in God. In this context it is telling that the book does not end with an answer to the question whether the wager between God and the Devil was just, but with the issue of Job's subjection to the rule of law. In this case it concerns a famous duality embedded in the sovereignty of God. God is both the one to define and posit the law, and the one who can step outside of the law. Consequently, Job's subjection is a double or a total one. He has to answer to God's rule of law – additionally he has to accept the state of exception enacted by God.

God embodies *supreme* law, then, to which even the Devil is subjected. We are not dealing here with the average conceptualisation of law as recorded, foreseeable, known beforehand, and common. The two pertinent and opposite questions are whether Job is asked to obey God's law without reservations, or whether God embodies justice and acts justly. Both questions are explicitly the topic of nigh relentless arguments between Job and his friends. They ponder the question of how, in a divine order, a decent man, leading a decent life, is dealt with unjustly and needs to accept this despite all odds. By implication, their discussion indicates that there is also an argument suggested between these men and God. At some point in the story (*Job* 9:32–35), Job cries out that he wished there would be a mediator, an arbiter or a judge between him and God. Job's lamentation implies

[27] The latest is that on 6 June 2020, a US District Court 'ordered Energy Transfer LP to shut and empty the largest pipeline from the North Dakota shale oil fields within 30 days, in a big win for the Native American tribes who have fought the line's route across a crucial water supply': pgjonline.com/news/2020/07-july/us-court-orders-dakota-access-pipeline-shut-emptied.

that another – perhaps more just – law could rule. The text does not offer one clear solution in return. Rather, it forms the interface between two kinds of logic, one on the side of law and the other one on the side of justice. These logics embody distinctly different positions, but nevertheless intersect. In the process they affirm, disturb and thereby propel one another to open up the possibility of a solution. Such a solution consists here in the possibility of another judge, another kind of law and justice. In fact, Job proposes a judge outside of God, a judge that would limit God's sovereignty. This possibility is mobilised from the side of the desire for justice, following one logic and provoking an answer from the other one. Yet, were this possibility to be realised, it would imply that both God and Job would have to answer to a counter-law, one that follows its own logic and would have different practices and implications (more on this in chapter six). The story does not push it that far. The disturbance involved is cut short when Job subjects himself to the regular order that is in place with God as the seal and source of law.

God and the Devil are experimenting to find out who and what it is they are dealing with and how they can judge it. It is no coincidence that the term 'trial' originally means 'experiment' or 'test' (the Anglo-French *trial*, is based on the verb *trier*: 'to try', 'to pull out'). Job is put to the test, then, and the Devil performs the nasty part of the law, in executing the test in practice. In this testing, God and the Devil form one system that has its origin in a distinct sphere but that rules or controls another sphere: the world of human beings. Both God and the Devil are traceable through their manifestation in this sphere, by what they do or say. This is the side of the law; it is a system with force that shows itself from some sort of outside when practiced. Law can be violently imposed, as if coming from an outside, because it is a system.[28]

On the other side we find the sphere of life as we know it, can sense it, can imagine living it, with people and animals in their relationships, in their individual and collective existence, in their communities and in the world they inhabit. We are dealing with characters who ask what justice means or where it can be found when they feel wronged. It is not an abstract thing to lose the 10 children you gave birth to – the children whom you cared for and who you thought and felt were yours. The story shows how people do not just wonder where justice can be found when they are dealt a bad hand, but also how they desire or long for it. By implication, justice is not just something to be discussed, as if it is predominantly a philosophical issue. It is something that is felt bodily and can be sought with the hope of it being established, or despite the despair that it will never be found.[29] The same bodily impact holds for any system of law, by the way. Laws do not just speak to the minds of people, but also to their hearts and bodies; affectively speaking, laws are both restrictive and productive.

[28] On this see for instance Austin Sarat and Thomas R Kearns, 'Making Peace With Violence: Robert Cover on Law and Legal Theory' in Austin Sarat (ed), *Law, Violence, And The Possibility Of Justice* (Princeton, Princeton University Press, 2001).

[29] On this bodily felt sense of justice, see Paul Ricoeur, *Reflections on the Just* (2007).

The story of Job serves to illustrate that there are several pairs of logic involved, in addition to the pair of reason and dream, when a system of law meets a realm of justice. These include the logics of fear and desire, of violence and empathy, or of completion and antinomy. Each of the following chapters explores a specific meeting of such pairs. Represented in a table, they look like this:

	Logic of the system of law	**Logic of the realm of justice**
Ch 1		
Ch 2	Fear	Desire
Ch 3	Tragedy	Comedy
Ch 4	Official	Officious
Ch 5	Person	Self
Ch 6	Completion	Antinomy
Ch 7	Violence	Empathy
Ch 8	Reason	Dream

When each of these two related kinds of logic will be worked out via a work of art or a cultural artefact that operates as an interface, we will come to see how the very same interface may also show possibilities of disrupting the relation between the two. A so-called third element is either positive, in the form of a promising possibility or solution on the horizon, or it is negative, in the shape of a materially real, disruptive element that can distort translation, that can thwart the meeting of the two spheres, that can cancel out both logics, or lead to an unresolvable impasse.

III. 'Thirds': Forces of Disruption and Impasse

The affective relation between the two spheres, and the argumentative process that results from it, is threatened by thirds that are not part of the dialogic, affirmative and disturbing relation. On the contrary, they disrupt it. Art is partly a productive interface for the meeting of the two practices and logics, as an interface that aims for coherence, even if it is to be achieved through disturbance. In the chapters that follow, examples are Milo Rau's *Congo Tribunal*, George Eliot's *Daniel Deronda*, and Valeria Luiselli's diptych of essay and novel, *Tell Me How It Ends* and *Lost Children Archive*. Art's interface can also embody an impasse, as is the case in Elfriede Jelinek's *Ulrike Maria Stuart*, Chibundu Onuzo's novel *Welcome to Lagos*, or, in my reading, Fritz Haeg's 'edible estates'.[30] Yet art's interface can lead

[30] The issue of impasse, and its current urgency, was central to Lauren Berlant, *Cruel Optimism* (Durham, Duke University Press, 2011).

to incoherence as well, facilitating forces of disruption that threaten both law and justice. Examples are Joost van den Vondel's poem about a water wolf or Nicholas Winding Refn's movie *Only God Forgives*. The fact that art's interface allows such disruptions to appear does not necessarily mean that art has the potential to disrupt society. Most of the time even disruptive art stays well within the limits of a given order. Art may become disruptive as soon as it comes to facilitate a state of obliviousness, or hallucination. Or art may produce apathy, when subjects are turned into zombie-like tools for ruling powers of either a public or private kind. There are currently debates, for instance, on whether games are forms of art that produce apathy or whether they are important tools in fighting it.

Etymologically, disruption harks back to the Latin *disrumpere*, which means 'to break apart, split, shatter, break to pieces'. Forces of disruption can either derail or black out both the rule of law and the struggle or desire for justice, or may lead to an unproductive impasse, as the temporal embodiment of a split. For instance, the feared other of both the logic of reason and of dreams is hallucination, precisely because there is no logic to it. If the Pharaoh had been hallucinating, Joseph would not have been able to make any sense of it. The propelling and productive dynamic between the logic of reason and of dreams is threatened, then, in times of hallucination – and chapter eight on *Only God Forgives* will argue that we currently find ourselves in one of these times. In this case, swirls of delusion threaten both the logic of reason and the logic of the dream, or lead to an impasse through which the two no longer productively relate. The MH17 case is telling, here: the number of alternative scenarios that have been brought into the world, the entire scope of lies, mystifications, secrecies, manipulated images, and perverse suggestions have deeply influenced people in the Netherlands, Malaysia, the Ukraine and Russia. Such alternative, hallucinatory scenarios are a threat to both the system of law and the realm of justice, and they are consciously used to create a lasting impasse.

In the story of Job, to give one other example, the disruptive force that threatens both kinds of practice and logic is not the Devil, for the Devil does not disrupt. He can never dethrone God; he can only act within the given limits. If there is a disruptive force at work, it could perhaps be traced to the two translations of a phrase uttered by the nameless woman mocking Job's misery and persistent faith: his wife. She either says 'Bless God and die' or 'Curse God and die' (the latter is the most common translation).[31] The coincidence of these opposing meanings, in a phrase uttered in the context of mockery, turns both into an example of cynicism. The cynical response is to never trust the rule of law and to never take for

[31] On the status of Job's wife, the translation of what she says, and her character's own literary history, see Michael C Legaspi, 'Job's Wives in the "Testament of Job": A Note on the Synthesis of Two Traditions' (2008) 127 *Journal of Biblical Literature* 71.

granted that life or God will treat one justly. Cynicism might be a disruptive force because it looks at both logics with suspicion, desires to dismantle them for their hypocrisy, trusts neither law or principles of justice, and can consequently break with all conventions. This happens when the reverence towards God is thrown overboard and a miserable and perhaps foolishly faithful man is simply advised to die. Cynicism may also lead to an unproductive impasse, as when entire populaces become cynical about a political or legal system. Still, when a cynic refuses to support an order, this may also be because such an order is unjust and will hinder a life of virtue. Moreover, the fact that the role of the cynic is ascribed to a woman, here, is reason for a suspicious reading. She might be a willful disturber (on which more in chapter seven). She might be someone questioning wrong conventions and moralities, or even a wrong supreme being.

A truly disruptive force in this story is God himself, who, as a radical sovereign, is able to act both arbitrarily and erratically. When in 1935 Carl Schmitt defined the sovereign as the power able to declare the state of exception in which authorities are no longer limited by law or demands of justice, this was the political analogy to divine sovereignty.[32] Yet, even for Schmitt, the sovereign was decisive for any system of law because it was precisely its incorporation in the law that allowed it to declare the state of exception.[33] This does not hold for God. He is above law and justice. If he gets angry, he may destroy (almost) everything he created. As the great creator he is also the great disrupter. This is also why one should oppose any theological, mysterious backing of a system of law (on which more in chapter three).

Whereas the term 'logic' indicates a process and structure with each step rationally linked to a previous one, the disrupting thirds do not follow such a process or structure. Instead, they indicate a state of disorganisation, an untrustworthy attitude; they connote erratic behaviour, or a dynamic that will have unpredictable outcomes. This is also why they can have, or have been considered by some to have, a liberating force. Perhaps so. If a given order is totalitarian and unjust, chaos can seem to be a liberating alternative. Yet the question then becomes whether such disruptions have led, historically, to liberation or to a more just order, or whether they could have potentially done so. Other questions relate to whether, by way of disruption, a somehow unjust order could not lead to an even more unjust order, or whether it could not lead to the disappearance of any kind of order altogether. There are certainly many beings on this planet, for instance, that would welcome the collapse of human order. The consequences are unknown.

[32] Carl Schmitt, *The Concept of the Political*, trans George Schwab (Chicago, University of Chicago Press, 1996).

[33] Schmitt, *The Concept of the Political* (1996) 7.

The thirds that are able to disrupt or derail the two forms of logic are elaborated in connection to works of art as well. Added to the table above, the list looks like this:

	Logic of the system of law	**Logic of the realm of justice**	**Disruptive third**
Ch 1			
Ch 2	Fear	Desire	Apathy
Ch 3	Tragedy	Comedy	Mystery
Ch 4	Official	Officious	Fictitious
Ch 5	Person	Self	Pack
Ch 6	Completion	Antinomy	Corruption
Ch 7	Violence	Empathy	Obliviousness
Ch 8	Reason	Dream	Hallucination

Take, for instance, a work of art such as the staged tribunal realised by Milo Rau in 2015 under the title *The Congo Tribunal*. In relation to it, we will consider how, from the side of the rule of law, there is always the fear for competing kinds of laws. Yet within a situation of lawlessness the desire for justice is equally prominent. What disrupts the logics connected to both fear and desire is apathy. If no one is able to respect the law, to care about the rule of law, or if everyone is too tired to fight against massive forms of injustice – like the ones that are taking place in Eastern Congo – both law and justice lose their force. Or, to give another example, with George Eliot's novel *Daniel Deronda* we will consider how law has to follow a logic of violence in its task to defend order, while the side of justice requires a logic of empathy. What threatens or disrupts both are collective forms of obliviousness. The theme of this nineteenth-century novel is the strife for an autonomous position of women and the strife for a safe Jewish homeland. In relation to both, the novel addresses a general obliviousness to the fate of women under patriarchy and an obliviousness to the fate of Jews, especially in Eastern Europe, where they were chased and slaughtered without the rule of law intervening and without any empathy from many in Russia or Europe. Obliviousness disrupted the logic of law and of justice in both cases.

In defining the disruptive thirds, I am not pretending they have some sort of objective status. Most people will agree that, for instance, apathy or obliviousness are disruptive to both law and justice. Yet for mystery, positions may differ. As we will find in chapter three there are those who think that mystery forms the divine or quasi-divine seal to the system of law. In chapter six we will see that there are those who defend corruption as the right thing to do in a society in which a fair distribution of public money is not functioning properly. And in chapter eight we will consider how hallucination can be a means that makes people feel that it is impossible to assess or find truth, regardless of its value. In all cases what I call 'disruptive thirds' are defended by those who profit from such disruption, be they people who think that the only order possible is a patriarchal one, people who think nepotism is the best way to organise society, or people who fare well with, say, 'intensifying' the lives of people in such a way that they do not care anymore about social justice as long as they have their chemically induced dreams. So, in defining the disruptive thirds, I take a position. The reader is invited to do the same, which may well mean that she disagrees.

As may have become clear, meanwhile, this study inscribes itself in what is called the field of law and literature, which could equally well have been defined as the field of law and art. What is this study's position in it?

IV. In Defence of Law, as a Defence of Justice

In the interdisciplinary field of law and literature, the two are mostly put into a relation of a sort of family or as one of questionable partners. Legal scholar Amnon Reichman, in a response to philosopher Martha Nussbaum's *Poetic Justice*, sketches the two fields as follows:

> Among these are theoretical claims – telling us something about 'the law' or 'legal education' – but also performative appeals, telling us how we should practice law (as lawyers and judges) and how we should teach (and learn) law. Specifically the book advocates the implementation of one of the Law and Literature movement's basic tenets, namely the incorporation of fine literature into the legal curriculum.[34]

Reichman hints at a relation between the two, here, that is especially productive from the side of the law. Literature is seen as simultaneously inferior and superior. It is inferior in its incapacity to follow the strict rules of reasoning and argumentation. Yet, it is superior in its capacity to make things imaginable, palpable, tangible and sense-able, or in its potential to promote empathy or ethical behaviour. Or, whereas law concerns a field that feels cold and instrumental, literature concerns one that indulges in the warmth of understanding.

The gendered nature of this relation was critically assessed by cultural studies scholar Greta Olson, who noted: 'This idealized image of literature is figured as initially suffering under the regime of rationalistic, masculinized law but then reforming "him" through the power of love'.[35] Indeed, within the idealised and gendered picture of the relation between the two fields, the field of law testifies to a strong humanist sentiment.[36] In this context the term interface, in its combining

[34] Amnon Reichman, 'Law, Literature, and Empathy: Between Withholding and Reserving Judgment' (2006) 56 *Journal of Legal Education* 296.

[35] Greta Olson, 'Law is not Turgid and Literature not Soft and Fleshy: Gendering and Heteronormativity in Law and Literature Scholarship' (2012) 36 *Australian Feminist Law Journal* 65.

[36] From the legal humanist side, one can think of studies inspired by James Boyd White, *The Legal Imagination: Studies in the Nature of Legal Thought and Expression* (Boston, Little, Brown, 1973); *When Words Lose Their Meaning: Constitutions and Reconstitutions of Language, Character, and Community* (Chicago, University of Chicago Press, 1984); *Justice as Translation: An Essay in Cultural*

'inter' with 'face', might tempt people to consider art as the face of a radical Other, as it was defined by French philosopher Emmanuel Levinas.[37] This face would be one that constantly questions human behaviour ethically and cannot be appropriated. Still, art is not the ideal place to look for justice, nor is it the better ethical other of law. Art can be unethical, perverse, criminal, evil and banal; to explain this away as actually a moral warning of sorts, or to disregard this capacity by saying that such work is not truly art, ignores the power and right of art 'to say all'.[38] Perhaps art has the potential of turning human beings into better versions of themselves. Art always has a rhetorical component. Yet, history has proven that precisely its rhetorical component could also turn art into a medium that instigated people's most abysmal behaviour.[39]

To counter an idealised picture of art, it is worthwhile to remember that poets have long been seen both as society's first legislators and as primary disturbers of societal harmony. The first may not only serve to indicate that literature and law share one dominant medium of symbolic order – language – it also indicates that art can very well stand on the side of the law, can make law, or can *be* law; like the biblical book of *Job*. When one considers collections of books like the *Tanakh*, *Bible*, or *Qu'ran* as works of fiction, they have had, and continue to have, immense legal force. One of the meanings of the *Torah* is, in fact, 'law'. This is why I do not consider art to be law's critical companion or law's comfortable partner in dialogue. I will not read art through its capacity to imagine or represent law and its principles, as happens in Anne Wagner and Richard Sherwin's *Law Culture and Visual Arts*. Nor will I consider art as it has been dealt with as a matter of concern in, or by law, as is the case in John Henry Merryman's *Law Ethics and the Visual Arts*.[40] I deal with art, including visual art, as an interface. Conceptualised as an

and Legal Criticism (Chicago, University of Chicago Press, 1990); *Acts of Hope: Creating Authority in Literature, Law, and Politics* (Chicago, University of Chicago Press, 1994). From the humanities side a paradigmatic figure is the already mentioned Martha Nussbaum with *Love's Knowledge: Essays on Philosophy and Literature* (New York, Oxford University Press, 1990); *Cultivating Humanity: A Classical Defense of Reform in Liberal Education* (Cambridge, Harvard University Press, 1997); *The New Religious Intolerance: Overcoming the Politics of Fear in an Anxious Age* (Cambridge, Belknap Press of Harvard University, 2013); *Anger and Forgiveness: Resentment, Generosity, Justice* (Oxford, Oxford University Press, 2016). In the early days, their position was severely criticized by Richard Posner in *Law and Literature: A Misunderstood Relation* (Cambridge MA, Harvard University Press, 1998).

[37] See, for instance, Emmanuel Levinas, *Time and the Other*, trans Richard A Cohen (Pittsburgh, Duquesne University Press, 1987), or *Humanism of the Other*, trans Nidra Poller, intro Richard A Cohen (Urbana IL, Illinois University Press, 2003).

[38] The quote was coined by Jacques Derrida, in French: 'le droit de tout dire'. See Derrida, *Sur parole: Instantanés philosophiques* (Paris, Éditions de l'Aube, 1999) and '"This strange institution called literature": An Interview with Jacques Derrida' in Derek Attridge (ed), *Acts of Literature* (London, Routledge, 1992). Derrida's position is summarized in Leslie Hill, *The Cambridge Introduction to Jacques Derrida* (Cambridge, Cambridge University Press, 2007) 108.

[39] On the rhetorical force in art see Arthur C Danto, *The Politics of Imagination* (Lawrence, University of Kansas, 1988). The Janus-faced quality of literature, its promoting both civility and barbarism, was central to Angel Rama, *The Lettered City*, trans John Charles Chasteen (Durham NC, Duke University Press, 1996).

[40] Anne Wagner and Richard K Sherwin (eds), *Law Culture and Visual Arts* (Dordrecht, Springer, 2014); John Henry Merryman, *Law Ethics and the Visual Arts*, 5th edn, co-authored with Albert E Elsen and Stephen K Urice (Alphen aan de Rijn, Kluwer International, 2007).

interface, art has an affirmative, disturbing or disruptive force with regard to issues of law and justice. This is a principally different paradigm to the ones outlined above. In the meeting of system of law and realm of justice, art does not systematically take one side. Rather, it brings the issue of taking sides to bear on audiences, across the ages, across cultures, and across all sorts of differences. It can then either promote or provoke choices, or lead to an impasse.

The provocation of choices or the possibility to rupture law's impasses is central to much of the work of legal scholar Peter Goodrich since the 1990s, on what he calls minor jurisprudences.[41] Looking, for instance, at the medieval courts of love, he traces a productive dynamic between established law and law's becoming, or forgotten genealogies, through forms of play. The minor functions in tension, here, with the major, as the child with the adult, the play with the serious, the lifestyle with the institution. Goodrich studies a dynamic that is inherent to the field of law, then, as when he states: 'If the minor is not to be entirely oppositional, if it is to take its place as part of the legal institution it requires its own positivity'.[42] Goodrich's examples, that is, are tangential to the realm of justice as it is treated in his study. Throughout his work, he is looking at aesthetic, playful modes of operation within a system of law. Yet it is precisely through these that a system of law may open itself up to the wider realm of justice. Or as Goodrich states:

> To cut a hole in the fabric of law is to insist upon more than law within the institution of legality. The hole, rend or tear that is made by the minor, by commitment to minority, thus turns minorist offices against the comfort of the constant and the habitus of habit.

With the latter terms, Goodrich may implicitly be referring to the work of French sociologist Pierre Bourdieu, whose concept of *habitus* is one that acts to ensure a system and its existing limits of law, be they legal or socio-cultural.[43] The question Goodrich asks, is how law's stability can be disturbed, as an opening gesture. In terms of art as an interface, this study comes close to Desmond Manderson's study *Danse Macabre: Temporalities of Law in the Visual Arts*.[44] In Manderson's case, art is considered in its potential to highlight principles of the rule of law, while opening up towards the wider realm of justice. If law is capable of injustices, for instance, this affects the realm of justice; and art is considered as the medium that makes this palpable.[45]

Goodrich and Manderson are paradigms for the Law and Literature movement, or Law and Humanities movement, as it marked itself in the legal field. From the humanities side as well, as the next chapters will make clear, there is a growing

[41] Peter Goodrich, *Law in the Courts of Love: Literature and Other Minor Jurisprudences* (London, Routledge, 1996). Since then other editions appeared also with the subtitle 'The Politics of Language'.

[42] Peter Goodrich, 'Major to Minor' (2017) 42.

[43] Pierre Bourdieu, *Outline of a Theory of Practice* (Cambridge, Cambridge University Press, 1977).

[44] Desmond Manderson, *Danse Macabre: Temporalities of Law in the Visual Arts* (Cambridge, Cambridge University Press, 2019).

[45] cf Desmond Manderson (ed), *Law and the Visual: Representations, Technologies, Critique* (Toronto, Toronto University Press, 2018) in which he proposes the phrase 'imaginal law' to indicate the intrinsic relation between images and issues of law, but also justice.

number of scholars involved in thinking through the relation between the law, justice and many forms of art. Often law is considered with suspicion and scrutiny, then. With respect to this, my study both connects to, and opts for an intimately critical relation with what is called critical legal studies.[46] The latter field considers law in its relation to the execution of power, noticing that systems of law have fairly often been unjustly serving powers, and with gusto. Critical legal studies has its origins in nineteenth-century legal realism, and developed itself through the civil rights movement of the 1960s and poststructuralist thought. Continuously, it has critically reflected on law's service to the state and disservice to justice. Many times, art has played a pivotal role in this reflection. If my study relates to this field of research in an intimately critical manner, this means it is intimately tied to and entangled in it, yet my position within this is adamantly critical. We are now witnessing situations in which functioning systems of law often prove to be a last stronghold against totalitarian or corrupting forces. This was not on the horizon in the 1960s and 1970s. Since then, it has become increasingly important, perhaps even urgent, to acknowledge the positive sides of a rule of law. Totalitarian forces need to be kept in check by law, or law should not only be used at will by totalitarian forces but also needs to serve those seeking the demands of justice to which totalitarian forces should answer. The issue here is not so much how to criticise, but how to commit one's self to a rule of law in light of justice.

V. Art, Annoyance and an Ethics of Affirmation

Conceptualising the role of art as an interface between the two forms of logic at stake in this study, is not to suggest that art is a driving force in an emancipatory process or a method of showing the masses how they can get the revolutionary they desire. If art has a role in relation to law or justice, in former or current historical contexts, it is to show how any system may turn into its own perversion; a perversion that consists in the fact that any act can be redefined according to the authority's wishes, mostly in the light of the demands of economy, societal order or history. From the side of justice, questions are: how can one resist becoming complicit or corrupt; or how can one have the courage to deviate in the name of justice when even the very attempt to resist might cost one's life? To bathe in the warm tub of complexities and indecision in the spheres of law and justice will not suffice. Law and justice are ultimately a matter of praxis, not of endless deliberations. Likewise, in this context, art as an interface is not something to be enjoyed.

[46] Both the Law and Literature movement and critical legal studies, alongside the position of mavericks like US American judge Richard Posner, are succinctly sketched in Lino A Graglia's review of Posner's *Law and Literature*, in (1989) 6 *Constitutional Commentary* 437. As becomes clear in this review, Posner, very fond of literature and rather critical about the Law and Literature movement, answered the question 'What has literary theory to offer law?' with a bland and dry 'Nothing'.

As we already noted, interfaces provoke choices, or they may lead to an impasse: a painful impossibility to choose.

The cases that follow are all considered within the larger frame of what Rosi Braidotti defined as an ethics of affirmation, an ethics that 'builds on radical relationality' and due to which the ethical core of subjects:

> [I]s not defined by their moral intentionality as much as by the effects of power, both repressive (*potestas*) and positive (*potentia*), that their actions are likely to exert in the world. The entrapping and the empowering modalities of power are always social, but they are neither dialectically linked nor mutually exclusive. They rather coexist as intertwined facets of the same process of subject formation.[47]

This quote may serve to indicate how this study aims to acknowledge or affirm two forms of power, two spheres, and two logics, without prioritising one over the other. An ethics of affirmation is not neutral, though. Systems of power that use morality to defend a status quo defined by massive inequalities clearly give priority to one over the other. They will give priority to the system of law, the rule of law, to defend the status quo. With an ethics of affirmation, then, the aim is not to achieve a balanced viewpoint. The aim is to posit an equal distribution of subject formation that does justice to an intrinsic multiplicity. Such multiplicity should not be fetishised, for an essential issue in the meeting of law and justice remains: 'Whose side are you on?' This is not a conceptual matter. In what comes, pivotal issues will be whose desires to live are allowed, and especially *how* they are allowed to live – or die.

French philosopher Jacques Derrida contended that true democracy and justice are not something one can ever *have*, like one can have one's revenge. Justice is not to be had; rather it consists in terms of an eternal promise; it is always *to come*.[48] Yet for Derrida, this eternally unfulfilled promise had its theological connotations. I defend another position. Perhaps justice can never be *had*, but it can be a promise that is fulfilled. There are many examples where the struggle for justice led to the opening or reopening of cases, with the promise of some form of legal resolution. To be sure, once that legal resolution is achieved, the question is always whether justice was served to the full for all those involved. Yet justice can never be 'full'. It can only be defined as more or less sufficient, satisfactory or felicitous. From the legal side, law cannot be satisfied with loose ends and is aimed at closure because it is systematic in nature. Any case works towards being closed, and if it is not closed on one level, it moves to a higher level, or the highest one. No one can open a case beyond the highest court of a country or the highest court of a federation. If one wants to appeal to an ever higher court, people will have to move to the margins of

[47] Rosi Braidotti, 'Non-Fascist Ethics: Learning to Live and Die as Affirmation' in Maria Hlavajova and Wietske Maas (eds), *Propositions for Non-Fascist Living: Tentative and Urgent* (Cambridge MA, MIT Press, Basic Series, 2019) 27.

[48] Jacques Derrida, *Deconstruction and the Possibility of Justice* (London, Routledge, 1993) 24–25.

the system or outside of the system, with its imagined courts, which were studied by Goodrich as minor jurisprudences.[49]

In terms of an equality that does justice to an intrinsic multiplicity, the practice of an ethics of affirmation is threatened by processes described recently by Peter Pomerantsev in *Nothing is True and Everything is Possible: Adventures in Modern Russia* or *This Is Not Propaganda: Adventures in the War Against Reality*. Such an ethics is threatened on a global scale by what Shoshana Zuboff defined as *The Age of Surveillance Capitalism*, a book with a telling subtitle: *The Fight for a Human Future at the New Frontier of Power*.[50] The affirmative and disturbing relation between law and what is just implies that all desiring beings are damaged by the playground of powers that consider forms of life to be first and foremost targets of manipulation or that deal with their subjects as mere puppets (and more on this in chapter six and eight). In any kind of totalitarian system, law and justice no longer productively relate. The realm of justice is cut short, in such cases, or is targeted by a system that is only legal in an instrumental or perverted sense of the term. In such circumstances, art has a substantial role to play. As interface, it will always open up both the system of law and the realm of justice. This is why all totalitarian systems have inevitably feared art or wanted to use it restrictively, for propaganda. This is why societies that want equal opportunities for all beings, as a matter of justice, need art's interface.

In the meeting of the spheres of law and justice through art's interface, friction is inescapable. If the working title of this study was *annoyance*, this was because all meetings of the spheres of law and justice come with friction that is sometimes solved but even if it is, never fully so. Annoyance etymologically falls back on Latin *in odio*, with the latter, *odium*, meaning hate or blame. The definition of odium is 'General or widespread hatred or disgust incurred by someone as a result of their actions'. The desire for justice may connote a love for justice, but it may equally well imply a hatred felt for those who can be blamed for the injustice done. Often such hatred is explained as a matter of unresolved trauma, as if people are not enlightened enough yet to see that hate does not lead anywhere. It is, then, as if fully realised justice can never involve hatred. Yet this is precisely the pivot: When is justice ever fully realised? For instance, due to the work of the South African Truth and Reconciliation Commission, installed in 1995 and operative between 1996 and 2002, perpetrators could evade punishment if they confessed what they had done and requested amnesty. Some argued that this could avoid civil war, others argued, and with good reason, that this very commission robbed them of their right to justice. Smack in the middle of the commission's work, lawyer

[49] Goodrich, *Law in the Courts of Love* (1996).

[50] Peter Pomerantsev, *Nothing is True and Everything is Possible: Adventures in Modern Russia* (London, Faber & Faber, 2015) and *This Is Not Propaganda: Adventures in the War Against Reality* (London, Faber & Faber, 2019); Shoshana Zuboff, *The Age of Surveillance Capitalism: The Fight for a Human Future at the New Frontier of Power* (New York, PublicAffairs, 2019).

George Bizos published *No One to Blame?: In Pursuit of Justice in South Africa.*[51] This was not a coincidence. The question whether people are to be blamed, can be blamed, or should be blamed is an affectively charged one. In many instances of injustice as a matter of 'unfinished business', hatred may be involved. As such, it is not incompatible with justice. Or, it can be but it need not be. The nice word for hatred is 'indignation'.

The French *ennui*, boredom, also falls back on *in odio*. Here, annoyance hints at the fact that many find struggles for justice annoying and at points tiresome, or boring. All those fighting for equal rights in the context of racism, gender, class, disabilities, animal rights, the environment and many similar causes, are often found troublesome and tiring and those in charge may consequently develop a feeling and response of *ennui*. I am writing this in the months of global protests against the killing of Afro-American George Floyd by a US American police officer in Minneapolis. Feelings of indignation or hatred are massive and widely shared. And Floyd's case is only one in a vast range of similar cases. In most of the cases authorities responded with ennui to the death of Afro-American citizens; in fact, some of the highest authorities still do. One could say a similar thing for European audiences that responded and respond with ennui to those fighting for the rights of thousands of Syrian refugees or African immigrants that drowned, and are drowning, in the Mediterranean.

The Latin poet Catullus wrote: *Odi et amo. quare id faciam, fortasse requiris. / nescio, sed fieri sentio et excrucior.* That is: 'I hate and I love. Why I do this, perhaps you ask. / I know not, but I feel it happening and I am tortured' (translation Leonard C Smithers). Catullus is pointing at the often-mixed feelings of love and hate, a mixture that may escape full explanation and may annoy any subject suffering from it. Likewise, the love for justice may imply hate or blame, even if this is not explicitly expressed. In general, those in power do not expect or accept people to feel hatred for injustices done to them in the past. They would love to see people let matters rest. If only it were that easy. If art is good at anything, it is in representing, even embodying, the ambiguous, the mixed and confusing simultaneity of emotions. One could seek the moral high ground, here, in promoting a pure love for justice. Yet such purity is bad fiction. All works of art in the chapters that follow accept the impurity involved when art acts as an interface for the meeting of law and justice. They register the impurity of human beings, in their loving and hating the dynamic between law and justice.

[51] George Bizos, *No One to Blame?: In Pursuit of Justice in South Africa* (Claremont, David Philip, 1998).

2

Logic of Fear vs Logic of Desire

Milo Rau's The Congo Tribunal *and the Care for Law*

'For as long as you call it civil rights your only allies can be the people in the next community, many of whom are responsible for your grievance. But when you call it human rights it becomes international. And then you can take your troubles to the World Court. You can take them before the world. And anybody anywhere on this earth can become your ally.'

Malcolm X, 'Not Just an American Problem but a World Problem'[1]

I. Absent Rule of Law and the Potential in Art's Interface

Between 29 and 31 May 2015, a theatrical tribunal was staged in Bakavu, the capital of the province South Kivu in Eastern Congo.[2] On the *Fragile State Index* by the Fund for Peace,[3] the Democratic Republic of Congo finds itself on the far end of the negative spectrum, past the red *alert* stage, indicating a state of lawlessness or absence of the rule of law.[4] In this violent and nigh lawless situation, the Swiss director, author and filmmaker Milo Rau (also initiator of the IIPM, the International Institute of Political Murder) established the Congo Tribunal.[5] It had as its purpose to find out who were and continue to be, directly or indirectly responsible for the decades of violence that have plagued Eastern Congo, and

[1] Malcolm X, 'Not just an American problem but a world problem, Corn Hill Methodist Church, Rochester, February 16, 1965', in *February 1965, The Final Speeches* edited by Steve Clark (Atlanta, Pathfinder Press, 1992) 192.

[2] For a complete overview of all performances in Congo and Berlin and for the documentary, see The Congo Tribunal at www.the-congo-tribunal.com. The project was also published: Eva Bertschy, Rolf Bossart and Mirjam Knapp (eds), *Das Kongo Tribunal* (Berlin, Verbrecher Verlag, 2017).

[3] Fund for Peace is an 'independent non-profit organization headquartered in Washington, D.C. with offices in Abuja, Nigeria, Accra, Ghana and Tunis, Tunisia' as it describes itself. The fund is supported by many companies, ministries and international organisations; see fundforpeace.org/who-we-are.

[4] See the 'Fragile States Index': fundforpeace.org.

[5] See IIPM: international-institute.de/en/news.

that have most affected the provinces Kivu and Tanganyika. The Congo Tribunal examined, that is, 'the causes and backgrounds to this, so far biggest and bloodiest economic war in human history'.[6] The focus of this chapter is how, in the absence of the rule of law, a legal space was filled in meaningfully by art, which, acting as an interface, attempted to amplify Congolese cries for justice while suggesting the possibility of an operative system of law.

The performance, or staged tribunal, followed a strict, regular and formal protocol. There was a head investigator: Sylvestre Bisimwa, president of the Congolese Bar Association. There was a president of procedures: the French-speaking Belgian Jean Louis Gilissen, an internationally well-known jurist, who was involved as a lawyer at the International Court of Justice (ICJ) and the International Criminal Court (ICC) in The Hague for decades.[7] There was also a jury, and victims and representatives of all parties involved were called before the court. The entire tribunal was repeated in Berlin from 26 to 27 of June 2015. Its theatrical structure is set out in Figure 2.1.

Figure 2.1 *The Congo Tribunal* in Berlin, 26/27 June 2015
Photograph: Daniel Seiffert

[6] See The Congo Tribunal: www.the-congo-tribunal.com.

[7] The ICJ is underpinned by the United Nations; the ICC is independent and is underpinned by the so-called Assembly of States Parties.

As the image shows, the entire event was quite literally staged. It did not take place in a court of justice, but in a flat floor space. Its theatrical set-up was completely transparent, in a Brechtian sense: everything was shown. Media was used not only to document the event but also to add a further element of theatricality through the use of screened images. In this case, for instance, the face of Gilissen is projected left and right.

In a review of the event, the British newspaper *The Guardian* wondered: was this the 'most ambitious political theatre ever staged?'[8] Subsequently, a documentary film was made about the event, that was screened throughout Europe and Africa. *The Congo Tribunal* was nominated for the Camera Justitia prize at the Movies that Matter festival in The Hague in 2018.[9] Yet the fact that the theatrical event had now become a documentary did not diminish its theatrical connotations. The documentary was framed theatrically; the filmed reactions of people became part of the total project. These were then used for exhibitions and for the website of the project. One of the issues for now is whether this focus on theatricality is coincidental or central to art's ability to function as an interface between the realm of justice and system of law.

The staged events, the film, the subsequent exhibitions and the website are paradigms of art's acting as interface, be it, in this case, with a twist. In the case of the Eastern Congo the question is whether a truly operative system of law, or the rule of law, existed or exists. The staged event and the documentary that was made of this event show that the realm of justice was very much alive, though. Whether it concerns the responses of Congolese people in the room during the staged tribunal, the cries for justice in the documentary or the responses of people in the Eastern Congo presented in the documentary, they all tell a clear story. Much available information, moreover, was already provided by a regional civil society platform called the Coalition of Civil Society Organisations in the Great Lakes Region (COSOC-GL). This platform was already looking for justice.[10] Clearly, the realm of justice was at work.

Yet what could art, as interface, mean if the realm of justice could not be connected to the counter-system of law since it was dysfunctional? The question can be answered by having a more specific look at the potential of the notion of the interface. In 2008 Alexander Galloway explored the nature of any interface

[8] Kate Connolly, 'The most ambitious political theatre ever staged? 14 hours at the Congo Tribunal' (2015) *The Guardian*, 1 July 2015, available at www.theguardian.com/world/2015/jul/01/congo-tribunal-berlin-milo-rau-political-theatre.

[9] Rau missed the prize; perhaps he wanted to stick to the theatricality of the tribunal to such a degree that his film lost some of its documentary qualities. Instead Alberto Arnout won with the documentary *Hasta los Dientes – Armed to the Teeth* (2018) on the battle for justice by family and friends of two Mexican students who were killed by the army. See Movies That Matter, available at www.moviesthatmatter.nl/english_index/festival/programma_en/filmprogramma_en/film_en/2406/armed-to-the-teeth.

[10] This NGO was called to life in 2011; see COSOC-GL www.facebook.com/faizykara.

in an article entitled 'The Unworkable Interface'.[11] Galloway's argument followed French philosopher François Dagognet, who considered the interface as a 'fertile nexus'. The 'nexus' was a trope in itself, that Galloway unpacked by introducing two other tropes. The interface is either a surface on which different spheres meet, or a threshold, door or window that functions as a gateway between the two. For both Galloway states:

> The interface is this state of 'being on the boundary.' It is that moment where one significant material is understood as distinct from another significant material. In other words, an interface is not a thing, an interface is always an effect. It is always a process or a translation. Again Dagognet: a fertile nexus. (939)

If we relate the different tropes to Rau's tribunal, one could say the stage was literally a surface that made a translation between two domains possible. The theatrical staging formed the surface by means of which the realm of justice came to be connected to the possibility of an official, legal tribunal. The stage was the interface, then, on which one significant realm met another. As a result an issue of translation was provoked. Yet if the cries for justice were to be translated into the materialisation of a legal case, the efficacy of any translation would be dependent on the functionality of the system of law it was being translated into. The interface as a surface might be dysfunctional as a result, since one of its connecting sides was missing.

The tropes door, window, or threshold connote something else, however. Here the question is whether the theatrically staged tribunal could somehow form the gate or entrée to a real tribunal. This is not so much a matter of translation but of transformation. Such a transformation cannot simply be a matter of going through the door, but a doorway can offer a perspective on another 'significant material'. The notion of transformation suggests, that is, the possibility of a working interface even if one side of the two 'significant materials' is missing. In such a case, the interface does not simply facilitate a connection, but forms the gateway between the one and the other by means of which one can possibly transform into the other. To specify how this works, Galloway distinguished between edges and centres. With the tropes of window, door or gateway, it is not a surface but a frame that is dominant, within which something is being presented. This frame is always media-specific and art has a particular role to play, here, since 'the edges of art always make reference to the medium'.[12] As if to confirm this, both the staged tribunal and the documentary that Rau made of the performance indeed emphasised the theatrical or cinematographic nature of the event and its registration. There is no direct translation or transition, such was the implication; to show something requires media and mediation.

[11] Alexander R Galloway, 'The Unworkable Interface' (2008) 39 *New Literary History* 931. The article was later reworked to become the first chapter of Galloway's *Interface Effect* (Cambridge, Polity Press, 2012).

[12] Alexander R Galloway, 'The Unworkable Interface' (2008) 939.

The performance of the Congo Tribunal was marked as staged and filmed by means of the organisation of the space and the transparency of the media used. In the case of the original tribunal, the space was formally a theatre, but, again, one with a twist. Here, the curtain, which usually acts as the veil between audience and stage, and can either be drawn open or closed, instead became the backdrop. As Peter Goodrich has shown, in his study of legal emblems that define law's 'lawness', legal emblems are 'theatrical devices', or 'dramatic machines' that define law's performance.[13] Things need to appear whereas much that defines the system of law also has to remain behind the curtains. Here, in contrast, people were looking at something that perhaps was initially taking place behind closed curtains but was now brought out in the open. Another inversion of theatrical devices was that the audience did not sit in the dark for this 'show' but was instead lit by artificial lighting that enabled them to be easily filmed. A camera was also present on stage and two screens were added at the front to show the audience what was being documented. Then, the motto above the frame was hard to miss and became a title of sorts: '*Verité et Justice*' ('Truth and Justice'). This title and the frame underneath it turned the scene into a tableau, and became referenced as such on the project's website.[14] This introduces yet another kind of genre-logic. Roland Barthes, in reflecting on Diderot's ideas on theatre and the tableau, defined the tableau, whether 'pictorial, theatrical, literary' as 'a pure cut-out segment with clearly defined edges, irreversible and incorruptible'.[15] Such a pure, irreversible and incorruptible cut-out segment coincides well with the unquestionable frame of the tribunal and its epitaph. Finally, yet one other generic logic was at stake in the documentary that was made of the event. This documentary begins conventionally, with shots from an airplane and the camera crew filming the aftermath of a shocking attack in the region. It subsequently becomes more cinematographic and reflexive of its form, when the staged event is presented using prompts such as a clapboard.

Both the staged event and the documentary reflected on their medium, then, and on how things were staged or captured. Such reflection provokes us to think about how the aesthetic of a given medium offers possibilities for, and confines how something is represented. Such a reflection also provokes us to think about the ways in which a medium relates to reality. For if medium-reflexivity emphasises the artificial nature of the event and its documentation, this does not mean that everything is fictional or unreal. The emphasis on the medium and its framing act is necessary in order to avoid mistaking the tribunal for a legal and official one; a mistake that would have vast consequences. Fearful of prosecution most

[13] Peter Goodrich, *Legal Emblems and the Art of Law: Obiter Depicta as the Vision of Governance* (Cambridge, Cambridge University Press, 2014) 83. Also see Peter Goodrich, 'The Evidence of Things Not Seen' in Peter Goodrich and Valérie Hayaer (eds), *Genealogies of Legal Vision* (London, Routledge, 2015) 53–78.

[14] For the 'tableau', see The Congo Tribunal: www.the-congo-tribunal.com/project.html#hearings.

[15] Roland Barthes, 'Diderot, Brecht, Eisenstein' in *Image/Music/Text*, trans Stephen Heath (New York, Farrar Strauss and Giroux, 1977) 70.

participants would not have appeared, as they did now because this was art. With respect to this, Galloway makes a move that is of relevance to our topic by introducing the notion of intraface. Using a specific game as an example, Galloway argues that its form of art is no longer in any sense *about* reality, or about unveiling reality's true status. Rather, that which is outside of art's frame, say social reality, is brought into the frame. In cases such as these, according to Galloway 'the "outside", or the social, has been woven more intimately into the very fabric of the aesthetic than in previous times'.[16]

This is enlightening, for instead of Rau's staged tribunal being a play about reality, it is a form of art that brings reality within the frame of the work. In the Congo Tribunal, the parties or individuals involved were not played by professional actors. The staged tribunal was no longer so much about reality, then, but came to enact reality. The result was that the staged event took on overtones of a game: less a matter of representation than a game *mimicking* the force fields of reality. Yet, this was a game in which real stakes were involved. One of the people questioned, for instance, was Adalbert Murhi Mubalama, mining minister of the province of South Kivu. The tribunal's enactment of reality contributed to his fall. Staged in 2015, the tribunal added force to the research conducted by the independent platform Global Witness since 2000. This research culminated in 2013/14 and led to a report called 'River of Gold' that was published in July 2016. The Congolese National Commission Against Mining Sector Fraud (CNLFM: *Commission nationale de lutte contre la fraude miniere*) then arrested the minister, and he was forced to resign.

So, if art's interface cannot be a surface on which two spheres can meet because one of the two is dysfunctional, it can still be a frame within which, or a gateway through which, the possibility of a functioning system of law is shown. This opens the possibility of a transformation. In what follows, I will be dealing with such transformations in relation to two counter-logics that nevertheless connect: the logic of fear in the system of law and the logic of desire in the realm of justice. The fear is that law will be lost, but also that existing laws are threatened by other, unofficially acknowledged ones. The desire concerns the installation of a meaningful system of law where there is none, or the replacement of laws that are felt to be unjust.

II. Law's Genesis, Fear of Law and the Nature of Courts

The coming into being of meaningful law was termed *jurisgenesis* by the US American legal scholar and lawyer Robert Cover.[17] As the qualifier 'meaningful' suggests, Cover was not simply concerned with new laws. His focus was rather on

[16] Galloway (n 11) 947.

[17] Robert Cover, 'Nomos and Narrative' in Martha Minow, Michael Ryan, and Austin Sarat (eds), *Narrative, Violence, and the Law: The Essays of Robert Cover* (Ann Arbor, The University of Michigan Press, 1995). The article was originally published in 1983.

how new laws have or acquire 'legal meaning'. Here Cover stated: 'legal meaning – *jurisgenesis* – takes place always through an essentially cultural medium'.[18] His contention should be read in relation to the legal and political system of the United States of America. Yet his analysis has a far broader scope. In the US system Cover traced a distinction between two opposing powers. On the one hand, there is the state that makes it possible for people with differing worldviews to live together. On the other, we find several smaller communities that are more distinctly homogenous, not compromise-oriented and self-regulating. Cover defined the first as an 'imperial community', the second as a set of 'paideic communities'.[19] The imperial community is characterised by a muted pluralism enabled by means of the rule of law. It is muted because all parties have to accept the supremacy of the state. Counter to what the term 'imperial' suggests, Cover calls the force of law 'weak', here. In liberal democracies the principles of law are 'system-maintaining "weak" forces'.[20] They are only aimed at making it possible for different communities to live together. In other words: members of the imperial community are less meaningfully involved in legal order because law is merely an instrumental system of obligations and regulations to them.

In contrast, paideic communities – communities that teach themselves how to live – are characterised by strong, particular and culturally determined desires and forceful laws in consequence. The term 'paideic' refers to the classical Greek and Roman term *paideia*, which describes the raising and training of young people to become citizens. According to Cover, paideic communities are unitary and in favour of an intensely normative life in a meaningful world: 'an integrated world of obligation and reality from which the rest of the world is perceived'.[21] To this purpose, they want to create laws with which they feel connected and that may produce 'normative mitosis': a splitting of worlds on the basis of different or disparate norms.[22] In this case, law is not something one should adhere to, but the embodiment of what Cover calls a *nomos*: 'a world in which we live'.[23] This is a world with norms and rules that are captured formally by means of narratives. Law, here, is 'a system of meaning rather than an imposition of force'.[24] According to Cover, new forms of law, laws that have meaning, are *created* by such paideic communities.

In the development of his argument Cover emphasised that he was not dealing with distinct societies that would either be wholly imperial or paideic. He was, rather, dealing with two 'attributes of all normative worlds'.[25] Within any imperial community, for instance, new laws can come to exist. Yet they will not connote

[18] ibid 103.
[19] ibid 105–06.
[20] ibid 105.
[21] ibid 128.
[22] ibid 128.
[23] ibid 96.
[24] ibid 105.
[25] ibid 107.

another kind of world, let alone a splitting of worlds. Their aim is to preserve an order. The imperial community lacks the intrinsic connection between *nomos* and narrative; the state is not 'a world in which we live'. Or, though some consider the state a fiction, its law is not a narrative 'system of meaning'. The state is institutionally installed to amalgamate multiple worlds, and contain them under a legally unitary whole. Yet as such, it still embodies, or stands for, a world in which a multiplicity of people are allowed to live.

Cover's distinction implies that art can work as an interface for both imperial and paideic communities, by translating the desires from different realms of justice to a system of law. Yet the interface will have a very different function and impetus for each community. The US Supreme Court, for instance, is a synecdoche for an imperial community that has the prerogative to create law.[26] It is a community that, ultimately, claims to be at the basis of the only officially acknowledged law, which is why Cover does not consider the production of new law to be an example of *jurisgenesis*. On the contrary, the imperial community is described by Cover in terms of the *jurispathic*, indicating the fear for other forms of law.[27] Though having its origin in a form of desire itself, then, the state comes to operate against all other forms of desire once in place. It operates to restrict different forms of social engagement and to preserve already fixed social norms. This is why the state fears multiplicity or law's plurality.

In the context of the state's fear for other laws, Cover comes to conclude with the following thesis:

> It is remarkable that in myth and history the origin of and justification for a court is rarely understood to be the need for law. Rather, it is understood to be the need to suppress law, to choose between two or more laws, to impose upon laws a hierarchy. It is the multiplicity of laws, the fecundity of the jurisgenerative principle, that creates the problem to which the court and the state are the solution.[28]

The terms Cover uses – *need* and *fecundity* – carry a strong affective charge. They connote, on the one side, the realm of the desire for justice, which is defined by needs and a fecund multiplicity. Yet the need for a court on the law's side is defined by a fear that finds its source in the desire for a state monopoly. Law requires officially acknowledged courts as the places where laws, the only valid ones, can be enacted and the decisions are based on which law is operate as the rule.[29]

[26] As dealt with in the previous chapter, James Boyd White argued that constitutional legal decisions rhetorically produce an ethical and political constituency; see James Boyd White, *Justice as Translation: An Essay in Cultural and Legal Criticism* (Chicago, University of Chicago Press, 1990).

[27] Gilles Deleuze and Félix Guattari developed a similar thesis on the state as a 'force of antiproduction', especially in *Anti-Oedipus: Capitalism and* Schizophrenia, trans Brian Massumi (Minneapolis, University of Minnesota Press, 1983).

[28] Cover, 'Nomos and Narrative' (1995) 139.

[29] The theatrical nature of the law's appearance through court is evidenced in many scholarly studies. See, eg, Judith Resnik and Dennis Curtis, *Representing Justice: Invention, Controversy, and Rights in City-States and Democratic Courtrooms* (New Haven, Yale University Press, 2011). Julie Stone Peters considers what happens to law's theatrical logic in contemporary circumstances in 'Theatrocracy Unwired: Legal Performance in the Modern Mediasphere' (2014) 26 *Law & Literature* 31.

Following desires for justice, however, it can never be the case that just *one* law is being created. There are always several, competing or different laws that do not add to one overarching system, because they organise differing worlds. Still, this fruitful multiplicity is regulated, controlled and countered; it is cut short by the state and its jurisdiction through the court. The latter forms the spatial heart of a hierarchical system that posits one law above all others.

Cover's analysis adds a specifically generic aspect to this dynamic. To him narrative, in its capturing of the *nomos* of a community, acts as the motor of the creation of new law. In contrast, in what follows I am about to argue that the generic form of theatre – constitutive for the court and, consequently, for both the practice of law and the actualisation of justice – is of equal importance. Firstly, people have to create a space in which not only the law can come to speak, but also its subjects. It concerns a space that is both open and closed, with specific formal, generic features, so that it enables people to publicly appear before a judge. Such a space should allow for witnesses to be heard, for parties to be accused, for a balanced judgment to be made. As Cover noted, such a space, once it has become an officially recognised court, can serve the superimposition of one law. The theatrical space that was first desired and needed has then turned into an officially recognised court. From there onwards it becomes the only space within which law manifests itself, with a supreme power granting itself the privilege to establish officially recognised judicial spaces. Yet this power transforms a generic space that was principally open into a closed one.[30] It does so not only institutionally, but also in terms of architecture.[31] In such cases, the radical openness inherent in theatre's origin can only still be felt through a dramatic potential. All the actors coming together carry with them the potential of the unexpected, the new. Whereas the architecture of courts embodies permanence, that is, the dramatic essence of theatre is always of the here and now. This is why, in origin, theatrical space and the generic form of drama connote multiplicity. They follow from the desire for justice, not only to enact law but also to create new laws.

The double nature of the court as a both open and closed one is relevant in a context that Cover did not address. When he focused on the productive splitting of worlds, he did not deal with what happens when the state's order collapses or is destroyed and the pluralism that was first tempered or muted by the state has now come to explode. Or worse, Cover did not ask what happens when the multiple worlds that specific communities inhabit according to a certain *nomos* are ripped to shreds, leaving little to hold on to because there is no inhabitable world left and all collective stories have been fragmented. The latter appears to be the

[30] The judicio-theatrical space is one example, here, of what Johan Huizinga defined in a study from 1938 as 'the magical circle' of any play, and specified as a 'sacred circle within which the judges are shown sitting' see Johan Huizinga, *Homo ludens: a study of the play-element of culture* (Brooklyn NY, Angelico Press, 2016) 77.

[31] See Linda Mulcahy, *Legal Architecture: Justice, Due Process and the Place of Law* (London, Routledge, 2010); or Resnik and Curtis, *Representing Justice* (2011).

case in Eastern Congo, where the artwork that is central to this chapter was first performed. Its aim was to operate counter to apathy, the third, disruptive element that threatens both the system's fear for other laws and the many, multiple desires for justice.

III. Apathy: The Threat to Law and Justice

Libraries can be filled with existing studies on notions such as empathy and sympathy, compassion, identification and affect (more on which in chapter three). Fairly few studies pay attention to their negative counterpart: apathy.[32] Most studies on apathy are to be found in the field of psychology and medicine, in which apathy is studied as an aspect of psychological illnesses and disturbances that range from schizophrenia to Alzheimer's, and from depression to possible effects of drug abuse. In the domain of literary studies, art history or the humanities in general, apathy has historically been predominantly studied in the context of the history of stoicism. Philosopher Laura Hengehold, for instance, traces the historical manifestations of *apatheia* or 'affect control' in relation to the latter. Such affect control would be of special relevance to judges, who should not be emotional in their verdicts, but should rather control them, in line with the stoic requirement. There is an important link to theatricality here. Ever since the first forms of theory on this generic form came into being, the regulation of passions has been of essence. This starts with Aristotle's *catharsis*, as the relief of too much emotional pressure or tension. It is taken up later by the classic stoics who wanted to consider the world in terms of a stage to be looked at, the *theatrum mundi*, in order to keep it at a distance. The stoic *apatheia* was reflective in nature, that is, and as such the opposite of regular apathy.

One other field that produced studies about the nature of apathy is that of politics. Political apathy or mass apathy was mentioned, for instance, in the later works of Max Scheler (1874–1928) who, in the context of rising Nazism, proposed that if political subjects stop to act, political apathy will inevitably lead to terror.[33] Since the 1960s there have also been studies on political apathy in the context of

[32] Just a few recent examples of the study into empathy are Jeroen Boomgaard, Rini Hurkmans, and Judith Westerveld (eds), *Compassion: A Paradox in Art and Society* (Amsterdam, Valiz/LAP, 2017); Martin L Hoffman, 'Empathy, Justice, Law' in Amy Coplan and Peter Goldie (eds), *Empathy: Philosophical and Psychological Perspectives* (Oxford Scholarship Online, 2012), available at doi.org/10.1093/acprof:oso/9780199539956.003.0015. A rare example of the study into apathy in the literary domain is Tony McCracker, *Apathy in Literature: A Discourse on Emotionless Characters and Concepts* (Hamburg, Ancher, 2014).

[33] See Max Scheler, *GW XIII, Schriften aus dem Nachlaß, Bd. 4: Philosophie und Geschichte* (Bonn, Bouvier-Verlag, 1990) 72. Not surprisingly, apathy was not taken up by Elias Canetti's study on mass behaviour, who focused on the opposite potential in masses, see *Crowds and Power*, trans Carol Stewart (New York, Farrar, Straus and Giroux, 1984), published in 1960 as *Masse und Macht*.

contemporary consumer society. The idea was that, since society was providing the well-to-do middle classes with everything they wanted, they no longer cared about politics.[34] In this context the theatrical nature of politics, so essential to the work of Hannah Arendt, was in danger of getting lost, because another generic form was taking over: that of spectacle. This might be the fascist or Nazi-spectacle with its overpowering and subjecting force, or it might be the consumer society of the spectacle as Guy Debord defined it, in which the theatrical reflection that is paramount to being able to act politically is hollowed out by another kind of spectatorship, one that works counter to political agency.[35]

Apathy in relation to the legal field is a major concern that needs to be addressed, but here too no extensive studies on apathy can be found. There are enough people, though, who note that apathy is the enemy of both law and justice, such as theologian Lesley Orr MacDonald or US American Senator Cory Booker. The latter stated that the 'opposite of justice is not injustice. It's apathy and indifference'.[36] The threat of apathy is considered in these cases by a feminist and a black Democratic politician. Both are very much aware of how systems of justice have been biased for centuries, not in the sense of failing to be impartial but in how these systems have been indifferent to the injustice done to those who fall outside of their remits. Yet whereas such indifference can be wilful (on which more in chapter seven), apathy is not in one's control. Like fear and desire, apathy is something that will overcome people. It concerns a fundamental lack of energy and by implication a threat to agency that results from something that is being done, affectively, to living bodies and beings.

A group of scholars studying apathy ecologically across species defined it as 'a quantitative reduction in goal-directed behaviour', a definition that, indeed, focuses on a measurable reduction in agency.[37] These scholars came to define five sub-domains of apathy, namely: self-care; exploration; social interaction; work/education; and recreation. Not all of these can be translated from human beings to other animals (in their case, rodents) but the first three can. And I would like to propose an additional sub-domain. In the last decades research has increasingly focused on the sense of fairness, an aspect of distributive justice common amongst primates.[38] My hypothesis is that apathy can be traced in an absence, not

[34] See Dale Southerton (ed), *Encyclopedia of Consumer Culture*, Vol 1 (Los Angeles, Sage, 2011) 235–36.

[35] Guy Debord, *The Society of the Spectacle*, trans Donald Nicholson-Smith (New York, Zone Books, 1994), originally published in French in 1967.

[36] Lesley Orr MacDonald, 'A Spirituality for Justice, The Enemy of Apathy' (2000) 8 *Feminist Theology* 13; for the quote by Cory Brooker, see Uptown Messenger: uptownmessenger.com/2019/01/sen-cory-booker-the-opposite-of-justice-is-not-injustice-its-apathy-and-indifference-full-video.

[37] Florin Cathomas, Matthias N Hartmann, Erich Seifritz, Christopher R Pryce, and Stefan Kaiser, 'The Translational Study of Apathy – an Ecological Approach' (2015) 9 *Frontiers in Behavioral Neuroscience* 241, available at doi.org/10.3389/fnbeh.2015.00241.

[38] See the work of Frans de Waal and his team: Frans de Waal, *Our Inner Ape: A Leading Primatologist Explains Why We Are Who We Are* (New York, Penguin Group, 2005); *The Age of Empathy: Nature's Lessons for a Kinder Society* (New York, Three Rivers Press, 2009).

of this sense of fairness itself, but of any kind of agency around or in relation to it. Apathy denotes a missing form of care, but also missing forms of desire or indignation. The absence of these, care or indignation, is captured by the phrase 'I don't care', which can easily become the phrase 'I could not care less', and this in turn can easily become numb silence. In the context of law and justice apathy is measurable in terms of an inability to care, then, an inability that can destroy a feel for law and a sense of justice. Additionally, it is measurable in terms of a lack of desire and indignation. The latter two can be assessed in how intensely people relate to things. Apathy indicates a lack of being related; it implies the inability to respond.

One specific disruptive third for both law and justice, as the case of the Congo amply testifies, is apathy. It is an apathy that does not just overcome people out of the blue. Neither is it the mass apathy that Scheler talked about, nor is it the luxury of apathy that was studied in the context of 1960s consumer society. This apathy was wilfully produced by actors who shunned the rule of law in order to be able to attain positions of uncontrolled power and make profits. The Global Witness 2016 report, 'River of Gold', is crystal clear about this.[39] As for wilfully produced apathy, in January 2018, UNICEF announced that there were 1.3 million people on the run in the eastern Congo, of which 800.000 were children, and in January 2019, the situation exploded, with outbreaks of Ebola and almost 13 million people living on the brink of famine.[40] The very phrase 'on the run', unfortunately, veils forms of agency. Who were these people running from, or rather: which parties were forcing them to leave or chasing them? People were on the brink of famine, yes: who brought them there?

Often the questions are answered in terms of 'consequences', like describing what happens as consequences of extremely violent conflicts that started after the end of the civil war in neighbouring Rwanda, which caused millions of deaths.[41] Still, as is often the case in wars, the conflict is related to forms of injustice that involve matters of interest, like minerals: tin, coltan (a source of tantalum) and tungsten. These are crucial for iPads and mobile phones, which is why they are also called 'conflict minerals' or 'engines of chaos'. The latter term suggests that the absence of the rule of law is not just something that is, coincidentally, lacking. It may be a produced absence that serves certain forces or powers, and to make this absence last, they need a populace's apathy, which is wilfully produced as well.

[39] The report is available at www.globalwitness.org/en/campaigns/conflict-minerals/river-of-gold-drc.

[40] See UNICEF, 'Humanitarian Action for Children 2019', available at reliefweb.int/sites/reliefweb.int/files/resources/Humanitarian-action-for-children-2019-eng.pdf. As for the situation in 2019, see 'Democratic Republic of the Congo: violence in Tanganyika and South Kivu fuels one of the world's worst displacement crises for children – UNICEF', available at reliefweb.int/report/democratic-republic-congo/democratic-republic-congo-violence-tanganyika-and-south-kivu-fuels.

[41] See 'How Many Have Died Due to Congo's Fighting? Scientists Battle Over How to Estimate War-Related Deaths' (21 January 2010) *Science*, available at www.sciencemag.org/news/2010/01/how-many-have-died-due-congos-fighting-scientists-battle-over-how-estimate-war-related. Estimates vary from 1,000,000 to 5,000,000 deaths for the period 1998–2003. Members of dozens of militia groups raped a number of women that has never been measured correctly.

To make the absence last, the dismantling of the practical functioning of courts comes in handy. One of the horrors palpable in the situation in the Eastern Congo, and in almost all cases of unregulated and relentless warfare, is that people have been so hurt and damaged that they no longer can care about anything except bare survival.

Apathy was countered formally, in the case of Rau's tribunal, by a performance that captured the theatricality of a court. There is a sharp distinction between the distancing power of theatre and the emotionless distance of apathy. In fact, the distancing power of the theatre might precisely be what is needed to counter apathy because it instigates conscious reflection. In the absence of the rule and practice of law, the Congo Tribunal showed how both law and justice are still possible through, or can be made sensible by, art. This is a different form of creation of law than the one of which Cover spoke. It is the creation of law that does not stem from a strong norm-world, a *nomos*, but from a strongly felt necessity or desire for a space of speech where the execution of law can take place. This site does not form a narrative, but physically hosts one, as a protected theatrical space in which a judge can intervene and place a verdict. It is a space that allows for a *mise en scène*, in turn opening up the possibility of a court by means of which law acquires the ability to act and speak. This in turn hints at law's grounding in theatricality.

IV. Theatre and Drama: *Dunamis* and the Judicial Mise-en-scène

Law is theatrical firstly, because, as French legal historian Pierre Legendre argued, language is theatrical. The fact that law is a matter of language is not an issue of dispute in this case – the issue as to why language should be *theatrical* in nature, is. As Legendre argues, language is not just a matter of communication, nor is it a tool that people can use at will. Human subjectivity is made through language and human beings appear to themselves and to others via language.[42] Everybody's so-called 'own' name is a good case in point, and one that is crucial to the law. One's name is not chosen but given, and as such will last a lifetime. The family name implies lineage, also crucial to the law. So, if it seems we *coincide* with our given name and family name, this is only a matter of something having become natural that is in fact distinctly artificial. Human beings do not conflate with themselves, that is, but always stand at a distance from themselves through language. It is this theatrical and symbolical distance to themselves, and the collective nature of it, that defines order.[43]

[42] Pierre Legendre, *Leçons X. Dogma. Instituer l'animal humain: Chemins réitérés de questionnement* (Paris, Fayard, 2017).

[43] Legendre's argument, much inspired by psychoanalysis, is comparable to the more anthropological take of Roberto Esposito, *Communitas: The Origin and Destiny of Community*, trans Timothy Campbell (Stanford, CA, Stanford University Press, 2010).

Secondly, from a certain historical moment onwards, the law comes to be enacted in the format of a theatrical dispositive.[44] As long as the judge is a mediator, she will simply split and bind the two parties in conflict. But from a certain point onwards court trials come to be staged – consequently, they require a proper stage. On that stage people enact certain recognisable roles according to distinct rituals.[45] Their dress will indicate what role they play.[46] Similar to a theatre play, a court case has several consecutive acts. There is drama involved, of people acting with one another, without their knowing the outcome of what they enact. Finally, and perhaps most basically: there will be an audience, that as such is only *pars pro toto* of the general public. This is not just a formal matter. The theatrical nature of the law is evidenced by the famous statement of Lord Chief Justice Hewart in 1924 'that justice should not only be done, but should manifestly and undoubtedly be seen to be done'. It is through its theatrical enactment that the law is not only able to work, but can also be seen to be working. This is a pivotal aspect of its legitimacy.

Thirdly, there are theatrical concepts that are at the basis of pivotal legal concepts. The very idea of a legal person is derived from Latin *persona* – the mask used by an actor. As the term may make clear one is not someone before the law as a natural being but as a being that has become a *person* because one is given a legal mask, by some sort of authority, as a result of which one is allowed to play a citizen's role and have a voice (and more on this in chapter five).[47]

Fourthly, it is often through theatrical means that people come to understand how the system of law functions on a practical level. A good case in point, and one example of training programmes in general, is the project Theatre of Law that The Royal Courts of Justice in London use for introducing young people to the legal system and issues of justice.[48] Students may come to act out the many different roles that appear in different cases in this project and as a result operate no longer as a uniformed and perhaps indifferent audience but as a well-informed, committed audience. One could argue that this form of theatre has been operative from antiquity onwards. It is through theatre plays that people have come to understand principal issues and procedures of justice. Consequently, the pedagogical power of theatrical enactment was central to the work of playwright and theatre maker Bertolt Brecht. This is evident in his distinction between major and minor pedagogy, and his alignment with the ideas on pedagogy of Paulo Freire and the

[44] For the European beginnings, see Sophia Papaioannou, Andreas Serafim and Beatrice da Vela (eds), *The Theatre of Justice: Aspects of Performance in Greco-Roman Oratory and Rhetoric* (Leiden, Brill, 2017).

[45] For all the theatrical requirements, see Goodrich, *Legal Emblems* (2014).

[46] Gary Watt, *Dress, Law and Naked Truth: A Cultural Study of Fashion and Form* (Oxford, Bloomsbury, 2013).

[47] On this see Hannah Arendt, *On Revolution* (New York, The Viking Press, 1963), or more recently, Edward Mussawir, 'The "method of dramatization" in the "law of persons"' in *Jurisdiction in Deleuze: The Expression and Representation of Law* (London, Routledge, 2011) 22–37.

[48] On this see National Justice Museum: www.nationaljusticemuseum.org.uk/education/educational-visits-london/london-theatre-law-key-stage-2.

theatrical performances under the name of Theatre of the Oppressed by Augusto Boal, who developed a specific kind of 'legislative theatre'.[49]

Fifthly and finally, theatricality implies an action that has an impact on an audience, both the audience present at the performance and the larger audience. In relation to this, the terms theatre and drama have often been confused. One such paradigmatic example of confusion in the field of law and literature is Richard Posner, who states:

> And while the legal trial may have a dramatic structure, and some celebrated trials may have performed a cathartic role comparable to what Aristotle assigned to tragedy, the essential spirit of law is not dramatic. Law's aim is to mediate, often to diffuse, but rarely if ever to aggravate, conflict. Most statutes represent compromises, and the vast majority of legal disputes are settled out of court.[50]

Practically speaking, Posner makes sense here: he is describing practices that have become dominant, namely all sorts of forms of mediation (on the dangers of which, more in chapter four). If most legal cases are now settled outside of court, and by implication outside of any form of public eye, this is decidedly non-theatrical: nothing is shown. Such cases may still be dramatic, but they do not entail an impact on an audience. Yet when a tragedy has a cathartic role, this is due to the fact that a drama develops in its being shown to an audience. It is in their being theatrically shown that legal cases do exactly the opposite of what Posner describes here. They may or will split audiences, not in order to aggravate conflict, but to do justice to the pain of conflict. This is what is at the heart of societal annoyance. Division marks the annoyance produced by the productive meeting between them. This was also Boal's point.

In terms of the theatrical impact on an audience, a distinction needs to be made between the theatrical impact of law on a society and the theatricality of courts themselves. The former was explored especially by Dutch legal scholar Willem Witteveen. His dissertation *Rhetoric in the Law: On Rhetoric and Interpretation, Constitutional Law and Democracy*[51] focuses on the persuasive power of language and its public and dramatic realisation. The latter would only gain in importance in later studies, such as *The Theatre of Politics: Public Rhetoric and the Passport Affair*.[52] In *The Imaginary State: Performances of Democratic Innovation* the

[49] Bertolt Brecht, *Brecht on Theater: The Development of an Aesthetic* (New York, Hill and Wang, 1964); Paulo Freire, *Pedagogy of Hope: Reliving Pedagogy of the Oppressed* (Lanham, Rowman & Littlefield Publishers, 2001), or *Education For Critical Consciousness* (London, Continuum International Publishing Group, 2005) and on the basis of Freire's work the 'Theatre of the oppressed': Augusto Boal, *Legislative Theatre: Using Performance to Make Politics* (London, Routledge, 1998).

[50] Richard Posner, *Law and Literature: A Misunderstood Relation* (Cambridge MA, Harvard University Press, 1998) 23.

[51] Witteveen, *De retoriek in het recht: over retorica en interpretatie, staatsrecht en democratie* (Zwolle, Tjeenk Willink, 1988).

[52] Witteveen, *Het theater van de politiek: publieke retorica en de paspoortaffaire* (Amsterdam, Amber, 1992).

political order was not only depicted as a director, but the theatrical way by means of which politics truly become politically active was key, namely in the hands of public action and public responsibility.[53] Here, Witteveen's argument was deeply influenced by Hannah Arendt, for whom theatrical impact was also key in politics and law. In *The Law as Work of Art: An Alternative Philosophy of Law*, Witteveen accordingly saw politics as a performance that was judged by 'the court of public opinion'.[54] And the latter study ends with a four-act play in which legal philosophers are portrayed as *dramatis personae*. Theatre, then, is used as a metaphor or a model. Witteveen, focusing on the theatricality of the political world in its relation to legal order, was less concerned with the theatrical nature of jurisdiction itself and more with the order of the law that depends on its public and collective reception.

In terms of the logic of genres, it is of relevance to note that Witteveen redefined the narrative nature of the law in depicting the jurist as a dramatic character, or actor.[55] The jurist was not a passive reader or only an interpreter, but an interactive entity that assisted in realising a collective story. Witteveen's four-act drama from *The Law as Work of Art* is helpful in understanding the nature of this story. This study ends with a monologue by legal philosopher Lon Fuller,[56] who argues that the metaphor of the law as work of art should be understood as work in progress; as an ongoing construction. By choosing the form of the drama, Witteveen implicitly made clear that the ongoing construction of law as a comprehensible narrative was dramatic in the sense that it should be understood as a string of actions with an unknown outcome.

The etymology of drama is rooted in the Greek verb *dran*, which means 'to act'. Drama thus concerns the development of acts and conflicts between actors. This development does not necessarily demand an audience; drama can take place behind closed doors. Theatre, on the other hand, stems from *theasthai*, or 'to behold', and is an issue of showing and seeing. In other words, theatre is about effects. Theatre is one paradigmatic interface, as a consequence, and drama another. Theatrically speaking, what is at stake is the construction of a scene that facilitates the relation between what is acted out and what is shown to and seen by an audience. Dramatically speaking, what is at stake is the realisation of a sequence of

[53] Witteveen, *De denkbeeldige staat: voorstellingen van democratische vernieuwing* (Amsterdam, Amsterdam University Press, 2000) 55, 74.

[54] Witteveen, *De wet als kunstwerk: Een andere filosofie van het recht* (Amsterdam, Boom, 2014). In the original: 'de rechtbank van de publieke opinie' (95).

[55] Witteveen's inaugural lecture was entitled *Balance of powers*, or: *Evenwicht van machten* (Zwolle, WEJ Tjeenk Willink, 1991). The reference to the jurist as an actor also explicitly recurs in *The ordered world of law: An introduction*, or: De *geordende wereld van het recht: Een inleiding* (Amsterdam, Amsterdam University Press, 2003) 288.

[56] Witteveen published a collection on Fuller's work: Witteveen and Wibren van der Burg (eds), *Rediscovering Fuller: Essays on Implicit Law and Institutional Design* (Amsterdam, Amsterdam University Press, 1999).

actions that facilitates the relation between what actors seemed to be and appeared to be in hindsight. In this context, Aristotelian drama was predominantly considered, unfortunately, a form of *plot*: actions and events that led to an inevitable end.[57] However, plot is a *narrative* construct. It concerns the way in which actions and conflicts are maneuvered as an understandable history with an outcome.

In our case, Milo Rau's tribunal was dramatic because of the very fact that it took place in the Congo and because of the events it enacted. The tribunal was dramatic in the sense that we did not know in advance how its dramatic interventions might perhaps contribute to a better functioning of the system of law or what the outcome of the acts performed would be.[58] Formally, it was theatrical because of its structure – the *mise en scène* – and because of the fact that it was publicly shown in a space that was theatrically turned into a court. Rau created a public space for speech and action that made jurisdiction *possible*. In this context a counterpart to the earlier mentioned *nomos* would be *dunamis*: the *ability* to act or speak. A specific *mise en scène* embodies the formal, basic organisation of jurisdiction from which its *dunamis* stems. A distinct fear of law is the fear to lose this space in the shape of courts and the power they embody. One specific desire from the realm of justice is that such a space exists at the very least. Apathy threatens both.

To counter apathy neither narrative nor drama suffice. Narrative implies an active logico-chronological framing of any dialogue and drama demands agency first and foremost. In both cases this is impossible in the state of apathy. To counter apathy we need theatre, because it embodies the potential of a space that facilitates and guarantees the ability to be silent – or to speak.

V. The Care for Law: *Jurisannihilatio* and *Juriscaritas*

The exhibition of The Congo Tribunal, organised in Stroom in the city of The Hague (Spring 2017), had as its subtitle: 'Where politics fail, only art can help' [*sic*] and was accompanied by the following statement by the maker:

> And with all the horrors shown in the film, it is important to me not to lose sight of hope. If The Congo Tribunal has proved one thing, it is that the truth can be found, no matter how complicated the connections are. And justice is possible, here and now. We just have to establish it.[59] [*sic*]

[57] Bertolt Brecht rejected drama precisely because it took the audience into a narrative and blocked critical reflection. See Brecht, *Brecht on Theater*, or Walter Benjamin, 'What is Epic Theater?' in *Understanding Brecht* (London, Verso, 2003).

[58] In the Dutch context the dramatic interruptions of law in society was central in a study entitled *Law and drama*: Hans Nieuwenhuis, Jan HA Lokin, Corjo Jansen, and Antoine Hol (eds), *Recht en drama* (Den Haag, Boom, 2014). This study did not explore the theatrical or dramatic nature of the law per se, but the dramatic development of the law through its intervention in society.

[59] See Stroom: www.stroom.nl/activiteiten/tentoonstelling.php?t_id=1018831.

The apathy produced in the Congolese populace is hinted at by the emphatically expressed desire 'not to lose sight of hope'. Indeed, if the desperate situation and feeling of apathy can be defined in one way it is not so much by the loss of hope (which may be temporary), but by the loss of any sight of hope. That being said, the simplicity of the statements that follow in the quote above would make any jurist smile: truth cannot simply be found, nor is making right and righteousness possible in the here and now merely a matter of realising justice. Any kind of superior smiles, however, are those that originate from the safe position of an established or functioning constitutional state, congruent with a functioning rule of law. In the Eastern Congo, people of flesh and blood longed for or thirsted for a form of right and righteousness, of justice, and they happened to find it through a work of art. That is to say: although right and righteousness were fundamentally absent, they were both still made palpable in a public scene, theatrically. This is a formal issue with crucial implications, especially in the fight against apathy.

Of the three generic forms that characterise literary texts – the narrative, the lyrical and the theatrical – the last form is of elementary importance for the structure and practice of jurisdiction. Narrative may play a part on several levels, for example in the reconstruction of the case, or in the explanation of the judge, but it does not constitute the situation of jurisdiction. The lyrical also has its place, for example in the sense that the law is constantly evoked or called upon by means of apostrophe. However, this still happens *within* the given theatrical situation. Theatre is what *constitutes* the situation that makes the legal procedure possible. This is due to the spatial organisation, but also due to the parts that are played out, the presence of an audience and the development of a sequence of actions in different phases. In this context perhaps the most important difference between narrative and lyrical speech on the one hand and the theatrical on the other is that only in the final situation a third party – a judge – can come in-between, as both a separate and separating agent.

Regarding the formal possibilities of this simultaneously separating and mediating agent, theatre historically precedes the legal and public enactment of law. The basic form of jurisdiction was developed in Athens centuries before Sophocles added a third actor or speaker to what had up until that point been a drama acted out by two alternating speakers. While actors could take on multiple roles, there were never more than two figures on the stage interacting with the chorus. With Sophocles, there could be three figures on stage. Formally, this meant that a third actor could not only listen, but also *intervene* in the action. This possibility was only partially realised in the basic form of jurisdiction as it existed in Athens since Draco's reforms from the seventh century BC. The formal structure of jurisdiction was a dual one: the accused had to defend himself before a public jury of deputies (varying from several dozen to hundreds), who then also passed a judgement.

This judicial situation formally resembles the first kind of theatre in Athens, where the chorus interacted with a character. This situation already became more complex when two characters entered the stage. The chorus could intervene formally, in that case, from a position *outside* the (world of) action. In other words: the chorus could comment but not intervene. With Sophocles, the intervention could occur by way of a character *within* the world of the action. A logical consequence was that the chorus leader could take part in the action, by intervening, as happens in Sophocles' *Antigone*, for example. Formally speaking, theatre laid the basis for a legal situation in which accuser and accused meet publicly before a judge: the third actor who does not comment from the outside, but intervenes.

When we talk about the creation of the law in both a historical and formal sense, theatricality is thus key. Firstly, the procedure is acted out in front of audiences that can judge the case for themselves, as it is presented in public. Secondly, the procedure is structured as a division of parties, with the crux of the matter being that the two not only battle each other (enough reason for drama) but that a third party can intervene to pass a judgement. When viewed this way, the law is formally 'complete'; it has found its solid, theatrical form in the form of a court with its procedures. Due to this solidity and its classical origins, the jurist, critic and theatre-maker Klaas Tindemans could view the theatricality of law as an archaic phenomenon.[60] The concrete cases that appear in front of a judge are a kind of reproduction that may still contribute substantially to the making of the law, but not so procedurally. All secondary rules are fixed and stable, contributing to the coercive force of courts.

Regarding this coercive power, Tindemans traces an important difference between the theatricality of law and drama in theatre. He argues:

> Theatre as artistic genre may be fascinated by the law because the juridical happening – a fortiori in its most theatrical appearances, such as lay-jurisdiction or an interrogation – is never optional, as opposed to dramatic art. The law *has* to change lives, theatre can only wish to do so. The law even has entities, such as bailiffs and prisons, that are meant to execute, guide or force the imposed changes in the lives of the involved. The theatre simply sends the audience away after the performance.[61]

These statements cannot simply be overlooked in relation to Milo Rau's tribunal in Eastern Congo. The question raised by Rau's project is: if a country finds itself in a situation in which secondary rules are not operative, if the rule of law has become optional, can theatre then reinvigorate the procedural creation of the law? As the Congo Tribunal attests, and urgently so, the theatrical form of jurisdiction may be fixed, but is not archaic. On the contrary, both the creation of law and the care for law depend on a perseverant care for a theatrical space of jurisdiction.

[60] Klaas Tindemans, 'De theatraliteit van het recht' (2017) 150 *Etcetera*, available at e-tcetera.be/de-theatraliteit-van-het-recht; in the original it says: '*archaïsch fenomeen*', 39.

[61] Tindemans, 'De theatraliteit van het recht' (2017) 39; in the original: 'Misschien is het theater als artistiek genre wel gefascineerd door het recht omdat het juridisch gebeuren – a fortiori in zijn meest theatrale verschijningsvormen, zoals lekenrechtspraak of een kruisverhoor – nooit vrijblijvend is, in tegenstelling tot de dramatische kunst. Het recht móet levens veranderen, het theater kan dat hooguit wensen. Het recht heeft zelfs instanties zoals deurwaarders en gevangenissen die de opgelegde veranderingen in het leven van de betrokkenen moeten opvolgen, bijsturen of forceren. Het theater zendt de toeschouwers na de voorstelling gewoon weg'.

In the context of situations such as the one in the Eastern Congo, and in relation to Rau's staged tribunal, I suggest we should complement Cover's statement quoted earlier by giving law's logic of fear its partner in dialogue, namely justice's logic of desire. This would be the result:

> It is peculiar that in everyday practice, the origins and justification of jurisdiction always have to be understood from the need and desire for justice. If lawlessness reigns or only the power of the strongest, or if any form of right has become arbitrary, then a basic call for the instalment of law is heard. It is the absence of laws, the wilderness of a *jurisannihilative* perspective, that creates the problem to which jurisdiction is the solution.

Opposite to Cover's *jurisgenesis*, the meaningful creation of law, we now add the dramatic *jurisannihilatio*, when law is made meaningless. The *jurispathic*, or law's fear for other laws, can consequently be complemented by a *juriscaritas*: the care or love for law, whether these be laws that are officially acknowledged by some sort of state or imperial community, or laws that originate in paideic communities. Courts are the theatrical spaces in which all four of these perspectives meet. The court is a theatrical space called to life by a desire for justice. As such, it is a space that needs to be maintained dramatically by people's care for law. This care is a persistent attempt to maintain law's meaningfulness.

New meaningful laws can be made in such courts though courts are also called to life on the basis of law's logic of fear. They testify to the defence mechanism of imperial laws against other laws and want to produce a collective fear of, and for, the one and only law as a consequence. Law's logic of fear is very much connected, here, to law's aspect of closure, whereas the logic of desire is very much connected to justice's wish to open up things. The two are intrinsically connected to two forms of drama that again have their own respective logics: tragedy and comedy. These are central to the next chapter.

3

Logic of Tragedy vs Logic of Comedy

Elfriede Jelinek's Ulrike Maria Stuart *and* Princess-dramas: Death and the Maiden

> 'Reviewing the literature on love I noticed how few writers, male or female, talk about the impact of patriarchy, the way in which male domination of women and children stands in the ways of love.
>
> ...
>
> There can be no love without justice. Until we live in a culture that not only respects but also upholds basic civil rights for children, most children will not know love. In our culture the private family dwelling is the one institutionalized sphere of power that can easily be autocratic and fascistic.'
>
> bell hooks, *All about love: New visions*[1]

I. Open or Closed: Tragedy, Comedy, Impasse

Whereas in the previous chapter the rule of law was missing and the question was how art can be the interface between two spheres if one of the two is missing, this chapter considers works of art that appear to mirror the very problem of this missing rule of law itself. In the work of Austrian author Elfriede Jelinek, systems of law are very much operative, yet their relations with realms of justice are filled with frictions. The issue is what happens if the realm of justice is unjust and art as an interface cannot offer a door, or a gateway from the side of the system of law to offer the possibility of justice. Then we find ourselves in an impasse. This issue is worked out in a play entitled *Ulrike Maria Stuart* and a series of dramas entitled *Der Tod und das Mädchen: Fünf Prinzessinnendramen* (*Princess-dramas: Death and the Maiden*).[2] These works do not so much describe an impasse, but

[1] bell hooks, *All About Love, New Visions* (New York, Harper Perennial, 2001) xxiv and 19.

[2] The *Princess-dramas* were first performed in 2002 and published in 2004; *Ulrike Maria Stuart* was first performed in 2006 and published in 2015.

rather perform an impasse, also in that they defy interpretation. They are clear examples of what Hans-Thies Lehmann coined 'post-dramatic theatre'.[3] With the term, Lehman indicates that familiar forms of dramatic theatre, driven by plot and mainly meant for passive consumption have been giving way to forms of drama that focus on processes of making meaning and demand a participatory audience. Such pieces do not so much provoke audiences or readers to make sense of them, but rather to engage with them, which might mean entering into, or feeling, the impasse. So, for anyone trained or used to reading plays by William Shakespeare, Nadine Gordimer or Derek Walcott, Jelinek's plays will be a confrontation. This does not mean her plays cherish the impasse they perform. The troubling issue the plays struggle with is how, for those suffering under the combined pressure of legal and symbolic weight, things can be opened up. To this order these plays use the friction between two major genres to create tension. These two genres also define the specific logics of the system of law and the realm of justice respectively: tragedy and comedy.

The tension between the two genres and logics is apparent in *Ulrike Maria Stuart*. The play's title immediately indicates that two historical characters, both dealt with by law, are fused: sixteenth-century Mary, Queen of Scots, and twentieth-century political activist Ulrike Meinhof. Jelinek's title straightforwardly alludes to a tragedy written by the eighteenth-century German author Friedrich Schiller (1759–1805), *Maria Stuart: Ein Trauerspiel*, or *Mary Stuart: A Tragedy*. Still, despite the explicit allusion to the eighteenth-century tragedy, Jelinek deals with tragedy by attuning it to its opposing genre, comedy. Her instructions make this clear: the characters should be worked out 'in a horrifying way, but also comical, to the point of being grotesque'.[4] This does not mean this is a tragicomedy, for that would alleviate the friction between the two genres. Such friction was still productive, as is attested to in classical antiquity and well into the Early Modern period, when programmes would always present tragedies and comedies together.[5] One reason for this may have been that this combination created an affective balance. Another reason may have been that the two genres are in friction with one another in asking a pivotal what-if question in opposite ways: tragedy deals with what has happened and can no longer be reversed, whilst comedy contrives to address what could happen and can be opened up. If the two are performed in one programme, the closure of histories and their possible opening are equally

[3] Hans-Thies Lehman, *Postdramatic Theatre*, trans Karen Jürs-Munby (London, Taylor and Francis, 2016).

[4] Elfride Jelinek, *Das schweigende Mädchen / Ulrike Maria Stuart: Zwei Theaterstücke* (Hamburg, Rohwolt, 2015) 9, in the original: 'auf erschreckende Weise, aber auch komisch, bis ins Groteske hinein'.

[5] On this see Martin Revermann (ed), *A Cultural History of Theatre in Antiquity*, Vol 1 (London, Bloomsbury, 2017). For the historical developments, see Betine van Zyl Smit (ed), *A Handbook to the Reception of Greek Drama* (Chicester, Wiley Blackwell, 2016). For the Early Modern period, see Martin White, *Renaissance Drama in Action: An Introduction to Aspects of Theatre Practice and Performance* (London, Routledge, 1998).

considered. By combining tragedy with comedy, Jelinek condenses this dynamic, both acknowledging and refusing the tragic closure of things.

If there are strong feelings involved in relation to issues of law and justice, these manifest themselves in a pronounced way when a case is closed or opened. Many will eagerly await the opening of a case, or long for the possibility that a case is brought to court. Others may fear precisely this. The closing of a case may lead to feelings of satisfaction and relief but also to feelings of bitterness and indignation. Legally speaking, people may understand and accept that a case needs to be closed, though still experience feelings of injustice when this happens. In terms of justice, people may suffer when a case succeeds in avoiding legal judgment. One could argue that feelings are more intrinsically part of the realm of justice, here, as they index personal indignations and attitudes in relation to what people feel to be just or unjust. Such an argument implies that feelings are not intrinsic to law. However, this chapter suggests otherwise. It contributes to a growing number of studies that deal with the role of emotions, passions and affect in relation to any system of law.[6] This could be a reason for joy, since it suggests that law is not just instrumental and cold, a characterisation that has most eminently been criticised by media scholar Greta Olson (see chapter one). As the term 'impasse' suggests, it might also be the case that affects operative in the system of law make it impossible to offer an alternative of justice to an unjust situation.

The system of law is defined in this chapter by the logic of tragedy and the realm of justice by the logic of comedy. These genres are not just formally defined. Both dramatic genres are deeply affectively charged because they deal with issues of closing down and opening up paradigmatically. In terms of reasonability, moreover, the two genres resemble one another in that both are investigative, and explore the status and limits of the real. Tragedy investigates the status of the real while nevertheless affirming that status. Comedy plays with the real in a provocative manner, which may disturb many, whilst for others this may offer a liberating alternative. Note that in defining the two thus, my definitions of 'tragedy' and 'comedy' differ from that of Hayden White in his famous study of the basic forms of emplotment in the writing of history.[7] To White tragedy is a form of historiography in which

[6] A concise summary of the debates and developments in this field is Robin West, 'Law's Emotions' in MNS Sellers (ed), *Law, Reason, and Emotion* (Cambridge, Cambridge University Press, 2017). According to West, scholars do not look enough 'at the emotions that both law and legalism produce, rather than the emotions that impact law, or that are censured, denigrated or regulated by it' 34. Yet one important moment in the field was Susan A Bandes (ed), *The Passions of Law* (New York, New York University Press, 2001). Recently studies involve Julia A Shaw, *Law and the Passions: Why Emotions Matter for Justice* (New York, Routledge, 2019); Heather Conway and John Stannard (eds), *The Emotional Dynamics of Law and Legal Discourse* (Oxford, Hart Publishing, 2016); or Greta Olson, 'The Turn to Passion: Has Law and Literature become Law and Affect?' (2016) 28 *Law and Literature* 335. In the context of legal education, Emma Jones emphasised the role of emotions in legal thinking and education, with *Emotions in the Law School: Transforming Legal Education Through the Passions* (London, Routledge, 2019).

[7] Hayden White, *Metahistory: The Historical Imagination in Nineteenth-Century Europe* (Baltimore, Johns Hopkins University, 1975).

the values of parties clash and prove to be irreconcilable. Comedy, for White, is a mode of writing in which a world is saved from disruption and its good order is celebrated.

I do not dispute White's position (or that of his source of inspiration, Northrop Frye), but rather choose to take seriously that the term 'comedy' is an indication of both the *comic(al)* and *comedic*.[8] The comedic can, but need not involve laughter, as Dante's *Divina Commedia* demonstrates (just as Nietzsche's *Gay Science* need not be much fun). Dante's comedy does offer an alternative order, though: man is not necessarily the tragic victim of the Fall; there is an escape. Yet plays by the French playwright Molière are not so much comedic as comical. His comedies did and do make people laugh and are far from a celebration of a world in good order. His piece *Don Juan* caused outrage because, to an orthodox religious audience, it seemed to open up the possibility of libertarianism. As for tragedy, what White identifies as the meeting of irreconcilable forces does occur, but this irreconcilability is not left unresolved. The tragedy of the genre lies instead in the elimination of alternatives. For instance, the tragedy with regard to the Catholic Scottish Queen, Mary Stuart, was not that her world proved to be irreconcilable with that of the Protestant English Queen, Elizabeth. The tragedy was that Mary was executed. Tragedy is the genre of closure.

An example of comedy's opening potential would be a play by Aristophanes (446–386 BC): *Bátrachoi* or *The Frogs*. It was performed in 405 BC, a time in which the utterly destructive and decades-long Peloponnesian wars had exhausted Athens. This in itself is telling: the comedy offered an opening during a situation of exhaustion, acting as a form of comic relief. Its comedic character did not depend solely on laughter, however. It may be amusing that one of the choruses consists of frogs, but the comedic aspect featured exists in the fact that comedy need not restrict itself to the limits of the real. The play's plot shows as much for it aimed at opening up history by calling back to life the deceased playwright Euripides, who had died a year prior to the performance. Instead, however, the much older playwright Aeschylos is brought back to life, through which the play uses both the aspect of the unexpected and that of mistaken identity in order to open up possibilities. In all cases the pivotal point is that comedy asks the what-if question by suspending the order of the real, or by means of a discrepancy. Comedy allows for the possibility that people can be brought back to life, that history starts anew, or that those who have no say in a given order get a presence and a voice. In an earlier play by Aristophanes, *Lysistrátē* or *Army Disbander* (411 BC), for instance, women are the main protagonists, even though in classical Greek society women were not supposed to act or speak in public.[9] The female characters act politically

[8] On this distinction see Frans-Willem Korsten, 'The Comedic Sublime in a Dynamic of Worlds: the Work of Frans Hals in a Dutch Baroque' (2016) 2 *Journal of Historians of Netherlandish Art* 8, available at doi.org/10.5092/jhna.2016.8.2.7.

[9] It is not surprising that *Lysistrátē* was taken up by contemporary feminists, as in the version of Germaine Greer and Phil Wilmot in 1999 under the title *The Sex Strike*. The play also inspired calls for

in this play by making the private very public: they openly declare that they will go on a sex strike to stop men from making war.

In contrast, tragedy poses the what-if question by taking the demands of representation within the order of the real as an unquestionable limit, whilst concurrently asking whether the occurrences that happened could not, or should not, have gone differently. A case in point is Schiller's *Maria Stuart*. The play's plot deals with the short period before the moment that the protagonist, the sixteenth-century historical figure of Mary, Queen of Scots, is executed. As a tragedy the play asks: should and could this not have gone differently? The answer is, as always, that perhaps it could have, but it did not, for the limits of the possible are the limits of a given order. Nevertheless, limits are tested when Schiller's play makes the two queens meet who historically never did: Mary and the English Queen, Elizabeth I.[10] Schiller was consequently accused of anachronism.[11] Yet the play did not go so far as to annul the execution. It was precisely because this was a tragedy that the reproach of anachronism could even be made. For comedy such a reproach would have been nonsensical.

Law sides with the tragic because law cannot and should not think or act beyond the limits of the possible and will always respond to the demands of representation in the context of the order that is given. Its working within the limits of the possible is functional with regards to how law either preserves or controls forces in relation to existing orders and authorities. From the side of justice, however, this strength of law is also a pitfall. It may hinder law's ability to act ethically, or it may block the actualisation of something new, an alternative. This has considerable consequences for the *Rechtsgefühle* of subjects, in what they feel not only to be legally but also ethically just, or what they feel to be possible or impossible. The element of change is central, and at stake, then, in these genres. In her study on comedy, Alenka Zupančič defined it as follows: 'Through different plots and situations, comedy is thus also a practice demonstrating that the Other (as the presupposition of sense) is no ideal or eternal and unchangeable in its form'.[12]

If Jelinek's *Ulrike Maria Stuart* is a paradigmatic example of the friction between tragedy and comedy, one reason is that the play radicalised Schiller's anachronism.[13] As art historian and philosopher Kathy Jo Saranpa argued,

societal sex strikes; on this see Stephanie McCarter, 'The Original "Sex Strike" Was a Farce and This One Is Too: A Classics scholar on the pitfalls – and potential – of basing your activism on "Lysistrata"' *Electric Literature*, available at electricliterature.com/the-original-sex-strike-was-a-farce-and-this-one-is-too.

[10] The two never met; or there are no records of such meeting, though they did exchange many letters. See, for example: Jane Dunn, *Elizabeth and Mary: Cousins, Rivals, Queens* (New York, Alfred A Knopf, 2004).

[11] On this see, for instance, Michael G Paulson, *The Queens' Encounter. The Mary Stuart Anachronism in Dramas by Diamante, Boursault, Schiller and Donizetti* (Berlin, Peter Lang, 1987).

[12] Alenka Zupančič, *The Odd One In: On Comedy* (Cambridge MA, MIT Press, 2008) 93.

[13] The performance was staged by Nicolas Stemann and concerned the first production of the play. On this, see Ortrud Gutjahr, 'Köniniginnestreit: Eine Annäherung an Elfriede Jelinieks Ulrike Maria Stuart und ein Blick auf Friedrich Schillers Maria Stuart' in Ortrud Gutjahr (ed), *Ulrike Maria Stuart; von Elfriede Jelinek: Uraffführung am Thalia Theater Hamburg in der Inszenierung von Nicolas Stemann* (Würzburg, Köningshausen & Neuman, 2007). The piece only appeared in print later, together with *Das Schweigende Mädchen* (Hamburg, Rohwolt Verlag, 2015).

Schiller's anachronism should be considered as a *counterlife*; the speculation of what could have happened that runs counter to what really happened.[14] In this context, she stated:

> Schiller's continued interest in revolutionaries and other usurpers can be seen in this light. His interest with the 'flashpoints' of history, the changing of systems and the distribution of power, must indicate an awareness of alternate possibilities [...] an ability to step outside of the limits of the possible.[15]

Yet this stepping 'outside of the limits of the possible' plays out differently in tragedy and comedy. Tragedy brings us to the moments during which a protagonist is confronted with the consequences of a step outside of an existing order, like Antigone. Comedy, in contrast, achieves moments at which we experience things happening differently. Schiller's anachronism was formally comedic, then, but caught within a tragic frame. Despite the potential of an opening up, the execution had to take place, not so much unquestionably but inevitably. Jelinek, in turn, radicalises Schiller's anachronism by fusing two historical actors: sixteenth-century Mary Stuart, and twentieth-century Ulrike Meinhof, a key figure in the German *Rote Armee Fraktion*. The two are both historically and spatially distinct, and symbolise radically different lives and political positions. Nevertheless, they find themselves as one in Jelinek's title and play. The effect of this anachronistic, preposterous or neo-baroque confusion is comedic.[16] That being said, the play is also tragic in showing how both characters were and are unable to escape the limits of the given order. That is the impasse.

The logics of tragedy and comedy have a disruptive counterpart in yet another genre: mystery. The latter's disruptive force consists in the fact that it short-circuits any questioning or investigation, as it presupposes an unquestionable authority. Mystery neither affirms, reflects, disturbs nor suspends. In between the fatedness of tragedy and the playfulness of comedy, the mysterious hovers between the absurd and the absolute. Of course, thinkers like Carl Schmitt and Jacques Derrida, albeit for different reasons, argued that mystery is at the basis of law.[17] Yet they confused

[14] Counterlife is a concept coined by Michael André Bernstein, *Foregone Conclusions: Against Apocalyptic History* (Berkeley, University of California Press, 1994).

[15] Kathy Jo Saranpa, *Schiller's Wallenstein, Maria Stuart, and Die Jungfrau Von Orleans: The Critical Legacy* (Rochester, Camden House, 2002) 139. Saranpa could also have involved David Lewis's ideas of 'possible worlds', with which Lewis indicated the independent existence of worlds that are either factual or counterfactual.

[16] In defining the bringing together of these characters as preposterous and neo-baroque, I take my cue from Mieke Bal, *Quoting Caravaggio: Contemporary Art, Preposterous History* (Chicago, Chicago University Press, 1999). As for the reception of *Ulrike Maria Stuart*, one article summarises the responses by quoting a review which suggested that the play was 'sehr lustig' (very funny), 'cool', 'spektakulär' (spectacular), 'amüsant statt brisant' (amusing rather than explosive)'; see Morgan Marcell Koerner, 'Beyond Media-Critique: Performance and Pop-Cultural Pleasures in Elfriede Jelinek and Frank Castorf's *Raststätte oder sie machens alle*' in Claude Desmarais (ed), *A Different Germany: Pop and the Negotiation of German Culture* (Newcastle, Cambridge Scholars Publishing, 2014) 121.

[17] Sergei Prozorov rightfully asks whether Derrida's deconstruction of Schmitt's theory of sovereignty 'contains anything that is not already present in Schmitt's work and whether the unravelling of these aporias is sufficient to somehow "debunk" Schmitt'. See Sergei Prozorov, *Foucault, Freedom and Sovereignty* (Abingdon, Ashgate, 2007) 87.

law with sovereignty, which is originally a theological concept, as they would willingly admit, and not an issue of law, but of power.[18] Or they confused order with the absolute, which is, historically speaking, nonsensical. Or, in taking refuge in mystery they scantly addressed its aspect of absurdity.[19] In terms of affect the genre of mystery produces awe and subjection, and these are of relevance to, and perhaps even necessary for, law. Yet, these affects are functional aspects, not fundamental ones. Most would not want to be in awe of, or subject themselves to, an unjust law. Let there be no misunderstanding: many did subject themselves as such, in the course of history. Yet they did so to their disadvantage. Or they were forced to exist under the power of mystery whilst resisting it. Jelinek's historical and literary characters prove the point. They also prove another point. Aside from what the systems of law did to them, were they allowed to fully live anyway, in what could have been realms of justice, but were not?

II. Culture-text and the Cohabitation of Symbolic Order and Law

In the title of Jelinek's play *Ulrike Maria Stuart*, the elision of one of the two's surnames cannot go unnoticed: Meinhof. Giving a subject a name is pivotal in two different kinds of order that are intrinsically connected, the legal and the symbolic one. Symbolically, a name places subjects in a lineage, like a family tree. Yet people are also born in legally defined territories, and alternatively may be placed through their parents and their blood as belonging to a state: the entity that legalises their name as a result of which they become legal subjects. If all this feels intuitively reasonable, as it has for centuries, it is due to the coalition between a symbolic and legal order. The symbolic one may connote particularity and affect whilst the legal one may connote universality and reason, yet the fusion of the two undermines such convenient oppositions. There is no *reason* to consider it reasonable that women are obliged by law to adopt the name of their husband, for instance,

[18] The connection between law and theology was pivotal in studies by Carl Schmitt, for instance in *Political Theology*, ed and trans George Schwab, foreword Tracy B Strong (Chicago, University of Chicago Press, 2006) and *Political Theology II: The Myth of the Closure of Any Political Theology*, trans Michael Hoelzl and Graham Ward (London, Polity, 2008). The same holds for Jacques Derrida, who was much inspired by the work of Emmanuel Levinas, here; for this see, Peter Goodrich and Michel Rosenfeld (eds), *Administering Interpretation: Derrida, Agamben, and the Political Theology of Law* (New York, Fordham University Press, 2019). On the theological confusion with regard to law and sovereignty, see Vincent Lloyd, 'Introduction' in Vincent Lloyd (ed), *Race and Political Theology* (Stanford CA, Stanford California Press, 2012); or Nehal Buta, 'The Mystery of the State: State Concept, State Theory and State Making in Schmitt and Oakshot' in David Dyzenhaus and Thomas Poole (eds), *Law, Liberty and State: Oakeshott, Hayek and Schmitt on the Rule of Law* (Cambridge, Cambridge University Press, 2015).

[19] One scholar who did take the absurdity of sovereignty as absolute power seriously, was Jens Bartelson, *The Critique of the State* (Cambridge, Cambridge University Press, 2001).

or that children by law have to take on their father's name. If this is conceived of as reasonable, it is because it *feels* reasonable; a feeling that is largely dependent on the symbolical order. This emotive component is the result of the cohabitation of any system of law with a symbolic order; an order that works by means of its own affective weight and that could potentially be a realm of justice, but need not be.

Previous to *Ulrike Maria Stuart*, Jelinek wrote the five *Princess-dramas* in which characters from different domains and genres come together, resonate with, or repeat one another. The fairy tale characters of Snow White, Sleeping Beauty and Rosamunde come to resonate with historical figures such as Jackie Kennedy and literary authors such as Sylvia Plath and Ingeborg Bachmann. The title of the pieces refers straightforwardly to a poem by Matthias Claudius written in 1774, that became famous due to Franz Schubert's 1817 composition 'Der Tod und das Mädchen', or 'Death and the Maiden'. Schubert would in 1824 reuse the title for one of the most famous string quartets in European history. Jelinek's sharing of this title is more than incidental. As her explicit reference suggests, the theme of the death of a girl or young woman is a cultural fascination, and a pattern that carries weight.

In the 1950s, for instance, French–Armenian singer and composer Charles Aznavour wrote, 'Une enfant' – 'A child', which was first performed by French iconic singer Édith Piaf. The song speaks of an adolescent girl who is seduced to leave her parents' home, only to then be found dead at the side of the road. It became a hit in England via Noel Harrison's version: 'A Young Girl (of 16)' and an iconic pop song in the Netherlands by way of singer Boudewijn de Groot in 1965.[20] The title would return in a play by Ariel Dorfman from 1990, in which a torturing doctor who raped his victim whilst listening to Schubert's music, meets the victim, with the roles now reversed. This, in turn, led to a movie by Roman Polanski in 1993. Apparently, it concerns what cultural analyst Maaike Meijer called a 'culture-text': a 'conglomerate of accepted, again and again recurring motives and modes of representation around a theme [...] that organises itself time and again in new cultural texts'.[21] This may also involve or affect historically real persons. At the end of her five pieces Jelinek explicitly mentions one. It concerns a young woman who was never allowed to have an independent life and became most famous for finding her death at the side of the road. In a postscript entitled 'The princess in the underworld (instead of an afterword)', Jelinek writes about the English princess Diana, who found her death at the side of the road in 1997, aged 36.

[20] The title of De Groot's song, translated by poet Lennaert Nijgh, was: 'A girl of sixteen'.

[21] In the original: 'conglomeraat van geaccepteerde, steeds weer terugkerende motieven en wijzen van representatie rond een thema [...] dat zich steeds weer organiseert in nieuwe culturele teksten', Maaike Meijer, *In tekst gevat: Inleiding tot een kritiek van representatie* (Amsterdam, Amsterdam Academic Archive, 2005) 33. This analysis is also key for Christina Kiebuzinska, 'Violence and Pornography in Elfriede Jelinek's "Princess Plays"' in Fatima Festic (ed), *Gender and Trauma: Interdisciplinary Dialogues* (Newcastle upon Tyne, Cambridge Scholars Publishing, 2012).

It would be foolish to consider all these examples in terms of singular cases, then, of women coincidentally struck by fate. It concerns a pattern or a type,[22] of a girl or a young woman who leaves the house and experiences what might happen to her as soon as she leaves the protection of the symbolic master. Retrospectively, Mary Stuart started getting lost once she had to leave her paternal home at age five to live in France. Having to flee the French house at age 16, she was then driven out of her own in Scotland by revolting noble men, and in England she was refused any home at all. Meinhof, in turn, figuratively and literally leapt out of a house. Dutch journalist Xandra Schutte summarised it as follows:

> On the 14th of June, Ulrike Meinhof did not just jump out of the window of that villa in Dahlem, she also jumped into illegality. On that day not only was Andreas Baader freed, it also saw the birth of the Rote Armee Fraktion.
>
> The question, of course, is why Ulrike Meinhof jumped. Or, put differently, why did a popular columnist, a producer of much praised radio- and television documentaries, a welcome guest at any of the fancy left-wing feasts in media-city Hamburg and mother of two children, choose terrorism?[23]

The last sentence is telling: how could a *mother* leave the house and choose terrorism with this leap? But of course, Meinhof first of all jumped into the unknown, by leaving a domestic and scholarly house that, so far, had protected her. In response to this, the law would ask what made her jump. Symbolically speaking, Meinhof's jump was a form of betrayal, as Schutte suggests: a betrayal to her children. In this context it is telling that children are a major theme in Jelinek's *Ulrike Maria Stuart*, just as the role that mothers are supposed to have.

Jelinek's dramas suggest that the death of (young) women is not incidental but, somehow, common. Law is far from neutral or innocent in this context. In the thousands of years of European history, law has been the gatekeeper of a symbolical, patriarchal order. It is no coincidence that in Jelinek's *Sleeping Beauty* the young woman is kissed awake by a prince called Mr Right. This is an awakening kiss that has principal connotations. In a sovereign state any subject needs to be subjected first in order to become a legal subject. Any legal subject is kissed into life by the state. Yet, if push comes to shove, this may also turn out to be a kiss of death. It is its power over life and death, or legality and illegality, that gives the nation state its

[22] On this repetitive pattern, see Dorothea Hauser, '"das stück, das tanten typen voraus haben": Zur Beziehung von Ulrike Meinhof und Gudrun Ensslin' in Ortrud Gutjahr (ed), *Ulrike Maria Stuart: von Elfriede Jelinek* (Würzburg, Königshausen & Neumann, 2007); also see Katharina Pewny, *Das Drama des Prekären: Über die Wiederkehr der Ethik in Theater und Performance* (Bielefeld, Transcript Verlag, 2011) 199–200.

[23] In the original: 'Op 14 juni 1970 sprong Ulrike Meinhof niet alleen uit het raam van die villa in Dahlem, ze sprong toen ook in de illegaliteit. Op die dag werd niet alleen Andreas Baader bevrijd, maar werd ook de Rote Armee Fraktion geboren. De vraag is natuurlijk waarom Ulrike Meinhof sprong. Of anders geformuleerd: waarom koos een populaire columniste, maakster van veelgeprezen radio- en televisiedocumentaires, graag geziene gast op de chic-linkse feestjes in mediastad Hamburg en moeder van twee kinderen, voor het terrorisme?'; Xandra Schutte, 'De Jeanne D'Arc van links' (23 June 2010) 25 *De Groene Amsterdammer*, available at www.groene.nl/artikel/de-jeanne-d-arc-van-links.

quasi-divine aura. Yet the name Mr Right obviously also has a symbolical meaning that suggests that women will have to wait until the right one comes along, as is the theme of the Sleeping Beauty and Snow White fairy tales.

The impasse consists, then, in the conflation of the two spheres, of a system of law and a realm of justice. The conflation is apparent in the work of an influential thinker in the field of law, and an expert on its architectonic build-up: French legal scholar Pierre Legendre. Just one example is his dealing with a specific Canadian criminal case from 1984, in a study entitled *Le crime de caporal Lortie: Traité sur le père* – *The Crime of Corporal Lortie: Treatise on the Father* – he presented his ideas about the system of law as an institution that is analogous to the family.[24] For Legendre, the state, both historically and symbolically, embodies the position of the father. This father is at the source of law and at the basis of the constitution of subjects, who are like children. Symbolically, this has its origin in patriarchy, and historically, in Roman law. To be sure, Legendre also noted in another study that law's reasonability has at times has been a safeguard against some of the idiocies or arbitrary natures of symbolic orders.[25] Yet this is why it is so disconcerting that he considers a legal order to necessarily be a paternal one.

In terms of architecture, Legendre is, however, spot on. Symbolically speaking, the space of the *domus* with the father/master as its head translates into: 'This is how we do things here'. There is no reason why the mother could not be at the basis of this phrase or any 'we' that would want to do things 'here'. Yet this is how it is; there is a mysterious quality to the phrase. In principle, the authoritative voice coming from the *domus* could be contradicted by voices coming from another space: the *agora*, the both real and imaginary public space where the *demos* meets. The *agora* translates into: 'This is what we agreed upon here'. The master/father could find a counter-voice, here, unless of course those allowed to speak in the *agora* or defined as part of the *demos* are, mysteriously and absurdly so, only father/masters. And then, the resulting resonance of these two spaces is strengthened when they come to resonate with yet another space: law's all-encompassing and quasi-absolute sphere, with God at its centre. Capturing and controlling everything in its embrace, this sphere affectively translates into: 'This is how it was given to us, here'.

When Sionaidh Douglas-Scott in her study *Law after Modernity* (see chapter one) suggests that law has considerable emancipatory power, she is surely right. Yet she may also be downplaying the affective force fields that rule many systems of law. Combined with the affective force fields that dominate realms of justice they

[24] Pierre Legendre, *Le Crime du Caporal Lortie, Traité sur le Père* (Paris, Champs Flammarion, 1989). Legendre's work has not been translated extensively, but Peter Goodrich made a reader: *Law and the Unconscious: A Legendre Reader*, ed and trans Peter Goodrich (Houndmills, MacMillan, 1997). On the case, also see David Marrani, *Space, Time, Justice: From Archaic Rituals to Contemporary Perspectives* (Abingdon, Routledge, 2018) esp ch 2.

[25] Pierre Legendre, *Leçons I: La 901e conclusion. Étude sur le théâtre de la raison* (Paris, Fayard, 1998).

cause tragedy to rule both spheres. An attempt to escape the double weight of these force fields may consist in the repeated performance of a play, which offers alternatives that cannot easily take place either within the system of law or the realm of justice. One of the explanations for why *Ulrike Maria Stuart* was performed without there being a published script may be that, in first instance, the play should not be codified.[26] Or, rather than the text being finished, and in this sense closed, the play needed to remain open as a performance. In this context, the element of reperforming or of thematic and textual repetition is a comedic one.[27] Jelinek strengthened the comedic element by fusing the two characters, making them rhyme with one another. She strengthens the element even more by making the text a repetitive one. In the absence of a real plot, the characters are caught partly in repetitive language, partly trying to find an escape by repeating things.

If this is an attempt to lift the impasse, there are two reasons why such lifting will not be easy. Let me turn in more detail to the characters that Jelinek is playing with. This is not to frame her text with a historical context that explains everything. If there is something to be explained, it is that performing repetitively is central when an impasse is involved, in an attempt to surpass it.

III. Mary Stuart and Ulrike Meinhof: Law's Domesticity and Mystery

Of all European rulers turned into literary and tragic characters, Mary Queen of Scots (1542–87) is a celebrated one. She is the daughter of the Scottish King James V and granddaughter of Margaret Tudor, who is the eldest sister of King Henry VIII of England. Mary becomes Queen at the age of six days, when her father dies in a delirium after being defeated by the English. At the age of five she is sent to the Catholic French court to become the future partner of the physically and mentally weak *dauphin* Francois II. She marries him in April 1558, aged 15. On the other side of the Channel that very same year, the Catholic English Queen, Mary I, child of Henry VIII's first and divorced marriage, also known as Bloody Mary because of her brutal persecution of Protestants, dies. Elizabeth, the lawful child of Henry's second marriage with Anne Boleyn, now takes the throne in

[26] On this perhaps principal performativity, see Gitta Honegger, 'Bodies That Matter', available at www.hotreview.org/articles/bodiesthatmatter.htm. Honegger mentions that at the time of the first performance of *Ulrike Maria Stuart* 'Jelinek's publisher, Rowohlt Verlag, sends out the script to theatres with a proviso that they are prohibited from distributing it beyond the production cast and crew. The implication is that each production must be considered the current text, and that only the producing theatres can be held legally responsible for its contents'. The title of the review is a reference to a study by Judith Butler, *Bodies That Matter* (London, Taylor and Francis, 2010), originally published in 1993. For Butler as well repetitive performativity holds the key to the opening up of closed systems.

[27] I am taking my cue here from the already mentioned Zupančič, *The Odd One In*, who talks about the possibility of repetition as '*constitutive* for the comic genre as such' 158, italics in original.

November 1558. She is 25 years old, and a Protestant. Yet according to the French King Henry II the lawful heir to the throne is his Catholic daughter-in-law, the Scottish Mary. During a tournament the splinter of a lance ends up in Henry's eye and he dies from the consequent infection in July 1559. Mary is now the Scottish Queen, is married to the French King, and holds a claim to the English throne. One and a half years later, however, Mary's weak husband dies and she is now an undesired young widow, despised by Catherine de Medici, who is mother to the very young Charles IX, for whom she will act as regent. The Catholic Mary has no other option than to return to Scotland, there marrying a Catholic cousin, Henry Stuart, in 1565. Less than two years later he is murdered, most likely by her third husband. Scottish lords now rise against her and force her to abdicate in July 1567 in favour of her son, James VI. She is put in prison but escapes, fleeing to England, where she is received coolly and is constantly moved from one well-guarded or isolated castle to another over the course of 19 years. Rightly or wrongly, she is accused of high treason, under the accusation of having plotted against Elizabeth, and is brought before an ad hoc court of 36 noble men in 1586. They condemn her to death. The beheading, on 8 February 1587, takes three blows; when the executioner lifts her head, so the story goes, it falls out of the auburn wig, revealing that Mary's hair had turned grey.

Still, Mary was not to disappear from the stage, nationally or internationally. Regardless of the veracity of the accusations made against her, the *Rechtsgefühle* of European audiences had been hurt by her execution. Almost 60 years after her death, the theatre giant of the Dutch Republic, Joost van den Vondel, writes *Maria Stuart, of Gemartelde Majesteit*, or *Mary Stuart or Tortured Majesty* (1646). He saw her as a Catholic martyr, and considered her an important political actor resisting a growing Protestant theocracy.[28] In 1684 John Banks presents *The Island Queens, or, The Death of Mary, Queen of Scotland A Tragedy*. Not performed for 20 years because of political reasons, it subsequently became one of the most frequently performed plays in eighteenth-century England.[29] Then, in 1800, in Weimar, Schiller inaugurates his *Maria Stuart: Ein Trauerspiel*, presenting a power game between Mary, holding the moral high ground, and Elizabeth, a political fox. The major question the play poses is: who is responsible, morally and legally, for Mary's death? This play inspires Gaetano Donizetti's opera *Maria Stuarda* (1835, Milan). In 2006, Elfriede Jelinek's piece *Ulrike Maria Stuart* is performed. In 2013 Netflix releases a four-season series on Mary's life: *Reign*. And in autumn 2018, Netflix again returns to Mary with the movie *Mary Queen of Scots*, based on a biography by John Guy, *Queen of Scots: The True Life of Mary Stuart* (2004).

[28] WAP Smit, *Van Pascha tot Noah. Deel 1: Het Pascha – Leeuwendalers* (Zwolle, WEJ Tjeenk Willink, 1956) 417.

[29] Jessica Munns and Penny Richards (eds), *Aspiration, Representation and Memory: The Guise in Europe, 1506–1688* (London, Routledge, 2015) 194; or Ritchie Robertson, 'From Martyr to Vampire: The Figure of Mary Stuart in Drama from Vondel to Swinburne' in Jeffrey L High, Nicholas Martin, and Norbert Oellers (eds), *Who is this Schiller Now?: Essays on His Reception and Significance* (Rochester, Camden House, 2011).

Mary Stuart finds herself, in Jelinek's play, fused with Ulrike Meinhof. The latter, born in 1934, becomes a well-known left-wing public intellectual in the post-war German Federal Republic, who radicalises after the assassination attempt on the left-wing student leader, and close friend, Rudi Dutschke. With Gudrun Ensslin and Andreas Baader she co-creates the Rote Armee Fraktion, which, alongside the Irish IRA, the Basque ETA and the Italian Brigate Rosso, is the most famous or infamous terror organisation in Europe at the time. She authors manifestos such as *The Urban Guerrilla Concept*, during her active period as urban guerrilla fighter from 1970 to 1972. She is caught and put in jail, a situation she had criticised before, in a movie called *Bambule*; German prison slang for prisoners who hammer on doors, metal pipes or bars in their cells as a form of protest.[30] Meinhof is found dead in her cell on 9 May 1976, hanging from a noose made of towelling attached to the prison bars.

Her death shocked national and worldwide audiences. As professor in German culture Sarah Colvin phrased it: 'The RAF shook West Germany in the 1970s not least because the population no longer knew whether it could believe in a *Rechtsstaat* or ethical government'.[31] The two terms juxtaposed by Colvin, 'Rechtsstaat' and 'ethical government', may suggest why Meinhof's death remains a matter of unresolved business. The state, in embodying the status quo, has to take the order that exists as an unquestionable point of departure. The Government, as a political entity, needs to be able to reflect on itself and its actions. So whereas Meinhof's death may be a closed matter legally or in terms of the state, it remains an open wound ethically or in terms of government. The web site German Guerrilla, to name just one, states: 'later investigations would uncover evidence that she had in fact been raped and strangled, and then hanged to make it look like she had killed herself'.[32] Who performed this investigation, the site does not specify. It cannot, in fact: there has been no official inquiry. In response to the request of Meinhof's lawyer at the time, an international committee checked all the information available and concluded that suicide was unlikely. Yet a conclusive assessment at a later stage did not take place. This assessment would also have been hampered by the fact that all fingernails had been clipped from her body and parts of it, like Meinhof's brains, had been removed – without authorisation, that is certain. As a result Meinhof is here to stay as a public character, and her case's appeal is not limited to Germany. Recently, for instance, she appeared in the Museum of Modern Art in New York, when Gerhard Richter's series of 15 paintings on the Baader Meinhof group, entitled *October 18, 1977*, filled an entire hall.[33]

[30] See www.youtube.com/watch?v=0kpooUb69SU. The movie should have been brought out in 1970. Because of Meinhof's process and the tense atmosphere in the country, it was not shown before 1994.

[31] Sarah Colvin, *Ulrike Meinhof and West German Terrorism: Language, Violence, and Identity* (New York, Camden House, 2009) 44.

[32] See 'The Stammheim "Suicides"' (4 October 2007) *German Guerilla*, available at germanguerilla.com/2007/10/04/the-stammheim-suicides.

[33] The title refers to the date on which Andreas Baader and Gudrun Ennslin were found dead in their cells.

Dutch/South-African painter Marlène Dumas made a painting of her in 2004, entitled *Stern*. Meinhof appears in poems (for instance by John Thorkild Ellison), songs (such as those by the anarchist punk band Chumbawamba), in historiographies (*Hitler's children*), novels,[34] and movies (like *Deutschland im Herbst, 1978*, or Rainer Werner Fassbinder's *The Third Generation*, 1979).[35]

If in Jelinek's play the relation between the Queens Mary and Elizabeth is anachronistically interwoven with the relation between RAF members Ulrike Meinhof and Gudrun Ensslin, surely this is a mixture of national and historical contexts. Intertextually, Jelinek was helped by the fact that the urban guerrilla fighters were often depicted by the media as 'terror queens' that had an ambiguous relationship with each other.[36] Yet Jelinek's fusion of the two different characters might be more related to how they, in being brought together within her play, appear to have a distinctly similar feel to them. Otherwise put, the play concerns characters that were dealt with by systems of law that were different in historical and political structure, but that had a distinctly similar affective impact.

Mary was a sovereign and anointed Queen and at the time this meant she could not be brought before a court within her own territory, and certainly not outside of it. She was above the law. Yet she had a good sense of the law's power and its limits. When she was brought before the improvised court of noble men, she complained about unjust procedures during her trial, since she was not allowed to consult her own papers and had no legal support. Yet her major legal point was a matter of domesticity. She had never been an English subject, so how could she be accused of high treason? As for Meinhof, she saw the court before which she was brought as one that was eschewing international principles of justice. For her, there was an intrinsic connection between Nazi Germany and the *Deutsche Bundesrepublik* (DBR), the German Federal Republic.[37] Meinhof teased or mocked law's domesticity, here, by pointing out the DBR's origin in, or continuity with the law of Nazi Germany. Or she attested to the mystery veiling law's relation to a symbolic order that had not changed with the transition from Nazi Germany to the DBR.

Mystery is explicitly dealt with in Jelinek's piece, *Death and the Maiden V*, subtitled *The Wall*. Here, German author Ingeborg Bachmann and American author Sylvia Plath find themselves together. Their coming together is not anachronistic, in this case, as they were historical contemporaries. Still, the two never met during their lifetimes. So, in being brought together, this might again be a matter of the comedic opening up of relations. Yet the space of agency is limited

[34] On this see, for instance, Julian Preece, *Baader-Meinhof and the Novel: Narratives of the Nation / Fantasies of the Revolution, 1970–2010* (New York, Palgrave MacMillan, 2012).

[35] The movie consisted of contributions directed by Alf Brustellin, Hans Peter Cloos, Rainer Werner Fassbinder, Alexander Kluge, Beate Mainka-Jellinghaus, Maximiliane Mainka, Edgar Reitz, Katja Rupé, Volker Schlöndorff, Peter Schubert and Bernhard Sinkel.

[36] Dana Bönisch, 'Of "terror brides" and "jihadi poster girls": how explaining "female" terrorism can only fail' (April 2015) *Kaput: Magazin for Insolvenz & Pop*, available at kaput-mag.com/stories_en/how-explaining-female-terrorism-can-only-fail.

[37] Colvin, *Ulrike Meinhof and West German Terrorism* (2009) 128–29.

by this wall, which the two start to climb over the course of the play, as if it is a mountain.[38] Having arrived at the top, they are confronted with mystery when they meet a 'creature' with his head in bandages, as a result of which it can hardly be heard. Nevertheless, it speaks:

> Simple it is, what you have asked me, but I will tell you nevertheless. These are the most horrible sentences ever expressed. This is why I emphatically beg for silence because I could not express them once again: Whomever of the deceased dead you allow to approach the blood, he will tell you truth. But whomever you forbid this, he shall return in silence. (my translation, FWK)[39]

Both character and text are mysterious, here, and sound akin to an oracle. The text is, consequently, partly absurd. Yet its implications are absolute. Any form of history connected to mystery or set in motion by it, is also cut short by it. Things have to go like this, it has already been decided. The future is locked. The 'why' can only be answered with a key to the riddle that has kept us caught in mystery's loop.

Mystery is principally different from myth, here, although the two are often used together or confused. Myth is involved in this piece when, immediately after the oracle, the piece ends with an 'airy woman's voice, may be a child, a schoolgirl from a town' who reads a passage 'absolutely in classic Greek' (100) from Hesiod's *Theogony.* This story is about how the earth, Gaia, invents a trick to disempower Ouranos; the overarching skies. Gaia gives Chronos, Time, a metal sickle with which he can castrate Ouranos. So he does. Yet drops of blood fall on the earth and from these the Furies are born (the hidden motor of legal order) and the Ash nymphs (who are at the basis of warfare as ash tree wood is used to make spears). The myth, here, is a narrative that precedes human history and order. According to the logic of myth, history is foreclosed in the sense that things are prearranged. There is nothing tragic or comedic or mysterious. Things went as they went. By analogy any legal order is mythical, when it deals with many things that are no longer questioned, such as the fact that one can own, sell and buy land that used to be no one's property. A myth is, as a narrative, principally something of the past, and as such myths are used by legal orders to avoid the production of new myths.

If law is marked by mystery, however, this translates the unknowable past into a known future. In its locking of the future, mystery does not so much found or ground law, but disrupts it, just as it disrupts the realm of justice. Mystery only serves the subjection of people, their being in awe. Whereas myth makes things

[38] There is a third female author implied in this piece, Marlen Haushofer, author of a novel entitled *Die Wand*, or *The Wall*, from 1963. On the role of this author and the theme of the wall, see Daniela Strigl, 'Gegen die Wand: Zu Elfriede Jelineks Lektüre von Marlen Haushofers Roman in *Der Tod und das Mädchen V*' (2006) 39 *Modern Austrian Literature* 73.

[39] Elfriede Jelinek, *Der Tod und das Mädchen I-V: Prinzessinnendramen* (Berlin, Berliner Taschenbuch Verlag, 2003) 140; in the original: 'Leicht ist es, was ihr mich gefragt habt, aber ich sage es euch trotzdem. Es sind die schrecklichsten Sätze, die je gesprochen worden sind. Deshalb bitte ich ausdrücklich um Ruhe, weil ich sie nicht nochmmal sagen könnte: Wem ihr jetzt erlaubt der abgeschiedenen Toten, sich dem Blut zu nahn, der wird euch Wahres erzählen. Aber wem ihr es verwehrt, der wird stillschweigend züruckgehn'.

appear as self-evident, then, mystery gives the incomprehensible or absurd not only an air of comprehensibility but of the absolute. Whenever people or entities resort to mystery, things are locked and thereby block the potential of both the tragic or comedic what-if question. This locking blocks any reflection on, or alternative to, what is. It is this blockage that Jelinek studies, not only with regard to systems of law but also with regard to the larger realm of justice and the ways in which both the system of law and the realm of justice are marked (or regulated) by similar affective forces. Having already dealt with a patriarchal symbolical order, I now focus on how this order lives in cohabitation with law, in law's relation to supreme power.

IV. The Weight of Law's Architectonic: Sovereignty

From all the political entities we currently live with or in, the sovereign nation state remains the most self-evident. Conjuring up a fictitious, brutal state of nature in which people were flying at one another's throat, Thomas Hobbes probably could not have predicted that his story, provoked by the brutal civil wars of the seventeenth century, was to be endlessly repeated as a defence of the state ever since. One dominant rhetorical function of Hobbes's story on the brutal state of nature was to veil the fact that the supposedly safeguarding alternative, the sovereign state, was as fictitious.[40] In the centuries that followed, it was not the last people living in natural conditions, but precisely those newly constructed sovereign states, that were flying at one another's throat, or at a multitude of colonial and ecological throats. This happened at the cost of vast numbers of subjects that sovereign states were supposed to protect. Yet ironically, once artificially constructed, the sovereign nation state became so real that it seemed, and seems, to have no alternative; it acquired a natural aura.

Still, sovereignty is one of the more intensely debated issues of the last few decades.[41] With regard to recent reconsiderations of sovereignty, Martin Loughlin, a scholar in public law, noticed a flood of adjectives that were being added to specify contemporary sovereignty: 'shared, mixed, divided, pooled, cooperative, floating, multiple, perforated, fragmented, reconfigured, complex, decentralized, agonal, and polymorphous are just some of the terms to have been affixed to the concept'.[42] According to Loughlin, not much clarity was gained with these

[40] The term 'fictitious' is consciously chosen; more on this in ch 4.

[41] International relations expert Jens Bartelson describes the current field in terms of a nominalist and a realist position. Nominalists consider sovereignty to be a flexible concept depending on situational and discursive definitions. To realists, 'conceptual change is much more like a thematic variation of an underlying core meaning that remains basically the same across time and space'; Jens Bartelson, 'The Concept of Sovereignty Revisited' (April 2006) 17 *The European Journal of International Law* 463, 465, available at doi.org/10.1093/ejil/chl006.

[42] Martin Loughlin, 'The Erosion of Sovereignty' (2016) 2 *Netherlands Journal of Legal Philosophy* 57, available at doi.org/10.5553/NJLP/.000048. Loughlin is building forth here on his 'Why Sovereignty?'

adjectives, as a result of which some scholars simply wanted to do away with the very notion of sovereignty itself. Here Loughlin's response was:

> But if we are confused about what is being jettisoned, avoiding use of the concept is unlikely to improve the situation. And if, as I suggest, abandonment amounts to a rejection of the modern edifice of public law, then those making that case are obliged to offer an alternative conceptual architecture to explain governing authority today.[43]

The tropes are telling: the 'edifice of public law' and 'conceptual architecture'. Despite being tropes, the terms 'edifice' and 'architecture' have a real function: to underpin governing authority. Loughlin's definition of sovereignty as 'the autonomy of the political domain' is marked and defined, that is, by an architectonic that guarantees the state's and Government's embodiment of supreme legal authority.

This architectonic seems to explain it all. Yet fairly little is explained when we consider that Loughlin is not able to say why it had, or has, to be like this. Instead he challenges those who criticise this construction to come up with an alternative. As long as the critics are unable to do so, the existing 'edifice of public law', is the only possible one. Mysteriously possible, then, since to Loughlin sovereignty 'expresses a principle of unity: it is an expression of illimitability, perpetuity and indivisibility. Any limit on sovereignty eradicates it, any division of sovereignty destroys it'.[44] Yet the question of what justifies or explains its indivisibility or absoluteness still remains unanswered, though the tropes of edifice and architectonic give a clear hint at such indivisibility and absoluteness.

The textual trope of law as a palimpsest emphasises a temporality that involves law's textual and archival history. Its temporality, that is, is imbued with textual layers and volumes that carry their own weight.[45] Yet spatially speaking, the system of law is marked by an architectonic. This architectonic adds another weight, of a persistence of space through time. Concerning this architectural persistence through time Giorgio Agamben stated: 'the *archē* is not a given or a substance, but a field of bipolar historical currents stretched between anthropogenesis and history, between the moment of arising and becoming, between an archi-past and the present'.[46] In his suturing of past and present, Agamben defines a spatio-temporal dynamic that embodies the stability of order. Yet it would be a mistake to only focus on a fundamental force (*archē*) marked by the to and fro between

in Richard Rawlings, Peter Leyland and Alison L Young (eds), *Sovereignty and Law: Domestic, Regional and International Perspectives* (Oxford, Oxford University Press, 2013).

[43] Loughlin, 'The Erosion of Sovereignty' (2016).

[44] ibid.

[45] Sigmund Freud, in *Civilisation and its Discontent*, considered Rome to be a palimpsest, thus fusing textual and architectural build-up. Rome was the architectonic metaphor here for the construction of a symbolic order. For law considered as palimpsest, see Bret D Asbury, 'Law as Palimpsest: Conceptualizing Contingency in Judicial Opinions', (29 July 2009) 61 *Alabama Law Review* 121; or Elizabeth Denlinger, 'The Palimpsest of Justice: Law, Narrative, and the Romantic Self' (10 September 2015) *New York Public Library* (blog), available at www.nypl.org/blog/2015/09/10/palimpsest-justice-pforzheimer.

[46] Giorgio Agamben, *The Signature of All Things: On Method*, trans Luca D'Isanto and Kevin Attell (New York: Zone Books, 2009) 110.

origin and present. The weight of the system of law is concrete, and determined by material spaces that have their own archaeological impact.

An archaeological approach shows a distinctly European idiosyncrasy with regard to the fusion of specific spaces and law.[47] 'Idiosyncracy' defines any kind of own (*idios*) on the basis of a mixture (*syncrasis*): a specific mixture of things that marks a particular and recognisable *own*. Even though Germany and France are both European countries, for instance, they differ because of the historically and conceptual relations each has between its system of law and its culture. Yet despite these differences, both systems of law were, and in part still are, also distinctly similar. What makes them similar is that one dominant origin of European law is the *oikos*, or *domus*: the private household.[48] When Roman public law was developed, it was by and large based on already existing forms of private law. With Roman Emperor Augustus, the figure of the *pater familias* was symbolically, politically and legally brought to a meta-level: the Emperor came to function as the father of the Empire.[49] Then, over the course of the Middle Ages and the Early Modern period, Roman law was used as the basis for international law and the development of conceptualisations of the sovereign state as a household.[50] The result was yet another instance of the mixture of space and law: the coincidence of the sovereign nation state with its lands redefined as territory. The coincidence made Patrick William Kelly contend, in his study on the fight for human rights, that activists 'face a significant challenge posed by the doctrine of state sovereignty. State sovereignty and its legal armor of 'domestic jurisdiction' had long warded off external groups from interfering in the domestic affairs of other nations'.[51]

As already discussed, law's contested or contingent roots in the symbolic order of the master of the house or the divine Father, provoked Carl Schmitt and

[47] The phrase 'archaeological impact or approach' connotes Michel Foucault's *The Archaeology of Knowledge*, trans AM Sheridan Smith (London, Routledge, 2002). Foucault's study, originally published in 1696, was inspired by Martial Guéroult's history of philosophy in which he asked what conditions made philosophy possible. It concerns unities that, according to Foucault are 'concerned not with the description of cultural influences, traditions and continuities but with internal coherences, axioms, deductive connections, compatibilities' 5.

[48] I mean especially the Latin *domus*, here. For a warning against a too facile similarity between *oikos* and *domus*, see Guy PR Métraux, 'Ancient Housing: "Oikos" and "Domus" in Greece and Rome' (1999) 58 *Journal of the Society of Architectural Historians* 392. For a historical overview, see David K O'Rourky, *Oikos – Domus – Household: The Many Lives of a Common Word* (Berlin, Peter Lang, 2013). On the relation between Roman private law and public and its importance for European law, see the work of George Mousourakis, *A Legal History of Rome* (London, Taylor and Francis, 2007) and *Roman Law and the Origins of the Civil Law Tradition* (Heidelberg, Springer Verlag, 2014).

[49] On this see Beth Severy, *Augustus and the Family at the Birth of the Roman Empire* (London, Routledge, 2003).

[50] On this see Randall CH Lesaffer, 'Roman Law and the Early Historiography of International Law: Ward, Wheaton, Hosack and Walker' in Thilo Marauhn and Heinhard Steiger (eds), *Universality and Continuity in International Law* (The Hague, Eleven International Publishing, 2011) 149–84; or Daniel Lee, *Popular Sovereignty in Early Modern Constitutional Thought* (Oxford, Oxford University Press, 2016) 18–19.

[51] Patrick William Kelly, *Sovereign Emergencies: Latin America and the Making of Global Human Rights Politics* (Cambridge, Cambridge University Press, 2018) 93.

many others to take their recourse to theology in order to defend and safeguard the patriarchal nature of law by proposing mystery to safeguard order.[52] I opt, however, to deal with law in terms of its jurisdiction, which was defined by Edward Mussawir as:

> [T]he pragmatic, active, and immanent plane on which law navigates its groundlessness. As soon as one places a 'subject' outside and transcendent to the term of law or rights … then one loses the perspective by which rights are uniquely connected to concrete situations.[53]

If this sounds too postmodern, allow me to refer to one of the more skilled, or flexible actors in Europe's political history: Jean-François de Gondi, better known as the Cardinal of Retz (1613–79). He never trusted any theological or mysterious underpinning of the state. The only thing that needed to be veiled according to him was the fundamental *dissensus* operative in any political body. In an analysis of Retz's famous memoires, cultural historian Malina Stefanosvka suggested that for him 'there is nothing mystical about the state's founding secret. Beneath the veil of tradition lurks nothingness'.[54] This nothingness is not nihilism. If we accept a radically immanent conception of law, law becomes contingent, dependent on situations, and therefore changeable. 'This is how we do things here' can change into 'This is how we did things here'. 'This is what we agreed upon here' may change when people consider that the 'we' did not include enough subjects or entities. 'This is how it was given to us here' may change when people say 'but we consider another given-ness now', or when they say 'but now we are someplace else'.

In this case sovereignty would have to be redefined and would lose its mysterious or architectonic underpinning. Such a redefinition is at stake when sovereignty expert Panu Minkkinen contends that higher or the highest law 'merely founds the authority to command whilst simultaneously setting conditions for the legitimate use of that authority'.[55] This dynamic is not a paradox. As media-archaeologist Bernhard Siegert explained, 'cultural techniques' work by means of media that are parasitical in how they work alongside what exists (as the name 'para-site' suggests). When authority and subjects are connected through law, law does not connect them directly, but sideways, via a medium. Media, in Siegert's analysis, create distinctions, and by implication some form of order, while retaining the

[52] Carl Schmitt, *Political Theology* (2006) and *Political Theology II* (2008), or Peter Goodrich and Michel Rosenfeld (eds), *Administering Interpretation: Derrida, Agamben, and the Political Theology of Law* (2019).

[53] Edward Mussawir, *Jurisdiction in Deleuze, The Expression and Representation of Law* (London, Routledge, 2011) 23.

[54] Malina Stefanovska, 'The Baroque Social Bond in the *Memoirs* of the Cardinal de Retz' in Massimo Ciavolella and Patrick Coleman (eds), *Culture and Authority in the Baroque* (Toronto, Toronto University Press, 2005) 221.

[55] Panu Minkkinen, *Thinking Without Desire: A First Philosophy of Law* (Oxford, Hart Publishing, 1999) 162.

potential to disrupt, or interrupt any connection.[56] When read in this light, law is a parasite that founds sheer power as authority. Yet law maintains the potential to condition and interrupt that authority. Sovereignty's mystery is clearly not defined by some sort of theological source, then. Mystery is not entirely absent also, however. It is now located in the phantom-like moments where law shifts from being a founding and connecting force to a conditioning or interrupting one – and back.

Mystery re-enters through a backdoor, moreover, when Minkkinen argues that sovereignty is characterised by two desires. On the one hand there is an *autocephalous* desire; a desire to concentrate law, power and self-knowledge in its own centre, or *head*: the original meaning of *kephalos*.[57] On the other hand, there is a *heterocephalous* desire that wants law to serve the domestication of power by helping power to organise the domus of power via its vertical structures. Now, *autocephaly* has its origin in the institutional organisation of, specifically, the Eastern Orthodox Church. It indicates a situation in which a bishop becomes head of his own region and need no longer report to a higher authority. As the head of a religious house, he is in charge of his verticality. Perhaps it needs no mentioning that this head is again a father who is given this authority by another father. Whilst the Orthodox Churches deny papal supremacy, they too work with popes and patriarch as heads. This brings us back, full circle, to the cohabitation of a patriarchal system of law and the realm of justice.

If Jelinek's plays, as interfaces, perform impasses, one of the reasons for the impasse is that for centuries the system of law has not offered a true, comedic alterative that could somehow transform the realm of justice in a more just one for women. The affirmation of both a system of law and the realm of justice, rather, led to a tragic closure of justice for many. This does not mean that women are only victims. Mary Stuart and Meinhof were clearly also perpetrators. Jelinek's interest in this duality of perpetrator and victim showed itself once more when she used the procedural documents of a trial to write *Das schweigende Mädchen*, or *The Silent Maiden*, which was performed in 2014 and published in 2015 alongside *Ulrike Maria Stuart*. This case concerned the *Nationalsozialistischer Untergrund* – the *National Socialist Underground* (NSU) that robbed 12 banks, executed two bomb attacks, and murdered 10 persons they considered to be non-German between 2000 and 2007.[58] Two men, Uwe Mundlos and Uwe Böhnhardt, were found dead in a burned camper in 2011. The only survivor, Beate Zschäpe, was brought before a court in München in 2013, and decided to remain silent or to pretend she did not know anything about the murders. She was convicted to life imprisonment

[56] Bernhard Siegert, *Cultural Techniques: Grids, Filters, Doors, and Other Articulations of the Real* (New York, Fordham University Press, 2015). Siegert was inspired by Michel Serres' study from 1980, *The Parasite*, trans Lawrence R Schehr, intr Cary Wolfe (Minneapolis, University of Minnesota Press, 2007).

[57] Panu Minkkinen, *Sovereignty, Knowledge, Law* (London, Routledge, 2009).

[58] One of the cases was investigated by Forensic Architecture; see ch 1.

on 11 July 2018. The case affected a general audience in several ways, and was the biggest criminal case in Germany since its reunification, both in terms of length and people involved. It took 438 days of court procedure; more than 500 witnesses were questioned.[59] This time the affective weight of the case was not due to the fact that the trio attacked the sovereign state or patriarchal society. Rather, the question was: what exactly was going on in the sovereign nation state's household with regard to what was made public and what remained secret? More specifically the issue concerned the relations between the NSU and German secret services. The female protagonist that remained, in this case, refused to speak; yet another impasse. Impasses are annoying. Yet they are not mysterious. They provoke the question of how things can be adequately closed or productively opened.

Reflecting on the NSU case, legal scholar and editor of the *Legal Tribune Online*, Annelie Kaufmann, ended her report on the verdict saying: 'Whether the court was successful in convincingly explaining the structure of the organisation and its environment, is another question, that has been discussed for years by those following the process'.[60] Kaufmann suggests yet another impasse. The system of law was apparently unable to disclose things sufficiently enough to be able to close things definitively. The reason might be that there was much more going on than could be seen or checked by the public eye; also because there were powers in play that could manipulate information or conveniently hide it. In the next chapter this problem of visibility is central. In it, the closing capacity of law and the opening potential of justice are explored on the basis of the logic of the official and the logic of the officious. The first connotes law's closure, the second embodies the potential of things being opened up from the side of justice. The disruptive third is the fictitious.

[59] On the verdict and case, see Annelie Kaufmann, 'So begründet das Gericht Zschäpes Mittäterschaft: Das Urteil im NSU-Prozess' (24 April 2020) *Legal Tribune Online*, available at www.lto.de/recht/hintergruende/h/olg-muenchen-6st312-nsu-prozess-urteil-begruendung-mittaeterschaft-beate-zschaepe.

[60] ibid. in the original: 'Ob es dem Gericht gelungen ist, die Struktur der Organisation und ihres Umfelds überzeugend aufzuklären, ist eine andere Frage, die von Beobachtern des Prozesses seit Jahren diskutiert wird'.

4

Logic of the Official vs Logic of the Officious

The Force in Form and Forum in Valeria Luiselli's Tell Me How It Ends *and* Lost Children Archive

'Such a conflict acquires a political character, then, not because of the elementary political nature of the aims demanding to be heard, but simply because given the complex system of manipulation on which the post-totalitarian system is founded and on which it is also dependent, every free human act or expression, every attempt to live within the truth, must necessarily appear as a threat to the system and, thus, as something which is political par excellence.'

Václav Havel, 'The Power of the Powerless' *Open Letters: Selected Writings, 1965–1900*[1]

I. Officious: Meddlesome, Informal, Obliging, Passionate

Consider the Latin phrase *Quod non est in actis, non est in mundo*: 'what is not officially registered, is not in the world'.[2] The quote was mentioned by German legal philosopher and media scholar Cornelia Vismann in her study on legal files. She was certainly not alone in stating that any legal order without files or records is a challenge to any conceptualisation of law. In German files and records are captured together by one term: *Akten*.[3] Yet in English the two imply a distinction between the materiality of what has been registered (files) and the function of what has been registered (records). Records have been made throughout the ages, yet the materiality of files has changed considerably over time, from stone

[1] Václav Havel, 'The Power of the Powerless' in *Open Letters, Selected Writings, 1965–1900*, edited by Paul Wilson (New York, Vintage Books, 1992) 156–57.

[2] The quote is pivotal to Vismann's study entitled *Files: Law and Media Technology* (Stanford CA, Stanford University Press, 2008). The Latin phrase, as Vismann notes, is probably medieval in origin, 56.

[3] The original title of Vismann's study was: *Akten, Medientechnik und Recht* (Berlin, Fischer Taschenbuch, 2000).

to papyrus, lead, wax, parchment, paper, and now to digitally preserved records. Consequently, the ways in which these were kept in archives have also changed. In this context Vismann, whose study was much influenced by the work of Michel Foucault, could equally well have asked: 'what would law be without archives?' Law's archives, though not a subject of continuous reflection, are at its heart, and their use rests upon one prerogative: that all the documents that the archive is comprised of are officially acknowledged. In contrast, justice, considered as that which people feel to be just, does not have an archive with officially acknowledged records or records in files. First and foremost, justice needs memory. It may even mark memory, as when elderly people can still vividly remember an injustice they experienced during their youth, or when people feel the injustice of things that happened generations or centuries ago.[4] When justice needs to be done, however, memory in and of itself does not suffice. It is equally important that things can be brought forward. This implies that there at least needs to be something that was preserved and as a result can be shown, even if this something was, or is not officially acknowledged.

The difference between law's officially acknowledged documents and archives on the one hand, and the memory of justice and its respective forms of preservation on the other, was paradigmatically at stake in the official apologies voiced by Kevin Rudd, the Australian prime minister at the time, to indigenous peoples for the crime of the Stolen Generations on 13 February 2008. The 'Stolen Generations' refers to large numbers of indigenous children who, roughly between 1910 and 1970, had been taken away from their homes and families in order to be raised in white families, a process supported by political and religious authorities. The governmental apologies were vocalised in Parliament. Since the apologies were part of an official speech in Parliament, they were taken up in its acts. All this, of course, did not mean that injustices had not been registered before, for then the politico-legal response would have not been provoked. A pivotal step that led to this was the 'Bringing them Home Report' from 1997, by the official committee under the umbrella of the Australian Human Rights Commission (AHRC).[5] The report was official, yet the committee based this report on both more or less official documents and, vitally, oral accounts that had never gained any official status. Nevertheless, these stories had preserved what had happened as a result of which the injustices could be brought to light.

[4] On this, see Klaus Neumann and Jana Thomson (eds), *Historical Justice and Memory* (Madison, University of Wisconsin Press, 2015). In the field of transitional justice, memory was also key. In the field of law, relevant memory studies focus on the official, legally underpinned orchestration of memory by nation states; see Austin Sarat (ed), *History, Memory and the Law* (Ann Arbor, University of Michigan Press, 1999), or on legal modes of dealing with injustices of the past, see Stiina Loytomaki, *Politics of Memory: Confronting the Past* (London, Taylor and Francis, 2015).

[5] The Australian Human Rights Commission (AHRC) was established by an act of Federal Parliament as an independent statutory organisation. See www.humanrights.gov.au/about; on the report, see www.humanrights.gov.au/our-work/bringing-them-home-report-1997.

The simplest way to define the opposite of offically recognised testimonies, stories or documents would be to call them unofficial or *informal*. Unfortunately, these terms fail to explain how such texts ever contained or acquired the force to affirm or disturb the system of law. The argument of this chapter is that unofficially registered or remembered instances of injustice are only able to affirm or disturb the political system or the system of law precisely because they have form, and in that sense are formal. Consequently, I use the term 'officious' to define remembrances, testimonies, stories, documents or other registrations.

The definition of 'officious' involves, according to the OED:

(a) Active or zealous in the exercise of an office; dutiful;
(b) Doing or ready to do kind offices; eager to serve, help, or please; attentive, obliging, kind;
(c) Unduly forward in offering one's services, or in taking business upon oneself; doing, or prone to do, more than is asked or required; interfering, intrusive;
(d) In diplomats' use (as distinguished from official): not directly bearing on official business; having the character of a friendly communication or informal action on the part of a government or its official representatives; informal, unofficial.

Hence, the officious may indicate the uncalled-for and not-asked-for, or in the context of this study, the annoying. It may indicate the informal in the sense of an 'off the record' registration that still has great influence on what is actually happening or even more adequately represents what is happening. It may indicate the kind, obliging or dutiful (though this is considered to be archaic or obsolete in other dictionaries).[6] And it may indicate the fiery, ardent, enthusiastic, and perhaps angry endeavour to do something; another indication of its annyoying force. The literary case central to this chapter proves and adheres to all the above-mentioned definitions of the officious, whether they be contemporary or obsolete.

Valeria Luiselli, a Mexican-born author now based in the United States, wrote two different works on a specific issue of law and injustice. Luiselli was much troubled by the US Government's dealing with refugee children who fled in snowballing numbers, particularly from the mid-American countries of Guatemala, El Salvador and Honduras, in 2014.[7] She wrote an essay on the issue, *Tell Me How*

[6] One source, here, is Merriam Webster, that gives as examples '*officious* people who are always ready to offer unasked advice' and '*officious* conversations between foreign ministers'. Other dictionaries define officious as 'meddlesome' or 'objectionably aggressive' or 'disapproving'.

[7] On this see, Muzaffar Chishti and Faye Hipsman, 'The Child and Family Immigration Surge of Summer 2014: A Short-Lived Crisis With a Lasting Impact' (2015) 68 *Journal of International Affairs* 95. The very qualification 'refugee' has its evident political, legal and ethical connotations. Legal scholars tend to speak of 'unaccompanied children', a phrase that led to the acronym UAC. See, for instance, Bill Ong Hing, *American Presidents, Deportations and Human Rights Violations. From Carter to Trump* (Cambridge, Cambridge University Press, 2019). Hing notes that in 'fiscal year 2014, the Department of Homeland Security (DHS) apprehended more than four times the number of UACs (about 73,700) than in fiscal year 2011 (about 17,100)' 57. Part II of his study is entitled 'Obama's Shame'; part III 'Entering the Trump Ice Age'. For a critical analysis, see Marcia Zug, 'The Mirage of Immigration Reform: The Devastating Consequences of Obama's Immigration Policy' (2015) 63 *Kansas Law Review* 953; or David Hausman and Jayashri Srikantiah, 'Time, due process, and representation: An empirical and legal analysis of continuances in immigration court' (2016) 84 *Fordham Law Review* 1823.

It Ends (2017) and a novel, *Lost Children Archive* (2019).[8] The essay's title, paradoxically, suggests a story, since the question 'Tell me how it ends?' suggests a narrative with a plot. It was, in fact, a question asked by the author's own daughter, who desired to know what happened to one of the children whom Luiselli had met during her work as a volunteer interviewing Spanish-speaking refugee children in New York in order to prepare their legal defence against extradition. The essay advances on the basis of the questions Luiselli had to ask to gather enough information for a successful handling of a case. Despite the title suggesting a story told to a child, then, the general content of the essay is much more formal in that it follows the format of a list of questions. In contrast, the novel's title, *Lost Children Archive*, explicitly suggests an archive, with all the historical and legal connotations this may entail. Yet the text is – despite its autobiograpical connotations – a matter of fiction. In its being a matter of fiction, the question then becomes how the novel, in following its title, is a sort of record, file or document, in the not only formal but also legal senses of those terms.

Legally speaking, both texts are officious in that they are 'off the record'. They help or make people talk about things that are important outside of the official political or legal sphere; or they tell a true story that could not be told officially. The works describe the reality of what was veiled by a legal euphemism: the Obama Government's formulation of a so-called 'priority juvenile docket'. The judiciary was allowed to give priority to groups of refugee minors in order to accelerate their extradition, as a response to the sudden surge in the numbers of children fleeing to the US.[9] Whereas previously minors would have 12 months to find a lawyer to defend them, minors were now only given 21 days.[10] Luiselli's verdict on this government measure is that it was the:

> [C]oldest, cruelest possible answer to the arrival of refugee children. Ethically, that answer was more than questionable. In legal terms it was a kind of backdoor escape route to avoid dealing with an impending reality suddenly knocking at the country's front door.[11]

[8] Valeria Luiselli, *Tell Me How It Ends: An Essay in Forty Questions* (London, 4th Estate, 2017), and *Lost Children Archive: A Novel* (New York, Alfred A Knopf, 2019).

[9] On the shift, see Liz Robbins, 'Immigration Crisis Shifts From Border to Courts' (23 August 2015) New York Times, available at www.nytimes.com/2015/08/24/nyregion/border-crisis-shifts-as-undocumented-childrens-cases-overwhelm-courts.html.

[10] Luiselli, *Tell Me How It Ends* (2019) 39.

[11] Luiselli (n 8) 41. To understand the cruelty involved, a helpful read may be the report of student Monica Valencia who met an 11-year-old girl she was unable to help: 'The reality for many undocumented children is that they will have to appear in court and represent themselves pro se. That is, if they do not find an attorney to effectively advocate for them and seek out legal remedies, they will have no choice but to face the immigration judge and the government attorney on their own. How can this be okay in our American system of justice? First, children and other undocumented immigrants I encountered do not speak English and do not understand the immigration process in its entirety. I don't understand the process completely myself, and I am a law student, so how can a three-year old, a seven-year-old, or even an eleven-year-old understand?' Quoted in Hing, *American Presidents* (2019) 94 fn7.

The distinction between the realm of justice and the legal system is made explicit here. The measure was ethically wrong, according to Luiselli, whereas legally speaking it was a trick, that is to say: strictly speaking it was not illegal because the law did not need to be changed. The trick was not to take away rights, but 'to give priority' to legally dealing with a certain group. This would de facto weaken their legal position, or reduce it to a nigh non-existent level.

It was the governmental provocation that made others act officiously in response, and Luiselli was one of those to join a new and rapidly developing movement. The required or necessary documentation that the essay and novel report on, and which they embody, funtions on the one hand as an affirmation of the judicial system. That system could and can still give children a chance to be safe. At the same time Luiselli's works are meddlesome, as they are not called or asked for by authorities. This is one of the definitions of 'officious' given above. The works function as forms of counter-documentation that aim to disturb the political system and the system of law, in order to lead both systems to a more ethical way of dealing with (possible) subjects. Considered from the viewpoint of the refugee children, Luiselli's works are kind, obliging and dutiful – another definition of officious. These children are fleeing violent circumstances, and have gone through horrifying journeys, protected by few, with a great risk of being abused, suffering hunger and thirst, in utter insecurity. Considerable numbers of these children disappear without a trace. For Luiselli, addressing the injustice done to these children, felt like an obligation and a duty, even if this may annoy the authorities, because 'being aware of what is happening in our era and choosing to do nothing about it has become unacceptable'.[12] Consequently, the texts have a tone of anger and fire, and are an ardent and passionate attempt to bring to light what is happening to thousands of unprotected children; yet another meaningful aspect of the officious.

In the context of the legal defence of refugee children, forms of registration and documentation are major themes in both the essay and the novel. Both texts also have a perverse twist to them. Having reached the border of the US, the children have to admit themselves to Border Patrol officers in order to be officially detained and recognised:

> If the legal proceedings don't begin now, their fate will be to remain undocumented, like many of their parents or adult relatives already in the United States. Life as an undocumented migrant is perhaps not worse than the life they are fleeing, but it is certainly not the life that anyone wants.[13]

So, the perverse twist is that the children are required to hand themselves in to be dealt with and to be officially recorded by a system that is aimed at throwing them out as quickly as possible. In order to avoid the latter, counter-documentation that

[12] Luiselli (n 8) 30.
[13] Luiselli (n 8) 20–21.

can become official when taken up in a legal defence is necessary, but this kind of counter-documentation first has to find a form in order to work officiously in the wider public realm of justice in order to eventually be considered official. Such counter-documentation may remain a weak force, since the 'undocumented' that Luiselli is referring to in the passage above, are legally 'undocumental' and so have not been hitherto recorded. The distinction between records and documents is pivotal, here, in the meeting of the system of law and the realm of justice.

II. Data Subjects: Records, Documents and Form

The history of the term 'record', based on the Latin *recordor*, is an ironic one. At the core of the term is the heart: *cor*. The verb meant to recall, to remember, to recollect, or to call to mind, something still captured in the phrase 'to remember by heart'. All these meanings are still palpable in the Spanish verb *recordar*. The form this remembrace attained could be either oral or literal. Only when it was taken up in the domain of law did the term 'record' come to mean what is recorded by writing, by means of a file, like in 'a written memorial made by a public officer authorized by law to perform that function, and intended to serve as evidence of something written, said, or done'. Thereupon, 'record' lost all of its meanings relating to the personal or the oral, of the heart. Both the original and modern sense of 'to record' were pivotal in the Australian case of the Stolen Generations. The Prime Minister's speech was important to Aboriginals in part because it made matters official. Yet perhaps more important was something not official, namely that things were recorded – said and heard – from the heart to the heart.

The distinction between hearing and seeing (and reading is a matter of seeing in this case) is pivotal because it concerns a principal cultural difference. For centuries, law has only officially acknowledged written records: acts that can be archived, retrieved, seen, re-seen, and read. Law is primarily literate, which is why Julie Stone Peters stated that law is 'a domain committed to the sanctity of the verbal text'.[14] Yet where does this leave oral cultures? Formally speaking, they would and will have their own forms of records, all oral in nature, and these could or would have authoritative status. However, these forms were not acknowledged by the (early) modern state. Many instances demonstrate how oral transmission lost its authoritative status once the legal system started to rely only on written texts.[15] Still, orally transmitted information, even when it was not acknowledged in the first instance by authorities, preserved its force because it had its own officious form that meant

[14] J Stone Peters, 'Theatrocracy Unwired, Legal Performance in the Modern Mediasphere' (2014) 26 *Law & Literature* 39.

[15] In the European context, the transition is described in Thelma Fenster and Daniel Lord Smail (eds), *The Politics of Talk and Reputation in Medieval Europe* (Ithaca NY, Cornell University Press, 2003), esp Thomas Kuehn, 'Fama as a Legal status in Renaissance Florence'.

things could be presented publicly.[16] Such bringing forward required and requires a form of publicity, on which more below.[17] For now, the form of what is to be made public is at stake: records and documents of whatever kind, in both an official and officious context, or in a literary or an oral one.

One prime example of a possible formlessness in terms of records and documents are human remains in the desert. Before long, wind and sand will have covered them up. They can be brought forward formally only if they are found, photographed or analysed, described and thus registered. Luiselli talks about so-called 'death maps' in this context, offered by, for instance, the non-profit organisation Human Borders so that family members and friends can retrieve the location of the remains of their loved ones who had tried crossing the desert and did not make it. Concerning the (digital) registrations of these remains, Luiselli writes:

> Numbers and maps tell horror stories, but the stories of deepest horror are perhaps those for which there are no numbers, no maps, no possible accountability, no words ever written or spoken. And perhaps the only way to grant any justice – were that even possible – is by hearing and recording those stories over and over again so that they come back, always, to haunt and shame us.[18]

In terms of art as an interface, the generic term 'story' connects the two different domains of law and justice. Legal issues concern whether crimes have been registered and recorded, and whether they have been numbered and mapped. As a result of this the search can start for those who can be held accountable. The search for what happened to whom, by whom, will lead to the reconstruction of a narrative, a story with legal consequences.[19] Yet the issue in terms of justice is how we can ever deal justly with the horrors of the happenings that were not registered or reported, whether by word of mouth or on paper.

Here, stories are capable of bringing to life the horror of what has not been seen and subsequently is refused visibility. The 'hearing' that Luiselli is talking about in this quote cannot be a listening to someone telling a story; she deals with the horrors about which 'no words ever written or spoken' exist. If, for instance,

[16] On the reconsideration of the relation between literate (Western) and oral cultures in a colonial and decolonial context, see Michelle Grossman, 'When They Write What We Read: Unsettling Indigenous Australian life – Writing' (2006) *Australian Humanities Review*, available at australianhumanitiesreview.org/2006/09/01/when-they-write-what-we-read1-unsettling-indigenous-australian-life-writing; or Abraham Acosta, 'Orality and Politics in Latin America: Thresholds of Illiteracy' (2013) 13 *The New Centennial Review* 203.

[17] The element of theatricality implied here was dealt with in the previous two chapters.

[18] Luiselli (n 8) 30.

[19] The importance of narratives in legal procedures has been studied more intensely since the 1980s; see Peter Brooks and Paul Gewirtz (eds), *Law's Stories: Narrative and Rhetoric in the Law* (New Haven, Yale University Press, 1996). More recently Greta Olson gave an overview of the field in 'On Narrating and Troping the Law: The Conjoined Use of Narrative and Metaphor in Legal Discourse' in Michael Hanne and Robert Weisberg (eds), *Narrative and Metaphor in the Law* (Cambridge, Cambridge University Press, 2018).

a company of six – adults, children, or both – would set out from Mexico to cross the desert to the US, they could all die without anyone knowing. So as to be able to hear of what happened to them, we would need the imaginative ears of artists who can produce the stories that fictionally record what happened, that offer themselves to repetition and so come to haunt us, ethically. The verb 'to record' is a matter, here, not of recalling but of 'calling to mind'. It is more a matter of the heart than of the archive. This, however, does not mean that no archive is needed – it is required, if not officially, then formally.

If the very same word 'record', whether considered as a noun or a verb, connotes different forces in the system of law or realm of justice, the same holds for the term 'document'. Historically and functionally, the legal relation between the two was studied by Vismann in her tracing of a pivotal transition from rule by means of records to rule by means of documents, and back again to rule by means of records.[20] The transition from the first to the second takes place first in the sixth century with a vast 'decline of public record-taking'.[21] In the Roman Empire records came to be at the core of all administration, but this feature was lost due to the collapse of the Empire. The Frankish rulers that followed worked by means of documents. According to Vismann, records and documents follow a different *logic* (my emphasis).[22] Documents are aimed at preservation rather than transmission. Items are 'not stored in any central repository', but follow 'a distributive mode; they are kept by the recipient'.[23] As a result, both have a very different effect or work differently in terms of their affective reach. Documents are not produced 'for any particular administrative use; rather they are made to impress. Their letters are signs of power, their very appearance represents the authority of the issuer'.[24] Documents were handed out, then, without their being registered or recorded or archived in first instance.

Yet with the growth of centralised power from the twelfth century onwards, matters increasingly come to be officially registered and recorded again, this time in so-called registries. The shift coincides with a shift from parchment to paper. Another shift takes place in the period of the Enlightenment. Here, the setting up of records is systematised, especially in Prussia, and turns into something that makes subjects a subject, since they 'produce themselves by administering themselves, by establishing a feedback with their own action'.[25] This subject formation is pivotal to the nature of history, since only 'what is no longer volatile can become history'.[26]

[20] Vismann, *Files* (2008) chs 3 and 4.
[21] Vismann (n 2) 71.
[22] Vismann's translator notes that in the German original of the study she used *Urkunde* as a general term that has specific equivalents in English as charter, deed or certificate, but which also has as a general English equivalent in 'document' (Vismann (n 2) 175 fn 2); the term 'logic' is mentioned on 71.
[23] Vismann (n 2) 72.
[24] ibid 72.
[25] ibid 112.
[26] ibid 113.

To Luiselli, and in the context of the issues she is grappling with, it is of necessity that things are recorded so that they may form the material for a history that changes negligible beings into subjects, both in a legal and historical sense. In this context both records and recordings, or documents and documentation, play a pivotal role, in a both affirming and disturbing dialogue with the system of law. Whereas the law derives its legitimacy through the archive with its records, the term documentation entails a certain attitude towards an event. That is to say: documentation is always *directed*, and the archive is a storage. Luiselli's documentation persists, here, in its adherence to the documentation that the children had to show – in that sense Luiselli's work is a mimicry of the process. As for the records that Luiselli is working with, they function as a different back-up. They are not so much signs of what has officially been registered, but precisely of what has not been registered.

The dynamic between documents and records can be traced in the case of a refugee adolescent named Manu, who is interviewed by Luiselli on the basis of a long list of questions. Manu's answers again morph themselves into a story:

> [I]t's a story condensed in a very specific, material detail that has continued to haunt me: a piece of paper that the boy pulled from his pocket toward the end of his interview, the creases and edges worn. … the document was a copy of a police report he'd filed more than a half year ago. The report stated, in three or four typewritten sentences, all in capital letters and with some grammatical mistakes, that the subject in question raised a complaint against gang members … threatening to kill him.[27]

The fact that the original file against the gang members must have been recorded in Manu's country of origin is one important element, here, be it one with little force. In any US handling of the case, the court was not going to check this. The force of the copy resides in the fact that it has become a document, 'kept by the recipient'. Its official status has become a sign of authority. Consequently, the document can become a piece of evidence in a legal argument that the boy fled his country because his life was threatened, which would be a pivotal element in getting a permit in the USA. As proof for this threat, the copy could be officially registered as document, to then be formally recorded and filed.

Yet in describing the legal handling of cases, and by participating as translator, the literary author Luiselli is also searching for forms of documentation and recording for the public domain and within the realm of justice. The status of documents and records is different, here, though the search for form is equally pivotal. Combining an essay with a novel (and formally speaking, a curious one), Luiselli implicitly makes a statement. The two different genres, in their having distinct forms, have differing affective forces. The first is more argumentative in nature, the second more narrative; the first intends to convince people, the second aims more at identification. Moreover, the two works can be considered, differently, as record, document or a mixture of both. The essay describes the documents required to attain a successful legal defence and to that order the essay documents

[27] Luiselli (n 8) 42.

Luiselli's activities as a translator. In contrast, the novel can be seen as the record of a fictional journey. The dominant thread in the novel is a family – wife, husband and their two respective children – travelling by car to the south-west of the USA. The husband has set out on a project to record sounds, or rather echoes, of the last free native people in the USA: the Chiricahua Apaches. Hence, the novel is not only the recording of a journey, but forms of recording is its major theme. It is one, moreover, that relates to another theme in the novel: histories lost.

In the back of the family car we find several boxes, storage spaces for professional and personal items: the husband has four, the wife, the boy, and the girl all have one. At some point, later in the evening, the wife, who is the major but not the only I-narrator, has a peek at them:

> It comes to me that maybe, by shuffling around in my husband's boxes like this, once in a while, when he is not looking, and by trying to listen to all the sounds trapped in his archive, I might find a way into the exact story I need to document, the exact form it needs. I suppose an archive gives you a kind of valley in which your thoughts can bounce back to you, transformed. You whisper intuitions and thoughts into the emptiness, hoping to hear something back. And sometimes, just sometimes, an echo does indeed return, a real reverberation of something, bouncing back with clarity when you've finally hit the right pitch and found the right surface.[28]

Evidently, this archive is an officious one. It is personal, though it also contains records of a people lost. The records filed in the box archive are described as sounds. This is partly due to the fact that the husband indeed collects sounds. The more general point is that records need to speak or be listened to in order to be heard. Should this be the case, they do not just sound one by one: they resound, collectively. As a result, they may be combined, or can be arranged to form the basis of a story. This story, as a generic form, does not reside in them. It resides in the one living with or going into the archive. She has to turn the required story into a document: 'the exact story I need to document'. As the term 'exact' suggests, this cannot be a neutral document, though it does need precision. As a story or novel, it needs a congruous pitch and texture. Hence, the novel is the record of a journey in which recordings are being made that have to turn into a document. This document has to transform volatile matters into a history that can be brought forward and sent out, as a document to the readers.

Luiselli's essay and novel both bring forth something. Whether it concerns the essay or the novel, they bring forth subjects based on data, both official and officious ones. There is a porous distinction here between characters with whom we can easily identify (like the family traveling south) and refugees seeking data that could protect them legally. Records and documents are needed to produce data subjects: subjects validated through data. That the border with literary documented characters is porous is attested to by the fact that Luiselli also wants to tell the stories of those who died without being registered. By means of telling

[28] Luiselli, *Lost Children Archive* (2019) 42.

their stories, these people come back to life because people inside and outside of the system of law are provided with 'data'. Stories give shape to unrecorded, unregistered histories which, in turn, are meant to become data also in a more public sense of the term. They seek publicity. The question in terms of both law and justice is: what kind of publicity is used or manipulated by whom?

III. *Öffentlichkeit*, Publicity and Forum

Terms come with their consequences. In Dutch and in German, for instance, the public nature and testability of legal cases is indicated by comparable terms: *openbaarheid* and *Öffentlichkeit* respectively. Both can be translated as 'publicity'. In both Dutch and German, and in both systems of law, the English term publicity is a loanword that produces a pivotal distinction. As the German Duden dictionary indicates, the noun *Die Publicity* means 'the way in which things become known by means of news media in public openness'.[29] Apparently, there is *Öffentlichkeit* on the one hand and publicity on the other. The same distinction is made in Dutch, and has been accentuated by legal scholars studying the relation of law to publicity in terms of both the law's principal openness to the public and in terms of its being made known to the public via the media. The two imply radically different modes of public visibility and have alternate implications, not only for the way in which legal order is perceived as legitimate, but also for the ways in which issues of justice can be brought forward.

A study of the Dutch situation by legal scholars Marijke Malsch and Hans Nijboer notes that in daily practice, only a small amount of case material is actually made publicly visible. About 90 per cent of all criminal cases in the Netherlands are resolved outside the courtroom by means of dismissal, penalty orders, administrative punishment, or various other forms of transaction.[30] The situation in the USA is similar. At present, the majority of US criminal cases is determined on the basis of plea bargaining.[31] This is not to say that cases settled outside the court are not public. They are, in the sense that they are open and can be checked, but they lack the public visibility and collective testability that characterise the cases that are taken to court. Still, the tiny portion of cases resolved publicly, openly and visibly in court are pivotal – as Marsch and Nijboer argue – for the way citizens perceive the legitimacy of cases in particular, and for the legal system in general, particularly in the criminal law context.[32]

The title of Malsch and Nijboer's study was 'The visibility of the law'. Not only by way of legal mediation is this visibility threatened. Globally, criminal

[29] In the original: 'durch Medienpräsenz bedingte Bekanntheit in der Öffentlichkeit'.

[30] Marijke Malsch and JF (Hans) Nijboer, *De zichtbaarheid van het recht: openbaarheid van de strafrechtspleging* (Den Haag, Kluwer, 2005) 4–7. The figure of 90% they give is from 2005; the situation has not changed much since then.

[31] George Fisher, 'Plea Bargaining's Triumph' (2003) 109 *The Yale Law Journal* 868.

[32] Malsch and Nijboer, *De zichtbaarheid van het recht* (2005) 1.

cases are increasingly dealt with outside of the public eye. This concern has been addressed by the London-based collective Forensic Architecture. Established by Eyal Weizman in 2010, Forensic Architecture is a fluid group of architects, artists, filmmakers, investigative journalists, scientists and lawyers. Some results of their collective research were published under the title *Forensic Architecture: Violence at the Threshold of Detectability* (we will deal with the bureau's work in more detail in section IV). For now, the point is Weizman's return to the etymological origin of 'forensic'.[33] The term is derived from Latin forensic, which means 'of a forum': a place of assembly, or a public place. Historically, the term indicates the place where legal cases were handled: the *forum*. This historical origin points to a pivotal aspect of the handling of law and justice, namely its openness. In this context, the aim of Forensic Architecture is 'the production of architectural evidence and … its presentation in different fora, both political and juridical'.[34] The several forums are open to the public in different ways, however, and demarcate the realm of justice and the legal system. Figure 4.1 presents some of these as they were shown at the exhibition at BAK, Utrecht, October 2018 (see chapter one).

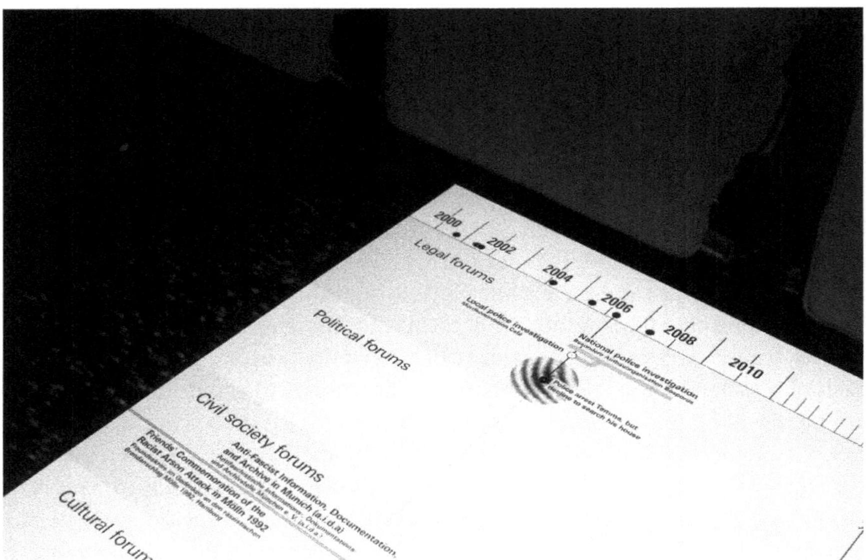

Figure 4.1 Forensic Architecture, *77sqm_9:26min* (2017)

Installation with three-channel video, 25:54 min, reenactment video, 15:14 min, carpet with floor plan, and diagram, installation view Forensic Justice at BAK, 'basis voor actuele kunst', Utrecht, 2018–19, photograph: Tom Janssen.

[33] Eyal Weizman, 'An Impromptu Glossary: Open Verification' in Maria Hlavajova and Wietske Maas (eds), *Propositions for Non-Fascist Living: Tentative and Urgent* (Cambridge MA, MIT Press, Basic Series, 2019) 144.

[34] Eyal Weizman, *Forensic Architecture: Violence at the Threshold of Detectability* (Cambridge MA, MIT Press, Zone Books, 2017).

As the selection of forums may make clear, Forensic Architecture is not just geared towards the publicity, or making open, of legal cases. The public handling of matters is related to different forums and this is decisive for law's *Öffentlichkeit*. Current forms of publicity, for instance, may be incompatible with, or operate contrary to law's *Öffentlichkeit*.[35] In the case of the refugee children, it was key to deliver their cases to a national and international audience that could help disturb the implemented system of law. Luiselli's work is one extended attempt to do just this, and different forms of media and different forums are needed to make this disturbance productive. Yet these media and forums also have their own agenda. For instance, the prospects of trial-by-media have become an immanent danger in recent years.[36] Another threat is that the law's *Öffentlichkeit* is no longer really open to the public because of the media's selectiveness. This is nothing new. One could argue that for decades, or even centuries, the media have mainly targeted juicy court cases. Yet the dynamic between *Öffentlichkeit* and publicity has been intensified with the rise of social media. The result may be a loss of visibility and openness, if only because most mainstream media is either in the hands of private parties that use publicity for their own profit, or in the hands of groups or agencies whose aim is not to inform but to wilfully manipulate information.

In *Lost Children Archive*, husband and wife are not just on a journey for the sake of the husband's project. The wife has had to renounce her dealing with the refugee children crisis in order to join her husband. However, this does not mean that she has given up on her activism. In fact, the novel gradually weaves in two histories: that of the couple's son and daughter moving 'down' south and the influx of refugee children moving 'up' north. This will culminate in the penultimate section of the novel, entitled 'Echo Canyon', which precedes the final part 'Document'. Both introduce another type of I-narrator. In this case the son is telling ('Echo Canyon') or talking by means of a recording ('Document'). Thus, both chapters, about family affairs and children traveling through the desert to seek asylum, are told from a child's perspective. In 'Echo Canyon' the couple's two children get lost and meet a group of refugee children in a rusted and deserted train car on some lost track in the desert. In 'Document' we receive a farewell note from the son to his sister now that the pair is separating.

Prior to getting there, however, the wife is constantly checking the media that are supposedly reporting on the refugee children. It is here that we encounter the flip side of publicity, with thwarted echoes and recordings. The fact that law needs to be publicly seen and tested was famously phrased by Lord Chief Justice Gordon Hewart in 1924: 'justice should not only be done, but should manifestly and undoubtedly be seen to be done'.[37] The phrase became far more famous than

[35] Malsch and Nijboer (n 30) 100–06.

[36] In the Dutch context, the issue was addressed by, for instance, Ybo Buruma, 'Invloed van de media op de rechtspraak' (1997) 20 *Trema* 305. Also see Marc S Groenhuijsen, 'Openbaarheid en publiciteit in strafzaken' (1997) 27 *Delikt & Delikwent* 417.

[37] *R v Sussex Justices, Ex parte McCarthy* [1924] 1 KB 256, [1923] All ER Rep 233.

Hewart's essay 'New Despotism' from 1929, in which he argued that the political powers of the executive were encroaching upon the legal system in such a way as to come close to subordination.[38] Such encroachment counteracted the requirement that justice must be seen to be done in the sense that legal responsibility has to be brought out in the open, in some kind of forum, in order to appear for the public eye and be put to a public test. Not only Hewart or Forensic Architecture, but also Luiselli noticed that this public *test* is increasingly threatened nowadays. This is partly because of secrecy, and partly due to manipulation and lies: the contemporary threat to law and justice consists in the intense multiplication of documents and records that are false, or, one could say: fictitious.

IV. The Destructive Fictitious and the Test of Fiction: Forensic Architecture

As French philosopher Jacques Derrida noted, literature is most certainly equipped to 'play the law', capable of 'playing at being the law', and as such capable of 'deceiving the law'.[39] Behind this argument is Derrida's assertion that the foundational myths of law and the mystical foundation of its authority depend on the act of *fingere*, a verb that connotes fictionalisation in both the etymological and common senses of the word. Etymologically speaking, the verb *fingere* initially means 'to shape' or 'to form'. Only later did it come to denote 'to pretend'. In its ability to make something appear or materialise, literature is analogous to law and to theatre. Law has to emerge theatrically from the domain of the invisible into the domain of the visible. In this context, fiction poses the possibility and difficulty in representing realities, or is a negotiation with reality that can be both affirming and disturbing. In contrast, the role of the fictitious is neither affirming nor disturbing, but rather disrupting, and it is this role that is highlighted on two levels: on the level of documentation and recording per se, and on the level of those who base their verdict on them.

The fictitious attempts to escape testing. Both in systems of law and in realms of justice, things need to be tested, hopefully without bias, and from differing sides. In her study *The Test Drive*, Avital Ronell considered that 'essentially relational and not static, testing admits of no divine principle of intelligibility, no first word of grace or truth, no final meaning, no privileged signified'.[40] In the realm of law and

[38] The very phrase 'new despotism' was not new. It was brought forward by Alexis de Tocqueville, *Democracy in America* (1840). In his case, De Tocqueville hinted at the potential that democracy would end up in securing the lives of people against any risk (a clear case of clairvoyance, so it appears). As for the phrase that became more famous, the Switzerland-based independent website *Justiceinfo*, funded by the Fondation Hirondelle, has it as its motto; www.justiceinfo.net/en.

[39] Jacques Derrida, 'Before the Law' in Derek Attridge (ed), *Acts of Literature* (London, Routledge, 1992) 212.

[40] Avital Ronell, *The Test Drive* (Champaign, University of Illinois Press, 2005) 9.

that of justice, or in the context of the handling of cases, this results in the refusal to take a final meaning (or a mystery) as a presupposition. In the case of a jury system, for instance, peers will base their decision on a case on the particular laws they adhere to. They will not do so on the basis of an imperial or royal, let alone totalitarian, word. And they will have to decide on the basis of their own judgement, not on the basis of manipulated and biased media information. In search of a truth that needs to be established, actors enter into the dramatic process of a test in the etymological sense of the word: in order 'to experiment' or 'to put to proof'.

The search for truth by means of a trial or test is formally embodied in the jury as icon or synecdoche of 'the people'. As the American Bar Association discloses on its website, under the heading 'Dialogue on the American Jury: We the people in action':

> The right to trial by a jury of one's peers is a cornerstone of the individual freedoms guaranteed by the U.S. Constitution's Bill of Rights. In a criminal case, trial by jury places twelve citizens between the power of the government and the rights of the accused. The government cannot take away someone's right to life, liberty, or property until it has convinced those twelve citizens of that person's guilt beyond a reasonable doubt.[41]

Again, a forum is at stake, in which the case has to appear. Yet what appears has to be checked by actors who, due to their diversity, alleviate in principle (though fairly often not in practice) any kind of bias. Consequently, legal jurisdiction can be overruled by a podium occupied by ordinary citizens: 'peers'. By implication peers also operate in the realm of justice. Here too, affairs are brought out in the open by means of media that need to be checked and judged.

In the context of contemporary forms of publicity, Julie Stone Peters makes a fundamental distinction concerning the issue of how law should be assessed and made to work. It concerns the distinction between what Plato called *theatrocracy* and *nomocracy*; the rule of public theatre versus the philosopher's rule of law on the basis of a given *nomos*. At stake is not just a biased opposition between the uninformed and pathetically inclined multitude and the well-informed, rational and individual philosopher. Plato was more concerned with what he called the excess of theatre and its possibilities for deceit. To counter this threat, he argued for the preservation of a rule of law that would answer to measure and reasonability. Still, at the end of her assessment of the status quo, Stone Peters calls Plato's distinction 'an ideological ruse' because the individual philosopher or lawgiver does not exist.[42] In the case of nomocracy, law does not appear quasi-magically

[41] 'Dialogue on the American Jury: We the people in action', American Bar Association (2016), available at www.americanbar.org/content/dam/aba/administrative/public_education/resources/dialoguepart1.authcheckdam.pdf.

[42] Stone Peters, 'Theatrocracy Unwired' (2014) 58.

from one source, but is always the result of informed people acting not just with one another but in the eyes of one another. Still, as Stone Peters states:

> If the opposition between theatrocracy and nomocracy is false … it is nonetheless integral to the theatre of law, internalized as part of – indeed essential to – the experience of legal spectatorship. This opposition operates to sustain the ideology of law's separateness (its 'distinctive temporal and spatial borders,' as Almog puts it), and thus the distinction between law and not-law. Much of law's legitimacy is, in fact, vested in this distinction, but the barriers are difficult to maintain.[43]

There is an internal differentiation at stake in Stone Peters' description of the double constitution of the 'theatre of law'. In the first case, the pivotal question is: how does the law appear on some sort of public stage? In the second case, the pivotal question is: how is law acted out on some sort of separate podium? Both relate differently to spatial and temporal borders, and, more specifically, to what is on stage (in the forum) or behind the scenes. Put differently, they relate in distinct and separate ways to law's necessary visibility, its being rendered out in the open by the logic of public-ness, and its equally necessary invisibility, of which the archive is the telling paradigm.

Law has been topical in many forms of visual representation since the Early Modern period. Stone Peters argues that digital media implies a quantitative change which, due to its omnipresence causes a qualitative change with their 'plenitude of moving images'.[44] What she calls a digital theatrocracy perverts the domain of law, because:

> [I]n law, once the very epicenter of democracy, one can see the gradual infiltration of the vision machine: first the 19th-century diorama and panorama, then the photograph, then finger-printing techniques, then the infinitely replicating and increasingly surreal images that make up law today.[45]

The problem, here, is not so much the visual nature of representations, but rather their quasi-infinite forms of replication, the speed of those replications, and the ways in which these can all be manipulated. Due to the omnipresence of repeated, multiplied and manipulated digital images, the operations of law threaten to become the topic of spectacle. And spectacle runs counter to the very idea of law's *Öffentlichkeit*. Spectacle does not concern the ability to openly test something, but instead corresponds to the logic of the game, with winners and losers. In this sense, Stone Peters is correct that this 'erodes our faith not only in law's truth-finding capacity, but also in its stabilizing power'.[46] In other words: the spectacle is inclined towards the fictitious.

These issues are addressed by Forensic Architecture, in its response to the fact that an increasing number of ruling powers, official and officious, operate

[43] ibid 58.
[44] ibid 43.
[45] ibid 43.
[46] ibid 42.

in secrecy. While avoiding registration of what happens, these powers produce false or deceptive documents and records, and consequently pervert the forums on which truth is sought. The third that disrupts both law and justice, here, could be the formless, of which the undocumented and unregistered are but a few examples. Yet precisely because they are formless, they have no potency to disrupt. In a sense, undocumented and unregistered beings, whether they be oral or textual, do not exist. Disruptive are those so-called official documents or procedures that are false or fraudulent; documents and records of crimes that have wilfully been destroyed; or the rapid circulation of scenarios that besmirch the status of epistemological authorities. I will use the term 'fictitious' here, as distinct from 'fictional', to mark not only the fact that things can be false, made up, or a sham, but to indicate the perversity that truth can be made to seem fictitious in any case. The fictitious is a matter, here, of trickery, lies and of the hidden, which is something other than secrecy.[47] In this context, Eyal Weizman makes a pivotal distinction between familiar modes of deception and 'ongoing attacks against the institutional authorities that buttress facts'.[48]

Fictitiousness threatens both official and officious entities seeking law and justice. The so-called unregistered or undocumented becomes fictitious, for instance, when things that have happened are only unregistered or undocumented because they are wilfully hidden. Luiselli mentions, in this context, how some US citizens in the border region use their right to carry arms to shoot so-called illegals without registering these killings. It is their hiding of illegal executions under the right to bear arms that is deceitful. Within the system of law itself, Border Patrol officers may send a Mexican child back without having to document this, since children trying to flee to the USA from neighbouring countries are dealt with differently by US law. The very act of sending the children back is lawful, then, or legal. Yet in terms of justice, the non-documentation may be fictitious in its hiding dishonesty or deceitfulness. For how can one ever check whether this was really a Mexican child?

The pressures that fictitiousness enacts on counter-documentation are defined by Weizman on the basis of seven focal points that imply distinct criteria of action – politically, legally, ethically and aesthetically. We have already dealt with the first above: forum, *forensis*. The others are:

- counter-forensics;
- resisting dark epistemology;
- open verification;
- polyperspectivity;
- unlikely common;
- evidentiary aesthetics.

[47] For this distinction, see Charles Barbour, 'The Secret, the Sovereign, and the Lie: Reading Derrida's Last Seminar' (2013) 3 *Societies* 117, available at doi.org/10.3390/soc3010117.
[48] Weizman, 'An Impromptu Glossary' (2019) 148.

Without there being an explicit connection between Luiselli's work and that of Forensic Architecture, it is remarkable how Luiselli's work deals with all these focal points and responds to the criteria involved.

The issue with counter-forensics is that any questioning of institutional authorities may seem to bring wilfully manipulative forces and justice-seeking ones into the same space. Yet even though both may make use of the same media and techniques, the motivations are radically different. Manipulative forces use media to twist facts and truth; in a counter-act justice-seeking ones have to use the very same media to find the facts and report on them. Luiselli's essay is an example of counter-forensics, here. Then, whereas the manipulation of facts by powers has long been widely known, dark epistemology is more perverse. Weizman notes how powers can thwart facts in an 'attempt to cast doubt over the very possibility of there being a way to reliably establish them at all'.[49] If dark epistemology is successful, truth becomes irrelevant. In a counter-act, and resisting this attempt, the entire list of questions that Luiselli deals with is about finding facts that lawyers can use to base their case on. With open verification, Forensic Architecture aims to find an alternative to *veritas* or the truth established by an institutionally underpinned authority. The establishment of truth needs to be a practice, which is conveyed by the fact that verification is rooted in a verb; establishing truth should be a practice that should be open to anyone. Verification is the opponent of the fictitious, and the 'anyone' is embodied in Luiselli, who is neither trained as a lawyer nor an investigator. She calls herself a documentarist, not someone who makes documentaries, but who establishes documents.[50] In this context it is telling, formally speaking, that a pivotal role in the novel is attributed to a polaroid camera, not a digital one. The images of the second can be manipulated, the images of the first cannot.

As for polyperspectivity, unlikely common, and evidentiary aesthetics, they all concern the essay as well but the novel first and foremost. Polyperspectivity indicates that any case will have multiple perspectives, both in terms of verification and in terms of the parties involved. This is precisely what the novel as a genre is famous for, in the language of Bakhtin: its polyphony and polyglossia.[51] The unlikely common indicates that the practice of verification will have to end up in a public document that may involve many different actors, perhaps surprising ones, like lawyers and activists meeting and working together with documentarists and novelists. The final characteristic, evidentiary aesthetics, concerns the capacity to sense and detect in a variety of ways, in terms of aesthetic sensibilities. I would like to turn this one around, as well, into the *aesthetic evidential*. All the seven characteristics somehow have to be at the heart of aesthetic forms. These are forms that can be used both in how we deal with cases in the present and in

[49] ibid 150.

[50] As Luiselli puts it: 'Documenting just means to collect the present for posterity', *Lost Children Archive* (n 8) 103; see also 55, 349.

[51] Mikhael Bakhtin, *The Dialogic Imagination: Four Essays* (Austin, Texas University Press, 1982).

a possible future. It concerns forms that are capable of outliving injustice, or at least have the potential to do so, not so much for the sake of justice per se, but for their potential to affirm and disturb the system of law for the sake of justice.

If, in the case of Luiselli, we witnessed someone using art to fight injustice, we now move to more ambiguous forms of art; or to art that is straightforwardly serving what, at least to some, can be called injustice.

5

Logic of Personhood vs Logic of Self

Threat of Packs in Vondel's 'Water-wolf' and the Shift of Commons into Property

'Perhaps the furies can get their due only when conceived from a point of view that attempts to be inhuman itself, as can happen at the discursive extremes of science and poetry, those twin attempts to expunge the reciprocal and human point of communication.'

McKenzie Wark, 'Furious Media'[1]

I. Personhood, Self, Pack and the Legal Need for Dissection

Both the affirmation and disturbance that define the dynamic between legal personhood and different forms of self in the realm of justice were apparent on 16 March 2017 in New Zealand. On this day a river and its surroundings, conceptualised by the Māori peoples as Te Awa Tupua, acquired legal personhood by an act of Parliament after 140 years of protests and struggle.[2] The Māori peoples, or the Iwi, felt the river to be part of their bones as an ancestor.[3] In the modern, Western or legal frame of mind, this implied a lineage and rights. So, within the frame of legal order, the concern could only be resolved by giving the river, legally named Whanganui since colonial times, legal personhood.[4]

[1] McKenzie Wark, 'Furious Media' in Alexander Galloway, Eugene Thacker and McKenzie Wark, *Excommunication, Three Inquiries in Media and Mediation* (Chicago, Chicago University Press, 2014) 157.

[2] See Eleanor Ainge Roy, 'New Zealand River Granted Same Rights as Human Being' (16 March 2016) *The Guardian*, available at www.theguardian.com/world/2017/mar/16/new-zealand-river-granted-same-legal-rights-as-human-being.

[3] For a both legal and anthropological analysis of the relation between the Maori and their land, see Andrew Sharp, 'Blood, Custom, and Consent: Three Kinds of Māori Groups and the Challenges They Present to Governments' (2002) 52 *The University of Toronto Law Journal* 9.

[4] On this see Liz Charpleix, 'The Whanganui River as Te Awa Tupua: Place-based law in a legally pluralistic society' (October 2017) 184 *Geographical Journal* 19, available at doi.org/10.1111/geoj.12238. Within four days after the New Zealand Act of Parliament, Justices Rajeev Sharma and Alok Singh from the High Court of the Northern Indian state Uttarakhand followed suit, judging that the holy rivers Ganga and Yamuna were to have 'the status of a legal person with all corresponding rights, duties and liabilities of a living person.' See *LiveLaw*, www.livelaw.in/first-india-uttarakhand-hc-declares-ganga-yamuna-rivers-living-legal-entities.

This was the element of affirmation; the decades of protests were a matter of disturbance. Both had been fuelled by the injustice felt to be done to the river's self, Te Awa Tupua, and the collective selves surrounding this forefather. Obviously, the Whanganui river was not considered a legal person by the Iwi. They had sensed the river to be some sort of self, though, in a world that felt like theirs. This self was now brought into law's sphere, a sphere that by granting personhood to a river and its surroundings (as 'an indivisible and living whole'), enlarged its span.[5] Tellingly, a history of appropriation preceded the moment of ascribing a legal identity to the river. Prior to the year 1848, Māori peoples living next to the river had enjoyed rights and responsibilities over it. This changed in 1848, when the Crown purchased 86,200 acres of land bordering on the river and, later, allowed steamers to use the river, which destroyed fishing grounds and polluted the river. The entire issue started, then, when an entity defined and protected by legal personhood, 'the Crown' – a synecdoche for the state in all its aspects – turned the commons of others into state property and gave rights to alien actors who did not respect the river as a self.

The ability to create a *ficta persona* is fundamental to any legal system that grants itself the power to give rights to persons and to protect their existence and property. The *ficta* refers back to the etymological origin of *fingere*: to make. It concerns law's foundational power to be able to craft things, such as turning an entity into a person. It also connotes the familiar element of fiction. The made person is real, legally speaking, but is not real like a physical person is. Legal personhood depends on two rhetorical or literary tropes, here: personification and anthropomorphism. The first gives entities some sort of recognisable human characteristic, or face. The second replaces the comparison that is characteristic for metaphors by the power to give something a name that, by consequence, gives this something a humanlike identity or a status. When the river was given legal personhood, for instance, it acquired an officially acknowledged human quality that was in line with the fact that the river was already considered to be a forefather. This is an instance of personification. At the same time, the river was no longer *compared* to a person by means of metaphor, because it had *become* a person: an instance of anthropomorphism.[6]

The term 'person' is derived from the Latin *persona*, or mask. This hints at the fact that a legal mask is layered onto the faces of legal subjects or to the non-existent face of collective entities to define their legal identity. If a corporation is turned into a legal person it does not get a face. Still, as a person it can now face the law.[7] The last phrase is again suggestive, for does law have a face then? The Latin phrase 'prima facie' suggests as much. It indicates that, legally speaking, one has to have a case. Anybody can

[5] Te Awa Tupua (Whanganui River Claims Settlement) Act 2017, Pt 1, sub-pt 2, s 12, available at legislation.govt.nz/act/public/2017/0007/latest/whole.html#DLM6831458.

[6] The role of the latter in the legal system was central to a study by Barbara Johnson, 'Anthropomorphism in Lyric and Law' (1998) 10 *Yale Journal of Law and the Humanities* 549.

[7] See ch 1, and see Hannah Arendt, *On Revolution* (New York, The Viking Press, 1963) or Edward Mussawir, 'The "Method of Dramatization" in the "Law of Persons"' in *Jurisdiction in Deleuze, The Expression and Representation of Law* (London, Routledge, 2011) 22–37.

be accused of anything, but the question is when there is sufficient cause for a case. The phrase indicates that, before anything has been officially scripted, at law's *first sight* there has to be substantial evidence. Yet this *prima facie* always relates to the real, embodied, faces of actors working within a system of law. They have to decide whether there is a case or not. The system is filled with real persons and faces, then, as when accused and witnesses are required to confront the judge, face to face. This may be why people speak of 'facing justice' in its meaning 'facing the law'. Yet if a corporation is brought to court, the only real faces appearing will be of its lawyers. The corporation as a legal person has no face.[8] Or, its face is only a suggestive metonymy, here, which highlights that law cannot but deal with persons.

As opposed to the logic of personhood from the side of a system of law, there is a logic from the side of the realm of justice that is hinted at by the phrase that people have a 'sense of justice'. Instead of alluding to an externally applied persona, this phrase presupposes a 'within', as an ethical potential. In terms of subjectivity, the sense of justice connotes a self, then, whether an individual or collective self. The term 'self' finds its etymological origin in Germanic languages and in all of them indicates a sense of particular identity, be it individual or collective. This self is pre-legal, which does not mean it is *natural* in any essentialist definition of the term. Human selves are deeply culturally determined. Yet they also indicate something that is present from birth. It is at the heart of what Hannah Arendt defined as 'natality', by means of which she indicated the potential in any self to act freely. This potential is not just free in and of itself; any human being is thrown into a specific world and shaped by it. There is a fundamental belatedness to any self, consequently. Yet with each birth a new self starts to act, as a result of which the belatedness can make way for the new – a new that may even surprise the selves that had started something.[9]

The New Zealand example of the Whanganui river seems to show that from the side of the realm of justice a battle was won.[10] A less optimistic analysis is that from the side of law, a logic of personhood will from here onwards come to disturb the logic of self that characterises, or characterised, a particular world and realm of justice. If art as an interface connects two spheres, both will affect the other and the directionality of change will not be one way. The long-term consequences of the river's shift from being a self to being a legal person can only in part be predicted. Yet in the course of this chapter I will come to argue that for instance in the Netherlands the dry-milling of waters, the taking of the commons and their legalisation as private

[8] On the discrepancy between the meeting of real or natural individual and vulnerable persons with artificial invulnerable ones, see Frans-Willem Korsten and Bennett Carpenter, 'Corporate personhood as inhuman: the paradigm of asbestos cases and Dracula' (2014) 84 *Quaderni* 'La radicalité ouvrière en mots et en actes' 13.

[9] On the paradox of newness and belatedness in Arendt's natality, see Natasha Levinson, 'Teaching in the Midst of Belatedness: The Paradox of Natality in Hannah Arendt's Educational Thought' (2005) 47 *Educational Theory* 435. Levinson deals with the paradox as it appears in Hannah Arendt, *The Human Condition* (Chicago, University of Chicago Press, 1998) and Hannah Arendt, 'The Crisis in Education' in *Between Past and Future* (New York, Penguin Books, 1977).

[10] The complexities and struggles involved are also central to Buaventura de Sousa Santos, *The End of the Cognitive Empire: The Coming of Age of Epistemologies of the South* (Durham, Duke University Press, 2018).

property, has also redefined a collective sense of self, over the course of centuries. New forms of artificial legal personhood have come to be experienced as somehow 'natural'. And the natural environment of the Netherlands has been reconstructed and legally redefined in such a way that this first disturbed, then affirmed new kinds of self. Law's power to turn natural beings into persons may seem to be an empowering move. In part, it is. Yet the being or entity turned into a person also becomes something else through its becoming a legal person.

Some consequences can be felt when we compare law's powers, here, with artistic or scientific modes of personifying natural beings, or nature. One paradigmatic example is the early modern picture that appeared on the frontispiece to Gerard Blasius's *Anatome Animalium* (The Anatomy of Animals) from 1681:

Figure 5.1 Frontispiece to Gerard Blasius, *Anatome Animalium* (1681)

The inscription above the temple of Isis, the goddess of nature, asserts that Nature could never be unveiled. This was sublime in the eyes of Immanuel Kant.[11] The inscription showed that nature was beyond measure. However, as soon as some entity is turned into a person, the result is measurability, whether literary, scientific or legal. In this case, the sublime, as the inexpressible and unmeasurable, is brought down to earth by way of this frontispiece. Tellingly, nature is unveiled by a figure that carries three instruments: a smoky oil lamp (on her head), a lens (in her left hand) and a scalpel (in her right hand). This enlightening and enlightened figure connotes the scientific shift from Early Modern to modern. Nature begot a face and a body, and a distinctly female one at that, as is indicated by four breasts. These can be read as metonymical, since multiple breasts are typical in animal species that are related to mankind in terms of evolutionary continuity and ecological contiguity. They are a metaphor in their indicating of nature's nourishing abundance. Symbolically, they may indicate monstrosity. Nature may be unveiled, then, but this does not mean it loses its threatening potential.

Nature's independent potential or its indestructible force is countered by an artistic armour of genres and tropes that is both complex and simple. Anthropomorphism is at work when Nature is given a name or a human body. Allegory, and by implication metaphor, is at work when nature is transposed into a goddess-queen, carrying a staff and ruling the animals of her kingdom. Personification is at work when all animals are given faces that show a distinct satisfaction with their being subject to this queen, including of course the usual suspect in the upper right, where a gluttonous snake is about to eat a dragonfly. The immensity of nature, its sublime quality, or its monstrosity, is countered, that is, by changing an order of almost infinite relations into an order with perhaps fictive, but nameable, and measurable entities. If, as a result, nature is no longer compared to a person but has become one, this is a person that can be faced, controlled, analysed and dissected.[12]

The element of dissection is highlighted by the small figures to the left and right below. The cherub to the left is busying itself practically with dissection. The figure to the right appears to have lost its wings, as a result of which it resembles a grown-up child, that both embodies man's capacity to learn and man's capacity to see, to depict and represent what he analyses and, to that order, needs to dissect. This child faces upward to both the object of study, dissection and depiction – nature – and to its great instructor, the figure of the sciences. The latter appears as

[11] Immanuel Kant mentions the inscription – 'I am all that is, that was, and that that will be, and no mortal has lifted my veil'– in a footnote to *The Analytic of the Sublime* in the Critique of the Power of Judgment from 1790. For a critical reading of Kant's footnote, see Barbara Claire Freeman, *The Feminine Sublime: Gender and Excess in Women's Fiction* (Berkeley, University of California Press, 1995).

[12] On the origin and history of personified Nature, lactating the world and with multiple breasts, see Mechtold Modrsohn, *Natura als Göttin im Mittelalter: Ikonographische Studien zu Darstellungen der personifizierten Natur* (Berlin, De Gruyter, 1997), or Katharine Park, 'Nature in Person: Renaissance Allegories and Emblems' in Lorraine Daston and Fernando Vidal (eds), *The Moral Authority of Nature* (Chicago, University of Chicago Press, 2003).

a distinct figuration of the term 'Enlightenment', due to the enlightening candle on her head, the lens and the scalpel. In its probing into the dark, the human gaze grasps and grabs. Tropology and the capacity to dissect go hand in hand, in the anthropomorphisation of an entire life-world.[13] The result is, on the one hand, that all interactions between man and nature become no different from the average interaction between persons. On the other hand, nature has now become a body that can be dissected. The first option connects well to the dominance of commerce in contemporary Western thinking, or as legal scholar Carol M Rose in her study on the commons stated: 'Commerce still seems to be our quintessential mode of sociability'.[14] The second option connects to the brutal forms of exploitation that have been characteristic of colonialism and capitalism, especially since the nineteenth century.

Obviously, law's way of dealing with nature is not the same as this literary-scientific one. Yet the underlying logic is similar. If nature is turned into a person, this makes it legally possible to define it as an entity in terms of its components, attributes and properties. In this context it is perhaps surprising that in the Dutch 'Law on the protection of nature' (*Wet natuurbescherming*, or Wnb) the rather basic term 'nature' is not defined. Neither is a human being, by the way, or an animal. As said, law does not deal with selves. Nature is defined, instead, on the basis of a legal dissection, in terms of its definable components. Dutch nature concerns those areas appointed or designated as 'nature', and concerns all those nameable environments or animals that fall under the protection of the law. Even wolves may fall under this protection. In fact, in 1979 the Bern Convention agreed that all European countries should protect them. In a follow-up, the Habitats Directive of the European Union of 21 May 1992, demanded that Member States see to it that the wolf has its specially designated areas of life.[15] Well, look at that: 'its specially designated areas of life'. It does not sound like a space that a pack could live with. If wolves were still sufficiently prevalent in Europe to be living in packs, they would roam freely and not care about (legally directed) designated areas.

With the force of the pack we meet the third that can disrupt the logic of personhood and the logic of self. Both the logic of personhood and the logic of self may change over time, but at some instance in time they connote and need stability, whether based on established customs or legally defined rights. Both are threatened by forces that transgress or destroy stability, such as the force of packs. Packs are on the move, much like waves, and in this capacity they are a trope of fluidity.[16] Packs do not consist of identifiable selves, but consist of a multiplicity

[13] On the role of lenses in relation to knowledge production in the Low Countries, see Svetlana Alpers, *The Art of Describing: Dutch Art in the Seventeenth Century* (Chicago, University of Chicago Press, 1983).

[14] Carol M Rose, 'The Comedy of the Commons: Commerce, Customs, and Inherently Public Property' (1968) 53 *The University of Chicago Law Review* 711.

[15] Council Directive 92/43/EEC, available at eur-lex.europa.eu/legal-content/EN/TXT/?uri=CELEX%3A31992L0043.

[16] The legal problems in dealing with fluidity are very much connected to the difficulty philosophy has in dealing with it. On this see René ten Bos, *Water: Een geofilososche geschiedenis* (Amsterdam, Boom, 2014), that is: *Water: A Geophilosophical History*.

with interchangeable selves and interchanging selves. Because packs are multiple and moving, it is impossible to give them a stable mask and turn them into an individual legal person.[17] Rather, they embody modes of infuriation. The cute little animal in Figure 5.2 proves as much.

Figure 5.2 A Polish *Cricetus cricetus* presented on a website on the situation in Limburg, the Netherlands

Photo: Agnieszka Szeląg[18]

The Dutch version of *Cricetus crecitus* has its habitat in the southern tip of the Dutch province of Limburg, where the soil consists of *loess*, which is what the animal needs to dig its corridors and build its nests. *Cricetus cricetus* is also known as the Eurasian hamster or common hamster. Unlike its Syrian, Russian or Chinese cousins, it never became a pet. It did change its habits, though, due to human activity. Following the development of large-scale agriculture, it spread westward from Asia, and came to be considered a farmland pest. Consequently, a familiar trope was called upon when looking for incentives to kill it. The Dutch name of this common hamster is 'Korenwolf': Cornwolf or Wheatwolf. The trope suggests

[17] Richard Iveson, 'Deeply Ecological Deleuze and Guattari: Humanism's Becoming-Animal' (2013) 4 *Humanimalia: a Journal of Human/Animal Interface Studies* 20, 36.

[18] Source www.groenkennisnet.nl/nl/groenkennisnet/show/Limburgse-hamster-nog-steeds-ernstig-bedreigd.htm. The website tells us that the animal is still very much threatened with less than 200 hamster burrows left.

that *Cricetus cricetus* hunts in packs that come in waves, threatening not human life itself but human life support. Consequently, for decades, its elimination was not legally underpinned, just as the killing of mosquitoes is not forbidden by law but dealt with as a matter of common sense. Only when so few of them were left that they could almost be singled out as individuals did they come to fall under the protection of law.[19] The creature was on the brink of extinction in 1999 and reintroduced by means of a breeding programme that depended on the last living animals caught alive.[20] So, if *Cricetus cricetus* leads a precarious existence now, it is at least protected by law.[21]

Symbolically speaking, packs are considered demonic. One famous example from popular culture are the Gremlins, in which one *mogwai*, or evil spirit, turns into a pack after having been given water.[22] As philosopher Richard Iveson explains: 'The reason for this demonic propriety is that pack animals, in contrast to both the pet and the model, form a multiplicity that presupposes contagion rather than filiation and involutions rather than hereditary production and sexual reproduction'.[23] With this contention, Iveson aligns himself with Gilles Deleuze and Felix Guattari, who argued that in terms of societal order, from a human perspective, any animal is potentially pack-like (as if every animal is a potential *mogwai*).[24] The animal pack embodies the potential of a becoming, and the radically open ended. Whereas previously the system of law was defined as tending towards closure and the realm of justice towards opening (see chapter three), the open character of the latter is not just that of the pack. Packs may disrupt anything, including realms of justice. And perhaps I need to repeat that in this study the realm of justice is not the realm of what is universally considered to be just. If, within a given realm of justice, people consider it to be just that anything that threatens them – even if it is animal that stings without pain and causes mild itching – must be killed, this realm is in a sense also closed. Packs of any kind may disrupt such a realm.

[19] In the Netherlands the animal falls under the so-called 'Wet natuurbescherming' (Law for the Protection of Nature), which in turn has to answer to the European Directives.

[20] AT (Loek) Kuiters, Maurice JJ La Haye, Gerhard JDM Müskens and Ruud JM van Kats, 'Perspectieven voor een duurzame bescherming van de hamster in Nederland' (2010) *Alterra Rapport* 2022, Wageningen, available at edepot.wur.nl/163477.

[21] When finishing the manuscript of this study the news reported that it is on the verge of dying out, nevertheless. The animal is on the red list of the International Union for Nature Conservation (IUCN) that appeared 9 July 2020: 'The IUCN Red List has today surpassed 120,000 species, with 120,372 species now assessed. Of these, 32,441 are threatened with extinction'. So, *Cricetus cricetus* is not alone.

[22] *Gremlins* was a movie hit in 1984 (Warner Bros) directed by Joe Dante. It was followed by *Gremlins 2: The New Batch* from 1990 (Warner Bros), also directed by Joe Dante.

[23] Iveson, 'Deeply Ecological Deleuze and Guattari' (2013) 36.

[24] The chapter '1730 – Becoming-Intense, Becoming-Animal, Becoming-Imperceptible' in Gilles Deleuze and Félix Guattari, *A Thousand Plateaus: Capitalism and Schizophrenia*, trans Brian Massumi (London, Continuum, 2004). The pack animal is distinguished in this chapter from 'Oedipal animals' as the individuated ones with which human beings can identify in terms of sentiment, and so-called 'State animals' which are animals that are defined on the basis of their function as a result of which they act as models, like when a car's motor is defined in terms of horsepower.

So, if legal protection is given to wolves, whether the real ones or the figurative ones like *Cricetus critecus*, this must imply they are no longer moving in packs but are running out of space as a species. The pack that became one of Europe's favourite tropes of a threat posed to society and order, law and justice, is on the verge of dying out. This paradoxically serves to tell us that there are disruptive forces residing in systems of law and realms of justice that may come to connect through the interface of art. In the Low Countries, for instance, the threat of waters was culturally defined by the trope of the wolf pack. The trope called for elimination of this threat, and art, in different forms, was helpful in promoting this. One such art form concerned the ability to redefine lands and waters in terms of 'designated areas'. It was the art of mapping.

II. The Art of Mapping: From Centralisation to Ecological Territorialisation

The ability to dissect lands and waters depends intrinsically on the art of mapping, with maps that can be accepted as legal documents and taken up in law's archives. This art was developing with astonishing speed in the course of the sixteenth and seventeenth century. A paradigmatic example is cartographer Jacob van Deventer, who made a map of the province of Holland in the Low Countries in the years 1537–38. This map would become the model of representation of Holland in atlases for a century to come. Van Deventer was not a small player as cartographer; he was the first to put the idea of trigonometry systematically into practice. As a result, his maps were remarkably accurate.[25] It was no coincidence, then, that he became an imperial cartographer in the service of the Habsburg emperor Charles V, and later a royal cartographer in the service of Philips II. The latter commissioned Van Deventer, probably around 1558, to chart not only all the important Dutch cities but also their environments, obviously for political, military and legal purposes.[26] Philips clearly did not see the Dutch Uprising coming, that

[25] It is still a matter of debate whether Van Deventer used the ideas of mathematician Gemma Frisius (1508–55) or whether it was the other way around. Be that is it may, Frisius was a figure in his own right. He not only described the principles of the camera obscura, but also got Gerardus Mercator as his pupil first and collaborator later, and Mercator would be responsible for what is still known as the Mercator projection. Frisius's method of trigonometry was first formulated in a booklet entitled Libellus de locorum describendorum ratione, & de eorum distantijs inueniendis, nunquam ante hac visus from 1533: 'A booklet about ways of describing places and to determine their distances that have never been seen'. On all this, see Fernand Hallyn, *Gemma Frisius, arpenteur de la terre et du ciel* (Paris, Honoré Champion, 2008).

[26] Willy Ahlers, 'Jacob van Deventer, nieuwe ideeën en nieuwe vragen' (2014) 23 *Caert-Thresoor* 59; or Bram Vannieuwenhuyze and Jelle Lisson, 'De stadsplannen van Jacob van Deventer: Een schitterende bron voor de stads- en dorpsgeschiedenis' (2012) 4 *Bladwijzer. Wegwijs met Heemkunde Vlaanderen* 3.

would erupt only 10 years later. This culminated in an official moment in 1581 with the Act of Abjuration, by means of which the Low Countries bid farewell to their king, or tyrant. He could surely not have foreseen that after eight decades of war, the Dutch Republic would be officially recognised in 1648, with the peace of Westphalia. In the course of the 80 years of war leading up to this international recognition, maps were crucial for the countless manoeuvres, battles, sieges, the taking and reclaiming of cities. Still, Van Deventer's commission was first and foremost part of Philips' attempts to centralise the Government, both politically and legally.[27]

Both war and centralisation in turn begot an unexpected ecological analogy when, over the course of the same period, another battle was waged. In the Low Countries, and especially in the provinces of Holland and Zeeland, water was dominant over land. For one, the Dutch would never have been able to win their war against Spain without water. The latter provided refuge for the so-called sea-beggars who were pivotal players in the beginning of the uprising.[28] Waters formed a decisive battleground when in 1588 the Spanish armies in Flanders were prevented from reaching the so-called invincible Spanish Armada waiting at sea to invade England. Key cities were protected by grounds that could be inundated when cities were attacked. Waterways formed the heart of a rapidly developing economy, as pathways for the transport of goods. Here, in the context of the increasingly prosperous Dutch economy and the consequent need for (more) fertile lands, maps were imbued with a different connotation. Especially in the context of Holland's desires to gain land by removing water, mapping supported, if not instigated, ecological territorialisation.[29] There is some adequacy in the saying 'God created Earth, the Dutch created Holland'. Yet hidden in this innocent phrase we find basic issues of the meeting of the logic of personhood, of self, and of packs.

To trace this, I propose an in-depth look at three different versions of maps that all made use of an original by Van Deventer from 1537.[30] Two are shown in Figures 5.3 and 5.4.

[27] A central, codified law for the Low Countries (one of the first in Europe), entitled 'Criminal ordinance', was announced by Philip II in 1570; Ludwig von Bar, *A History of Continental Criminal Law* (1916; repr Boston, Little, Brown, and Company, 1999)); for a more general picture see Geoffrey Parker, *The Grand Strategy of Philip II* (New York, Yale University Press, 2000).

[28] Virginia West Lunsford, *Piracy and Privateering in the Golden Age Netherlands* (New York, Palgrave Macmillan, 2005).

[29] Amongst the many studies about the situation, see Gerard van der Ven (ed), *Leefbaar laagland. Geschiedenis van de waterbeheersing en landaanwinning in Nederland* (Utrecht, Matrijs, 2003), or more recently Siger Zeischka, *Minerva in de polder: Waterstaat en techniek in het Hoogheemraadschap van Rijnland 1500–1856* (Hilversum, Verloren, 2008). Europe-wide 95% of all lands that were milled dry can be found in the Netherlands; and half of all the polders in Europe; see 'De Beemster' *RouteYou*, available at www.routeyou.com/nl-nl/location/view/47224624/de-beemster?toptext=578609.

[30] The original map made by Jacob van Deventer from 1537/38 was lost in World War II, but there is a facsimile left, see nl.wikipedia.org/wiki/Bestand:1558_Hollandt_v_Deventer.jpg.

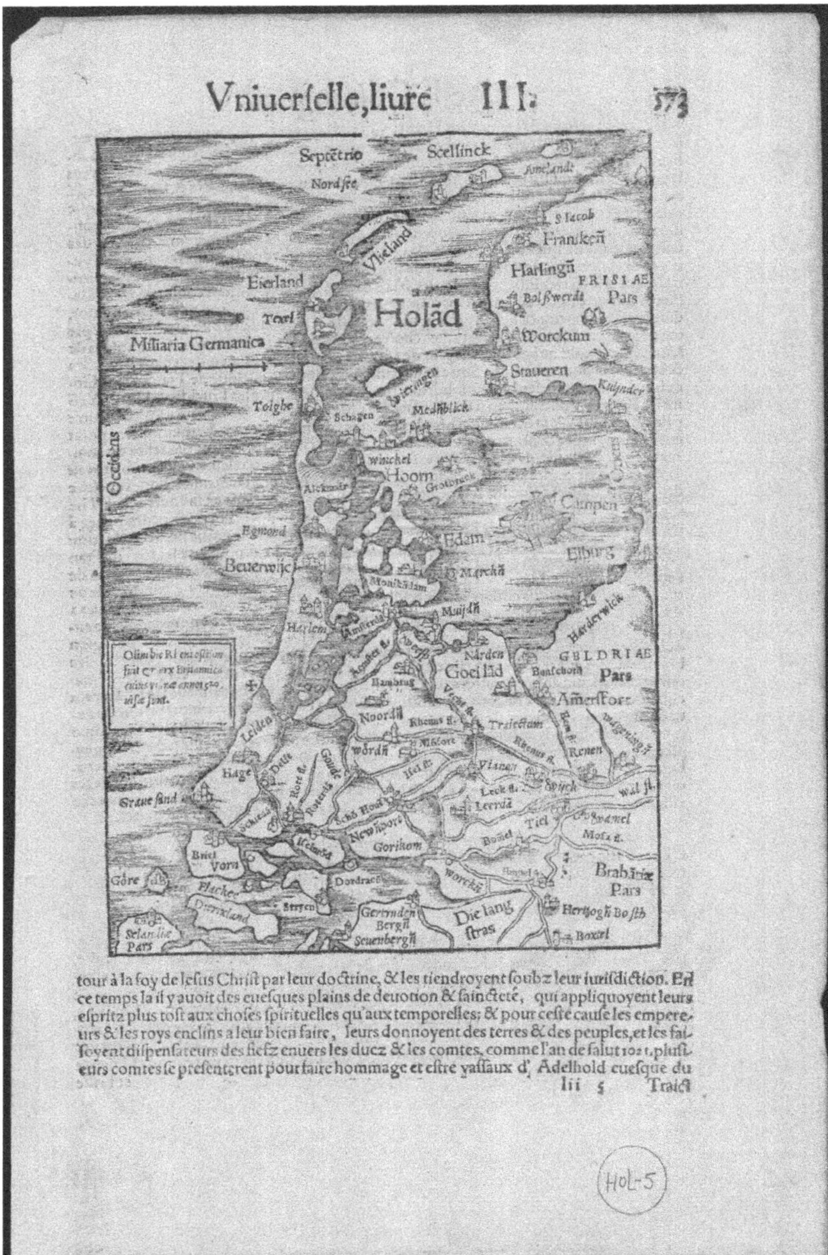

Figure 5.3 *Cosmographei oder Beschreibung aller Länder*

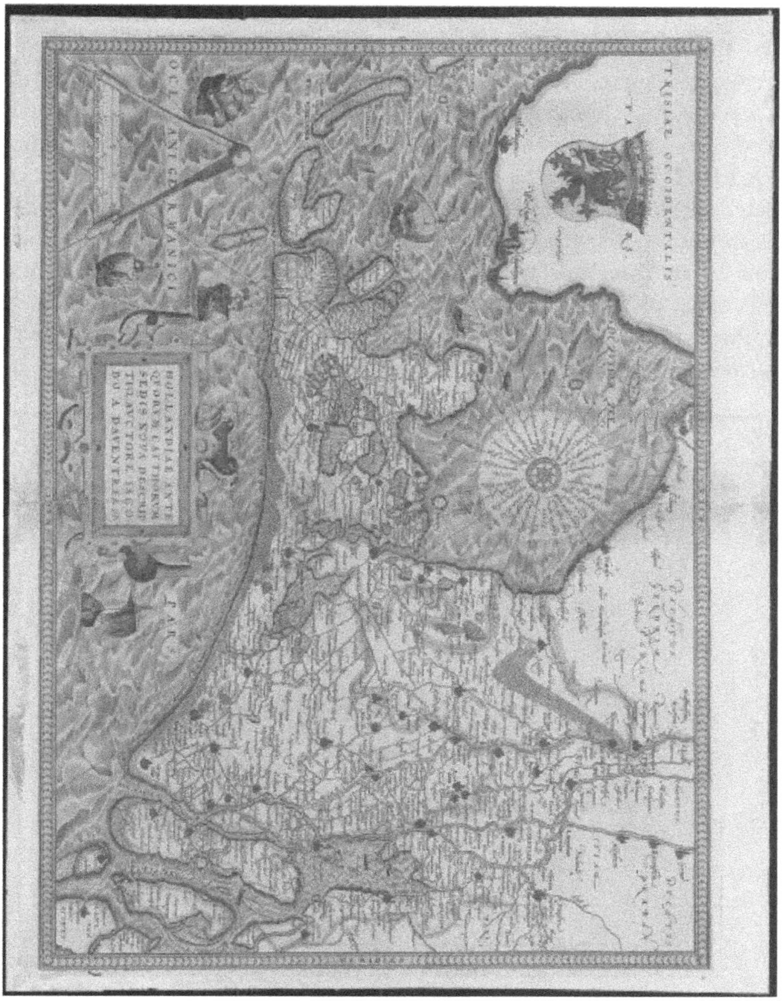

Figure 5.4 *Theatrum orbis terrarium* (first copperplate)

The image in Figure 5.3 was part of a German atlas from 1544 entitled *Cosmographei oder Beschreibung aller Länder*, that is: *cosmography or description of all lands*. The map was made by Sebastian Münster, published in Basel by Heinrich Petri, and finally reprinted in 1628.[31] The map in Figure 5.4, dated 1570, appeared in *Theatrum orbis terrarium* or *Theatre of the Sphere of the Earth*. In this case, the first copperplate edition was compiled by Abraham Ortelius, and published in Antwerp by Gilles Coppens van Diest. It was reprinted one final time in 1612 and is considered to be the first true world atlas.[32]

[31] The map shown here is based on the fifth, expanded reprint in 1550, but is taken from the 1578 reprint; see bc.library.uu.nl/nl/kaarten-van-holland-en-utrecht.html; its official title is 'Holand'.

[32] One version, entitled 'Hollandiae antiquorum catthorum sedis nova descriptio, auctore Iacobo a Daventria' can be found at objects.library.uu.nl/reader/index.php?obj=1874-348539&metadata=1&lan=en#page//15/27/85/152785649902439138109219780637837148035.jpg/mode/1up.

Visually or formally speaking, the maps give a radically different impression. In the first, the seas are fiercely zigzagging, visually more agitated than the land, with waters that appear teeth-like. In the second, the water bodies are more whirling and fluid, accentuating calmer circumstances. In the first, the bodies of water tend to be more vast or pronounced than the lands, as if the Low Countries should rather be called High Waters. In the second, the turbulence of water appears instead to translate itself onto land, as if the two are equally dynamic. In the first, land and waters appear to intersect. In the second, land and water are more intermingled.

Now let us compare Figure 5.4, the first copperplate, with Figure 5.5, the second copper plate. Here, the waves of the first plate are replaced by dots.[33] As a result, the waters in the second copperplate appear as an equally distributed light blue surface of tranquillity and silence.

Figure 5.5 *Theatrum orbis terrarium* (second copperplate)

The two maps in comparison also highlight another contrast. The waters of lakes and rivers have acquired a more strongly pronounced dark band on the map to the right, as if demarcating a border or a limit. The result is that the lands appear to be more secured, and more networked as well, now that the waters appear to be contained; many look more like functional waterways, connecting the network of cities. One other effect of the sea's appearance as remarkably tranquil in the second copperplate is that two instruments protrude more sharply: a compass rose in the centre of the South Sea, and a calliper in the upper left part. The compass rose gives the impression that we are looking into the human eye's controlling iris; with the calliper we are given this glimpse from the side, opening up to the world but also capturing it from a specific perspective.

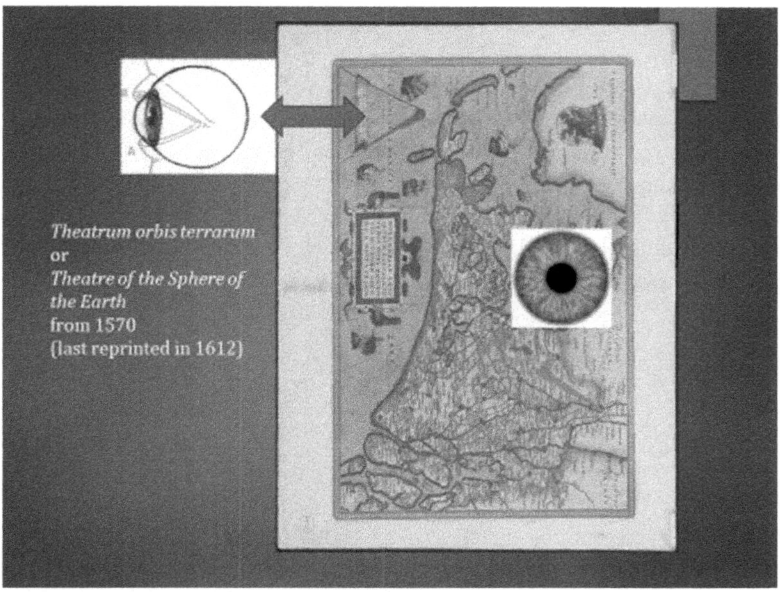

Figure 5.6 Visualisation of calliper and iris by the author

Both instruments conjoined are clear indices of a *cartographic gaze* that was defined by John Pickles as follows:

> The cartographic gaze is dominated by a commitment to modelling a God's-eye view, what Donna Haraway (1991) called the 'God-trick'. This transcendental position is both the view from above, an elevated two-point perspective bird's-eye-view, *and* an all seeing eye that views everywhere at the same time.[34]

[33] The map shown here is based on the print from 1570, but is taken from the 1595 reprint. Its official title is: 'Hollandiae antiquorum catthorum sedis nova descriptio, auctore Iacobo a Daventria'. For all this, and the replacement of waves by dots, see dspace.library.uu.nl/handle/1874/20401.

[34] John Pickles, *A History of Spaces: Cartographic Reason, Mapping and the Geo-Coded World* (London, Routledge, 2004) 80. See also: Doug Specht and Anna Feigenbaum, 'From Cartographic Gaze to Contestatory Cartographies' in Pol Bargués-Pedreny, David Chandler and Elena Simon (eds), *Mapping and Politics in the Digital Age* (London, Routledge, 2018).

The reference to Haraway, implicitly helps Pickles to emphasise the tension between a particular or situated position, and a position that claims to be, somehow, objective.[35] The representational in between, I want to argue, is a sphere. With the devices of calliper and compass, by means of both focused and framing focalisation, the world is captured in a theatrical sphere, as the title of the atlas, *Theatre of the Sphere of the Earth*, also suggests. So, whilst the compass rose and calliper may be placed in the represented waters, they are obvious indices to the fixed grounds on the basis of which these maps could be made so accurately. Precisely because they are placed in water, they act as indices to the ways in which the waters have now become dominated by the land.

In this context, the contrast between the third map (Figure 5.5) and the first (Figure 5.3), from the *Cosmographie*, tells us that water has come to be controlled. One specific example of this is a dominating piece of blue in the map of Holland from the *Cosmographei*. It represents a vast lake that no longer exists but harbours Amsterdam airport, Schiphol, at four meters below sea level. The name Schiphol might either mean ships' hell or ships' hall. The name is a residue of either dangerous waters that formerly brought ships to the bottom of the sea, or the indication of a place where ships could find protection against dangerous winds.[36] The airfield is located smack in the middle, that is, of what were either turbulent and treacherous waters, or a hiding place of rescue in the upper right of the 'Lake of Haarlem':[37]

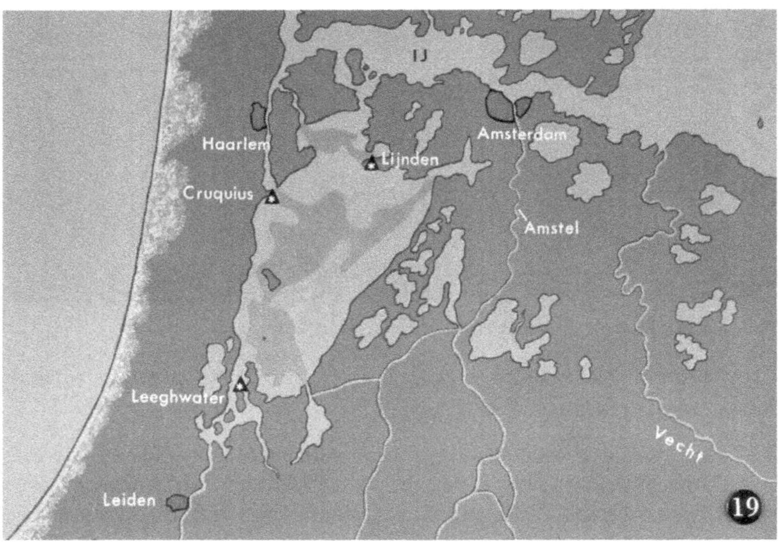

Figure 5.7 Map of the lake of Haarlem in the seventeenth century

[35] Donna J Haraway 'Situated Knowledges: The Science Question in Feminism and the Privilege of Partial Perspective' in *Simians, Cyborgs, and Women: the Reinvention of Nature* (New York, Routledge, 1991).

[36] For this see: 'Luchthaven Schiphol', available at nl.wikipedia.org/wiki/Luchthaven_Schiphol#Naam.

[37] For this map see *Rijkswaterstaat*, available at beeldbank.rws.nl/MediaObject/Details/333473.

As Figure 5.7 shows, this vast lake was separated from the North Sea by only a small ribbon of land, less than 10 kilometres in breadth. The lake directly joined the South Sea, which in turn directly bordered the North Sea. In a sense it was not a lake at all, then. It was an arm of the South Sea, reaching deep inland and nearly isolating Amsterdam from the rest of Holland. Consequently, the call for its drainage increased in intensity during the course of the seventeenth century, although it would take until 1849 before the process of dry-milling the lake would begin. Yet worked-out plans to remove the waters of the lake and turn the entire area into profitable lands or polders were proposed by the great water technician Jan Leeghwater (1575–1650) in his three-volume study *Book of the Lake of Haarlem* (*Haarlemmermeerboeck*) from 1641.[38] The art of dry-milling was much helped, in this case, by literature. It helped to promote the endeavour by making people feel what kind of pack needed to be countered and eliminated.

III. Waters as Wolf Packs: Tropes of Infuriation

Leeghwater had already made a name, not only in his work as architect, patent holder of a diving bell in 1605 or his support in the Dutch conquering of the key city 's-Hertogenbosch, but especially due to his innovative activities of dry milling the lakes of Beemster, Purmer, Wormer, Heerhugowaard, Schermer and Starn.[39] Leeghwater made a chart (see Figure 5.8) that depicted the situation if the Lake of Haarlem was milled dry. It also contained a poem, in the lower left corner, that called for its dry-milling.[40]

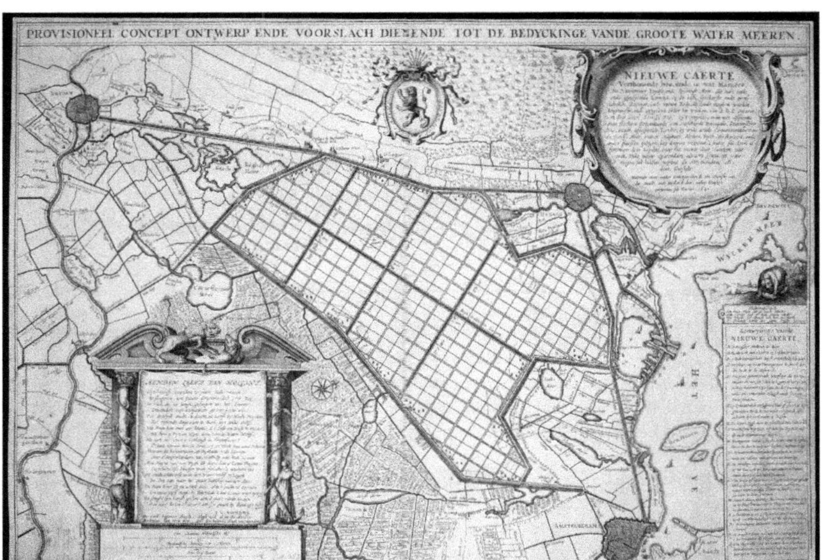

Figure 5.8 Leeghwater, 'Provisional concept plan and proposal with the aim of diking of the big water lakes'

For the reader's orientation: the north is almost to the right here, as is indicated by the compass rose at the heart of the map (so the map should be turned anti-clockwise once). The poem's text, on the left below, is captured in an architectonic frame that stands out against the background. It can be read as the gateway to a house, or a garden, or a gate offering a view into the future. Behind it, the organised space of the dry-milled lake is surrounded by already existing polders that hold the potential of the lake's future.

Within the inserted frame there is a poem (see Figure 5.9) made by the Republic's most influential author, its greatest playwright, satirist, and author of occasional poetry: Joost van den Vondel (1587–1679). On top of the frame, two animals are battling one another.

Figure 5.9 Detail from Leeghwater, 'Provisional concept plan and proposal with the aim of diking of the big water lakes' showing poem and the lion subduing the wolf

[38] Jan Adriaansz. Leeghwater, *Haerlemmermeerboeck: Beschryvinge wegens het bedyken en droogmaken van de Haarlemmer-meer* (1641); also see *dbnl*, available at https://www.dbnl.org/tekst/leeg001haer01_01. The engineer adopted his family name 'Leeghwater', meaning 'Emptied waters', when asking for a patent for a diver's bell.

[39] JG Roever, *Jan Adriaensz. Leeghwater: Het leven en werk van een zeventiende-eeuws waterbouwkundige* (Amsterdam, NV J Ahrend & Zoon, 1944); on the more general context of Leeghwater's works, see Cordula Rooijendijk, *Waterwolven: een geschiedenis van stormvloeden, dijkenbouwers en droogmakers* (Amsterdam, Atlas, 2009).

[40] The map can be found (and be enlarged) at *Allard Pierson, de Collecties van de Universiteit van Amsterdam*, available at hdl.handle.net/11245/3.3072.

A lion is fighting and defeating a wolf, here. He is not the only lion. In the upper middle of the map there is a lion that seals the entire plan. The two announce and illustrate the poem's major protagonist, the Lion – the symbol of the Dutch nation:

TO THE LION OF HOLLAND
To be chasing foreign enemies
To swipe your tail so bravely over Sea
Is vain, when your lung is consumed
Or is relentlessly wasted inside, and you, with a pained heart
Sigh and cough, and with vast clots spit woefully
Your rotting intestines out of your throat, into the waves.
What is the gain in plundering East and West with your claw
While this cruel Water Wolf is biting your heart
Who now aims to triumph over you before long
Oh, Land Lion, time you wake up, and awake with your roar
All moor peoples, the Kennemers, and Rhyneland's old masters
Together with Amsterdammers as the Lion's emergency force
Let one smother with a dike this animal that plagues you
Let the wind-lord fly in with his wings of mills
The fast wind-lord knows how to charge the Water Wolf
In the sea from which he never grows tired gnawing on you
Thus the Land Lion gains land, thus he draws gold from foam.[41]

The first lines hint at Dutch privateers on the world seas, who are metaphorically referred to as the sweeping tail of the Dutch lion, earning money with the chartered, politically and legally commissioned seizing of foreign ships. The sweeping tail seems to connote infuriation, yet this is legally countered by turning pirates into privateers. This shift connotes another historical transition. In the sixteenth century the lion was an icon of ferocity and cruelty, and only in the context of the

[41] For the original see Joost van den Vondel, 'Aen den Leeuw van Hollant' in Arie Jan Gelderblom (ed), *'k Wil rijmen wat ik bouw. Twee eeuwen topografische poëzie* (Amsterdam, Querido's Uitgeverij, 1994) 41; or *dbnl*, www.dbnl.org/tekst/vond001dewe04_01/vond001dewe04_01_0043.php: 'Uyt-heemse vyanden te sitten inde veeren / Te slingeren den staart Grootmoedich over Zee, / Is Ydel, als uw longh geslagen aen het Teeren, / Inwendich vast vergaet en gy met herte wee / Soo deerlyck Sucht en Kucht en Loost by Heele Brocken / Het rottende Ingewant te Keel uyt, inde Golff / Wat Baet het met uw Klauw al t'Oost en West te Plocken / Wat Baet het met uw Klauw al t'Oost en West te Plocken / Na dien u Byt int Hart dees Wrede Water Wolff / Nu uyt om over u Eerlangh te Triomferen / O: lant Leeuw Waeck eens op, en Weck met eenen Schreeu / Alt veen de Kennemaers, en Rynlants oude Heeren / Met d'Amsterlanders, tot noothulp van hun Leeuw / Men Sluyte met een Dyck dit dier, dat u Comt Plagen / De Wintvorst Vlieger met syn Moole wieken toe / De snelle Wintvorst weet den Water Wolff te Iagen / In Zee, van waer hy u quam Knabblen nimmer Moe / Zoo wint de Lant Leeuw Lant, soo puurt hy Gout uyt Schuym'.

Dutch Revolt did it acquire its positive connotations of strength, sovereignty and unity.[42] The lion, with its sweeping tail, is then warned that his efforts to defeat enemies or make an easy gain may be in vain if its lungs are meanwhile being wasted and consumed. Hence, the lion should redirect its claws to the enemy residing in Holland's lung, in a battle that could deliver equal profits. To this order, a pack animal has to be killed: the Water Wolf. The killing has to be done skilfully, using forces of nature that cost nothing and are working non-stop: the winds. Killing this animal is technically possible, by means of windmills and dikes. It is politically possible, if people come to concerted action. It is economically attractive, moreover, because there is the promise of profit. Watery foam that consists of nothing but bubbles can be turned into solid gold. One crucial element is left unmentioned, meanwhile: the gained land needs to be legally redefined.

The metaphor of consumption, and the coughing of clots that comes with this disease, bore a marked relation to reality: Holland was indeed losing land by physical clots. Its soil consisted of peat, and the waters would erode it away relentlessly. Such erosion was worsened by storm floods, of which the Low Countries witnessed an almost countless number. In this context, the wolf, as a pack animal is brought in as a metaphor. That metaphor was broadly shared. It underpinned, for instance, Hobbes' description, in *About the Citizen*, of the brutal fight of cities against one another.[43] It is clear that Hobbes was not an ardent student of nature, or of wolves. Yet he tapped into this broadly shared and culturally propelled anxiety. In the Low Countries, moreover, the trope of wolves hunting in packs was a favourite index for whipped-up masses of water, the backs of hunting wolves resembling the heaving of waves. As such, the two are both icons of infuriation, chasing prey whilst moving on, threatening the very grounds that form the stability of human existence: land, territory, property. In light of these, the waters as they are depicted in Figure 5.3 acquire a distinct connotation. The waters are presented in the form of teeth, connoting the teeth of wolves. This association between wolves and waters is not idiosyncratic or anachronistic. The trope of the water wolf used by Vondel was well known, and prevails up until the twenty-first century.[44] The formal expression

[42] On this shift, see Marijke Spies, 'Verbeeldingen van Vrijheid: David en Mozes, Burgerhart en Bato, Brutus en Cato' (1994) 10 *De zeventiende eeuw* 141.

[43] *De cive* was written in 1642 but published in 1651, see Thomas Hobbes, *On the Citizen*, (ed) Richard Tuck and Michael Silverthorne (Cambridge, Cambridge University Press, 1998).

[44] See Cordula Rooijendijk, *Waterwolven*; in translation: *Water-wolves: a history of storm floods, dike builders and dry millers*, or see Menne Kosian, *Droogmakerijen* (Amersfoort, Rijksdienst voor het cultureel erfgoed, 2017) 13. A newspaper article entitled 'The Dutch delta: an endless series of storm floodings' describes the sea as being 'vraatzuchtig': ravenous. The Dutch word 'vraatzuchtig' is hard to translate, but connotes an animal that devours its prey; see Jacob Hoekman, 'De Nederlandse delta: een eindeloze reeks stormvloeden' (31 January 2013) *Reformatorisch Dagblad*. One other example: the website of the waterboard Rijnland describes an important part of its history under the heading 'The water wolf subdued' ('De waterwolf bedwongen'), see www.rijnland.net/over-rijnland/erfgoed/artikelen-uitgelicht/de-waterwolf-bedwongen. Last but not least, an entire miniature world of the Netherlands, *Madurodam*, offers children a battle against this wolf by making them dry-mill the Haarlemmer lake, www.madurodam.nl/nl/het-park/waterwolf.

of the waters in Figure 5.3, in their connoting teeth, resembles that of a wolf eating its prey, as if gnawing away the land.

Art's interface is functional, here, as a means to animalise waters as a matter of infuriation. It is also capable of civilising the wind. The wind could be the premise of flooding, yes, but is personified here as the force propelling the tools that will help control the waters. Finally, art manages to allegorise human beings as the noble sovereign of all animals: the lion. This lion, in turn, is repersonified as either the company of Dutch privateers or a collective body of Hollanders, whose bravery, skills and techniques can make a profit. The literary play with animalisation, personification, allegory and metaphor has a distinct rhetorical goal. The person who asked Vondel to make the poem, Leeghwater, was far from naïve: he was experienced in draining lakes and knew it required investments to claim the land of such a vast lake. He also knew there were profitable fishing industries surrounding the lake that would oppose such endeavours, or authorities that would point to the importance of waterways as a means of access for the big cities. As such, Leeghwater needed literature to prepare the grounds and incentivise people to set out on a risky path.

The world proposed by Leeghwater and Vondel was caught in a theatrical sphere that was projected and framed by the human gaze and the power to name things; also legally defining them. Although waters were not mapped in as detailed a fashion as lands were, this did not mean they were not considered as under some form of custody. They would either belong to, or fall under the authority of, differing governing bodies, including counties, cities, and, in rare cases, even individuals. Yet apart from the latter, by and large the waters were public or common property. However, the endeavours to make polders out of waters turned this common entity into private, profitable property. This is why I consider the English verb 'reclaiming', as a term that indicates the dry-milling of lakes, as inadequate. The prefix 're-' suggests that the lands already belonged to someone. Well, they were not. To make them someone's, legal anthropomorphism was needed. It concerned not so much the literary trope of giving human qualities to non-human entities. Rather, it concerned the power to turn commercial bodies into legal persons with transferable property.

In first instance, commons can be seen as the spatial analogy to a lack of personhood because these spaces depend on a complex dynamic of use and sharing. Yet in terms of law the personalised distribution of both uses and actors is pivotal in order to define property. Now there is no denying that, since early modernity, what is common is considered to be some sort of property that is in need of protection. In the case of the Low Countries, for instance, much land was gained by different modes of empoldering through collective efforts. In order to make sure that parties looking for quick profit would not simply appropriate the lands gained, they were protected by law from some moment onwards, by means of the installation of waterboards. These were early modern forms of what would later be called cooperatives.[45] Still, most commons were pre-legal, essentially. There was not one

[45] The process starts in 1255 with count William II of Holland giving rights to the waterboard of Rhineland.

legal entity responsible for them and they fell under the customs and responsibilities of collective selves.

Commons are disturbing elements in the choice between use and property because they confuse the clarity of who *owns* them. The issue of ownership depends on the distinction between legal personhood and self, whether individual or collective. It also depends on the ability to delineate what is being owned. Well, many commons were not defined by stable borders. Depending on the culture, as the New Zealand example illustrated, some commons included many more beings beyond only human ones. They could, but need not, be defined by territory, as the first forms of newly gained lands in the Low Countries show. There were myriad forms, with inner and outer commons as prominent and recurring types (eg in the shape of pastures and wastelands), but also with different forms of the use of commons, like the rights to pasture and pannage. In all cases, people had no trouble dealing with them, sharing them, in practice. Ultimately, the legal redefinition of land started to become exceedingly prominent with regards to property, and by consequence, in terms of legal personhood. Collective and individual selves suffered from the consequences, especially when the European redefinition of the commons into private property coincided with a process of colonisation.

In Europe, and England especially, commons were first enclosed and then turned into property. How this was transposed onto the colonial domains is still the object of investigation,[46] but it was no coincidence that the best and brightest in Europe, like Hugo Grotius or John Locke, would spend much effort considering the commonality of land and property in indigenous lands. Allan Green argues that the general picture is significantly influenced by the fifth chapter of Locke's Second Treatise of Civil Government: 'Of Property'. According to Green, this text forms to the backbone of the view that 'enclosure rather than commons acted as the driving force' since Locke was the major 'proponent of both enclosure and colonizing and preeminent philosopher of property in land'.[47] The idea was that colonialists cut up the land first, physically, by means of hedges and fences and then declared it to be their own, legally. The other view, according to Green, is that 'dispossession came about largely through the clash of an indigenous commons and a colonial commons'.[48] Here, the first step was to define the commons of colonialists as legally rightful, although they had no rights, and to define those of others as based on customs. Thus, colonial commons were legally established, or given a recognisable legal face, and the commons of others were a matter of a somewhat amorphous tradition. This is how commons became legally defined, protected, defended and gradually enlarged as property; a concept that was alien

[46] See, for instance Allan Greer, 'Commons and Enclosure in the Colonization of North America' (2012) 2 *The American Historical Review* 365, available at doi.org/10.1086/ahr.117.2.365.

[47] ibid 366.

[48] ibid 366.

to those who could not even conceive of the idea that one could legally claim land as property.

The way in which human beings relate to nature in terms of justice can be traced in the history of the commons, then. It has been a topic of much concern in the last decades, especially in an ecological context.[49] Though law's power to turn entities into persons serves to enlarge issues of accountability, this power also implies a distribution of irresponsibility.

IV. The Veil of Irresponsibility, New Persons, New Selves

Despite law's public nature, where public is considered to be the opposite of private, its *idiocy* dominates since states depend on particularity: their privacy in the sense of their being on their own, which makes their very sovereignty possible. Even if in the modern study of law no ultimate sovereign power is to be assigned, since the higher or highest law is not one of command but 'merely founds the authority to command while simultaneously setting conditions for the legitimate use of that authority' (see chapter four),[50] this occasions fundamental problems, particularly with regard to ecological issues. In light of this, law not only struggles with anything that transcends the limits of the state by means of which its conditions are set, but also with the fluidity of water, of which we now know that it connotes the pack or the swarm. Law favours ground(ing). Its logic of personhood, with the state being the highest legal person, connotes the axiomatic link between sovereignty, lands and territory.

The dealing with water in terms of land is evidenced, for instance, in the first Article of the Water Framework Directive of the European Union (WFD), codified as 2000/60/EC. It dates from 23 October 2000 and states: 'Water is not a commercial product like any other but, rather, a heritage which must be protected, defended and treated as such'.[51] The speaking subject is the EU's authoritative body; its agents, the Member States, are supposed to act in protecting, defending and treating an object – water. This is not a commercial product like any other,

[49] The common denominator is the phrase 'tragedy of the commons' coined by biologist Garrit Hardin, 'The Tragedy of the Commons' (1968) 162 *Science* 1243. The phrase and the analysis have been heavily criticised since then, with fairly few attention being paid to the legal issues involved with the privatisation of the commons or the legal protection of inherently public property. Notable exception is Rose, 'The Comedy of the Commons' (1968). About the current problems, see, for instance, Stefan Partelow, David J Abson, Achim Schlüter, Maria E Fernández-Giménez, Henrik von Wehrden and Neil Collier, 'Privatizing the Commons: New Approaches Need Broader Evaluative Criteria For Sustainability' (2019) 13 *International Journal of the Commons* 747.

[50] Minkkinen, *Thinking Without Desire: A First Philosophy of Law* (Oxford, Hart Publishing, 1999) 126.

[51] Directive 2000/60/EC of the European Parliament and of the Council of 23 October 2000 establishing a framework for Community action in the field of water policy, available at eur-lex.europa.eu/legal-content/EN/TXT/?uri=celex%3A32000L0060.

but by implication a product nevertheless: a heritage. This, in turn, is a term that is used seemingly neutrally. Yet etymologically, heritage implies the elements of 'heir; inheritance, ancestral estate, heirloom'. As such it is related to water's counterpart, *land*. As heritage, then, water is an object that is analytically taken apart, visualised, and legally renamed as ground, which is indeed how the Dutch Law on the protection of nature (Wnb) defines water. Article 1.1.2 of this law states: 'In this law and the legal notices that define it the following is to be understood included: - land/ground: waters'.[52]

If we return to the maps dealt with above, it is telling that both mapping and law eliminate all the senses except the visual in order to be able to fictively frame, name and stage things.[53] In recent decades juridical interactions between script and image have been studied intensively, the pivot being that law's claim on superior reasoning based itself analytically on script and that, ultimately, it either fears the unruly, affective disturbance of troubling images or uses them to bring people to law's source of authority: script.[54] Despite the considerable insights that studies into this dynamic have produced, they have also been inclined to forget how visuality defines law through the elimination of other senses. To be sure, there is a major distinction, here, between law's capacity to give entities a face and the practice of the judiciary, in which the spoken word and aurality are equally important.[55] Still, if nature is unveiled and her face can be seen, as a result of which she can be considered a person, this has as its effect that the question of whether one could smell her, feel, hear, taste her, let alone intuit her is being short-circuited. Maps are not just representations with abstract, epistemological force; they affect people through their visual force that, in our case, facilitates the underpinning of property by legal persons. This affective force can be traced when frightening waters are turned into lands that are simultaneously and reassuringly reconfigured on the basis of a grid that works on a cartographic and legal level, as is shown in Figure 5.10.[56]

[52] Wnb, Artikel 1.1.2: 'In deze wet en de daarop rustende bepalingen wordt mede verstaan onder … – *grond:* wateren …' See: wetten.overheid.nl/BWBR0037552/2019-01-01.

[53] Maria Aristodemou, *Law and Literature: Journeys from Her to Eternity* (Oxford, Oxford University Press, 2001).

[54] The theme runs through most of the work of Peter Goodrich, from *Languages of Law: From Logics of Memory to Nomadic Masks* (Cambridge, Cambridge University Press, 1990), via *Oedipus Lex: Psychoanalysis, History, Law* (Berkeley, University of California Press, 1995), and *Legal Emblems and the Art of Law: Obiter Depicta as the Vision of Governance* (2013) to edited volumes such as Peter Goodrich and Christian Delage (eds), *The Scene of the Mass Crime: History, Film and International Tribunals* (London, Routledge, 2012), or Peter Goodrich and Valérie Hayaert (eds), *Genealogies of Legal Vision* (London, Routledge, 2015).

[55] On this, see James EK Parker, *Acoustic Jurisprudence: Listening to the Trial of Simon Bikindi* (Oxford, Oxford University Press, 2015) 32–33. Parker also offers a critique on those who, like Peter Goodrich, would want to posit a hierarchy between the visual and the aural in the domains of law.

[56] On the maps, see *Het Geheugen van Nederland*, available at www.geheugenvannederland.nl/nl/geheugen/view/minimap?coll=ngvn&identifier=ZZM01:B000768&pc=.

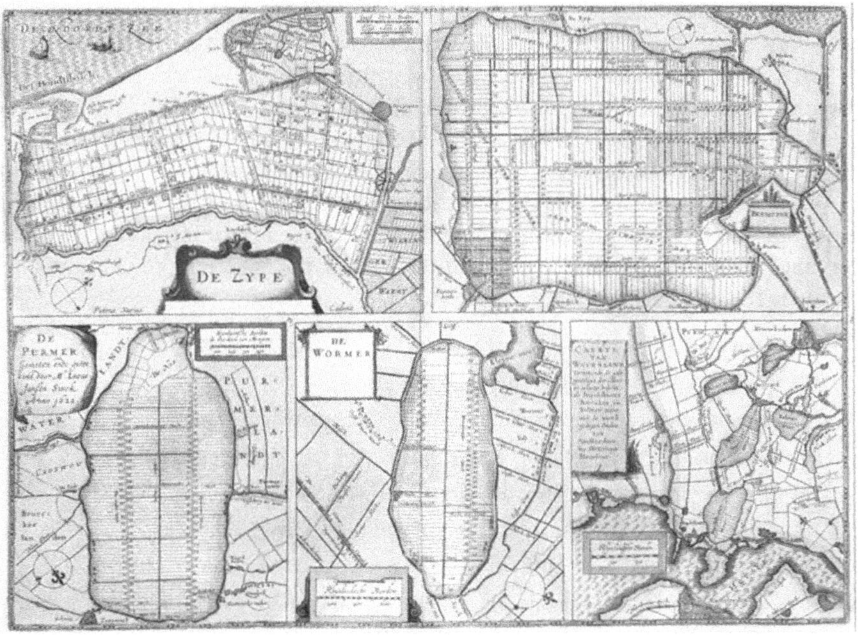

Figure 5.10 Chart of several famous polders made by P van der Keere and LJ Sinck and published by Hondius in 1633; de Beemster is at the top-right

By means of a simultaneous mathematical and legal grid, commons are being cut up, divided into first sellable and then rentable parts, that serves the endeavour of collectives of investors that worked on the basis of a so-called *octrooi*, a charter or concession, which would by implication turn them into legal persons. The charter would legally underpin their activities and would make sure that the gained common property would change legally into private property, on the basis of a monopoly, once the lake had been turned into land.[57] Charter and chart go hand in hand, here, and as such they allude to the fears that Vondel's poem was playing with. Underpinned by charters, charts and maps served to prescribe to land the iconic image of property – a much less frightening one than the fluid mass of the water wolf, though a no less aggressive one in many ways.

The transition from commons to private property needs a distribution of responsibilities. The kind of distribution at stake was specified by legal scholar Scott Veitch in terms of law's intrinsic irresponsibility.[58] In Veitch's reading of especially colonial transitions, law, in the service of politics, made sure that legal persons were no longer held responsible for what they had done to colonial selves, whether human or otherwise, once sovereignty had been transferred. In the case

[57] H. van Zwet, *Lofwaerdighe dijckagies en miserabele polders: een financiële analyse van landaanwinningsprojecten in Hollands Noorderkwartier, 1597–1643* (Hilversum, Verloren, 2009).
[58] Veitch, *Law and Irresponsibility, On the Legitimation of Human Suffering* (Abingdon, Routledge-Cavendish, 2007).

above, the water wolf may have been killed effectively, indeed providing others with considerable profits. As a result, no one asks any more: what about the waters? Or what about the (collective) selves living with or in these waters? This veiling of responsibility is a painful and powerful ability of law to distribute rights, obligations and competences. Anyone acting wrongly will be held responsible by law, unless, of course, wrongful acts are not defined as such, legally.

Law's veiling of responsibility is distinctly at work in the following piece, also by Vondel, on a lake that was claimed and gained at the beginning of the sixteenth century. The Beemster lake was milled dry, under the leadership of Leeghwater, between 1607 and 1612:

The Beemster

The wind lord, to spawn the sorrow of Hollands virgin
Since she had been damaged and infringed by storm after storm,
Dressed itself with wicks of mills and grinded, after much turning,
The Beemster into pasture, and discharged the lake into sea.
The sun, surprised, saw the clay still briny from the waves,
And dried them, and presented them with a festive cloth of green,
Embroidered with flowers, abundance of leaves, harvest and spikes,
And in decorating her hair cast it full of scents;
The source of cream and butter sprang from her breasts
Her fishy body became flesh, still virgin and fresh;
The crown on her forehead pushed itself through clouds
Like when luxury, on average, finds joy in height.
Here the greyhound hunts game, here the chariot takes a trip for fun,
People dance, people dine, in the merchant's wealthy quarter;
Here the golden age is laughing in sweet lust bowers,
Not afraid of any war, or of dangerous endeavours at sea.
You can make up Cypris, as she came to charm Cyprus,
I know *this* goddess was born from the foam of the sea.[59]

[59] For the original, see Joost van den Vondel, 'De Beemster' in JFM Sterck, HWE Moller, CGN de Vooys, CR de Klerk, BH Molkenboer, J Prinsen, J Lzn and L Simons (eds), De werken van Vondel IV (Amsterdam, De Maatschappij voor goede en goedkoope lectuur, 1930) 609; also see *dbnl*, www.dbnl.org/tekst/vond001dewe04_01/colofon.php: 'De Wintvorst, om den rouw van Hollands maagd te paeien, / Vermits, door storm op storm, zij schade en inbreuk leê. / Schoot molenwiecken aan, en maalde, na lang draeien, / Den Beemster tot een beemd, en loosde 't meir in zee. / De zon verwondert, zag de klay nog brack van baren, / En drooghdese af, en schonkse een groenen staatsiekeurs, / Vol bloemen geborduurd, vol lovren, ooft, en airen; / En, toiende heur haar, bestroide het vol geurs. / De room en boterbron quam uit haar borsten springen, / Het vissigh lijf wert vleesch, noch maagd en ongerept; / Haar voorhoofts torenkroon quam door de wolken dringen: / Gelijck gemeenlick weelde in hoogheit wellust schept. / Hier jaagt de windhont 't wilt, hier rijt de koets uit spelen, / Men danst, men banketteert, in 's Koopmans rijke buurt. / Hier lacht de goude tijt, in lieve lustprieelen, / Die voor geen oorloogh schrikt, noch kiel op klippen stuurt. / Verzier van Cypris, hoe zij Cypers quam

The literary process may be clear by now. It concerns the familiar mix of personification, allegory and anthropomorphism. The second line mentions infuriated winds. Yet they have now been civilised: they have been dressed by means of windmills. Through their work, the lake has been discharged into sea. As a consequence thereof, water has changed into pasture. It is made abundantly clear what fruits, what goods, what riches, what luxury, what fun people can have now that the lands are up for grabs. It is even made explicit who did the taking: those who were able to make the investment, people from the 'merchant's wealthy quarter'. A majority of actors is absent in the meantime: the farmers who did not and could not own the land they worked, but had to pay rent to the ones who had changed commons into private property; the fisher families whose habitat had been destroyed; the animals whose habitat had been destroyed.

Again, an individual person rises from the indistinct mass of waves: a virgin goddess that is a rival to the classical goddess Aphrodite, prefiguration of Venus, born on the coast of Cyprus. Yet, unlike readings that emphasise how the latter's birth from foam is made up, or mythical (whether it is the foam of Uranos's genitals or that of the sea), its birth is technological in this case. It is through art, considered both in terms of technique and literary imagination, that a fictive person is created that connotes another *ficta persona*: the collective of merchants that paid for its birth. This collective was charted, and became a legal person looking for manageable land as a result, that, once found, was in need of protection. Hence the perhaps strange line emphasising that all these wealthy people are not complacent. They are willing to take a risk (as any investor does) and they are willing to go to war to defend their property, if need be. Private property, legally speaking, depends on the element of exclusion, a so-called right that has to be defended.

The combined efforts of art, literature and cartography were that aesthetically, legally, and politically, waters came to affect people differently. They were no longer pack-like, but became mapped property, and by implication heritage. Law has been allying itself with ruling powers and the sciences in this massive historical process rather than joining the ranks of collectives of selves. This alliance is implied when Karen Barad, author of *Meeting the Universe Halfway*, reconsiders CP Snow's ideas on the split between the humanities and the sciences, the so-called two cultures, and states:

> [T]he entanglement of matter and meaning calls into question this set of dualisms that places nature on one side and culture on the other. And which separates off matters of fact from matters of concern (Bruno Latour) and matters of care (Maria Puig de la Bellacasa), and shifts them off to be dealt with by what we aptly call here in the States 'separate academic divisions,' whereby the division of labor is such that the natural sciences are assigned matters of fact and the humanities matters of concern, for example.[60]

bekoren: / Ik weet, dat dees Godin uit zeeschuim is geboren'. For an extensive interpretation, see Arie-Jan Gelderblom, 'Dichter bij een droogmakerij' in Eddy K Grootes and Sonja F Witstein (eds), *Visies op Vondel na 300 jaar* (The Hague, Martinus Nijhoff, 1979).

[60] Karen Barad, '"Matter Feels, Converses, Suffers, Desires, Yearns and Remembers" – Interview with Karen Barad' in Rick Dolphijn and Iris van Tuin (eds), *New Materialism: Interviews & Cartographies* (Ann Arbor, Open Humanities Press, 2012).

A distinct hierarchy is embodied in this division, which may explain why the legal disciplines have tended to betray their alliance with the humanities in a desire to serve the masters of fact. At the same time, considering the humanities in terms of their being the realm of care or concern implies a certain ignorance as to the historical role that the humanities, paradigmatically embodied in literature and art, have played in anthropomorphising the world in a manner that not so much served legal facts, but *produced* them.

Anthropomorphism is the pivot when mapping, art and literature are complicit with legal order. Carefully arranged, artistically prepared, imagined and mapped private and public spheres within which manoeuvrable legal puppets are allowed to play their role, have much helped to eliminate natural life-worlds and restrict or counter fluidity. The process was made possible by the ways in which the system of law and realm of justice were not just able to affirm but also disturb one another with new realities as a result. The Dutch Republic witnessed the birth of new legal bodies and new legal persons, internally and externally. It also witnessed the birth of new kinds of selves in relation to this. Peoples and other beings who had been living in or with waters for centuries, came to be used to living in lands that had either eliminated waters or had turned them into one vast, machine-controlled, useful and productive network.

Selves are not stable through time, nor are they natural. The historical process of gaining land and turning commons into private property on the basis of legal personhood has had a lasting impact on the Dutch feel and idea of a self. Currently, a considerable part of the Dutch collective self tends to respond with indignation as soon as one wolf enters the country, or when gained lands are returned to water. In March 2020, for instance, work was started on the de-poldering of a relatively small polder on the border with Belgium, the so-called Hedwigepolder. It was one of the last polders to be made in the Netherlands in 1907, and was family property from the beginning. After being inherited by three generations, it was to be returned to the waters of the Western Scheldt by order of the state, so that nature could be restored, as the state phrased it. This had taken decades of legal battles, up until the highest law council of the country. It remains a controversy until today.[61] The private owner of the polder was given 21 million euros in compensation,[62] which did not mean he gave up the fight; he filed two complaints with the European Court. That Court's verdict will come too late, but might, of course, lead to more compensation.

[61] The verdict of the High Council was given on 5 January 2018. ECLI:NL:HR:2018:7; see *de Rechtspraak*, uitspraken.rechtspraak.nl/inziendocument?id=ECLI:NL:HR:2018:7. It may be telling that in reports on the issue, the owner of the polder was described as someone 'fighting like a lion'; see *Omroep Zeeland* (22 May 2018), available at www.omroepzeeland.nl/nieuws/105903/Hedwige-kostte-levensgeluk-en-een-fortuin.

[62] This was due to a verdict by the court of Middelburg, 23 April 2020; see Rolf Bosboom, '21 miljoen euro schadevergoeding voor oud-eigenaar Hedwigepolder' (23 April 2020) *PZC*, available at www.pzc.nl/zeeuws-vlaanderen/21-miljoen-euro-schadevergoeding-voor-oud-eigenaar-hedwigepolder~ac14a2f1.

The idea of restoring nature made many angry, and also had passionate supporters. The passionate supporters won, but only because they had found the affirmation of the highest legal person: the state. It is just one other, rather poignant example of how annoying the confrontation between a system of law and a realm of justice can be, how annoying legal battles themselves can be, how annoying the final verdict was for a host of selves. The artificially claimed new environment came to fall, this time, under the heading of 'nature'. Only time will tell whether it will survive the effects of climate change, the contemporary feared pack-like force. It is caused, though, by a very human infuriation that, historically speaking, has been systematically veiled by legal personhood and was given the face of a reasonable person. The human infuriation implies, obviously, that humanity itself could well be considered a pack. If this is the case, it is itself the major threat to just legal systems or realms of justice that are worthy of that name. In the next chapter we will consider this idea by looking at corruption, first in human societies, then in an ecological context.

6

Logic of Completion vs Logic of Antinomy

Corruption and Well-being from Marek Hłasko, to Chibundu Onuzo, to the American Suburban Grass Turf and Fritz Haeg

'You live like Epicureans and sows. So the fat is in the fire.'

Martin Luther, 'Against Hanswurst'[1]

'[T]he greatness, but also the perplexity of laws in free societies is that they only tell what one should not, but never what one should do.'

Hannah Arendt, *The Origins of Totalitarianism*[2]

I. Corruption, Law's Completion and Antinomy

Corruption may be an ambiguous or slippery concept,[3] yet its negative connotations are easily understood in a legal context. Corruption is not only a criminal offence; it will also disrupt legal systems. If subjects cannot trust a judge or lawyer when both consider private gains preferable to upholding public standards; if the officer of justice answers to the uncle who gave him the job rather than to the law; if legally covered Mafiosi can buy the less powerful or powerless to help them veil criminal activities, or threaten them with consequences if they don't, the execution of law threatens to becomes a sham. In contrast, in the realm of justice one could at least ask why corruption would have to be a disruptive threat or whether it could not be somehow justified, or felt to be just. In this chapter we will deal with

[1] Martin Luther, 'Against Hanswurst' in *Luther's works: Church and Ministry III* vol 41, edited by Eric W Gritsch, (Minneapolis, Fortress Press, 1966) 211.

[2] Hannah Arendt, *The Origins of Totalitarianism* (Orlando, Harcourt, 1976) 467.

[3] Richard Mulgan, 'Aristotle on Legality and Corruption' in Manuhuia Barcham, Barry Hindess, Peter Larmour (eds), *Corruption: Expanding the Focus* (Canberra, ANU Press, 2012).

The Graveyard, a novel from 1958 by the Polish author Marek Hłasko (1934–69).[4] The novel was written in the heyday of totalitarian communism, when the Polish system of law was in full force but still simply translating what the party wanted. Would corruption not be a just, or at least understandable response to this totalitarian state? As I will argue, it might be understandable, yes; even functional in some sense. It would, however, still be a disruptive threat to any system of law or realm of justice.

The original meaning of corruption is a falling apart or passing away, as originally defined in Aristotle's *On Generation and Corruption*.[5] Here, corruption was a physical issue. Things fall apart; they always do. One of the most important modern laws of nature – the second law of thermodynamics, or the law of entropy – states something similar. I find this physical origin noteworthy because both systems of law and realms of justice consist precisely in their working against the law of entropy, which is why they are constantly at work and demand a lot of energy. Their aim is to keep an order intact, or to keep a realm functioning, with all the differences of interests and affects this connotes. To keep things in good order, both system and realm will constantly need to adapt or transform, but the goal remains the same: to avoid this falling apart. Yet this is precisely what corruption will cause, whether intentionally or not. The reason is that corruption is aimed at individual or private survival. This is what makes it understandable and functional. Yet if actors do not care about the collective, public or correlational whole of system of law or realm of justice, both will start to fall apart.

In what follows I aim to explore three different modalities of corruption's disruptive force. Corruption can become a matter of a collectively shared culture; it may be deemed functional, something that veils its disruptive force; and corruption can be a matter of unacknowledged (ecological) disruption. The latter is something that enlarges the realm of justice considerably, and might also enlarge the span of corruption as a criminal offence.

Two of the examples that follow – Marek Hłasko's novel in the Polish context of the 1950s and Nigerian Chibundu Onuzo's *Welcome to Lagos* from 2017 and set in our contemporary situation – deal with a perverse or corrupt system of law, on the level of the police, the level of law and the level of politics. There is an important difference in the meanings of perverse and corrupt, here, even though the Latin *pervertere* also means to corrupt. Etymologically speaking the one, *pervertere*, means to upturn or overthrow things. The other, *corrumpere*, means to destroy things. One other aspect is that perversion concerns the upturning of a somehow natural order, whereas corruption connotes destruction as a natural thing (as with Aristotle's *phthoras*). As a result, corruption may feel more natural than perversion. If ideology is characterised by its capability to normalise or naturalise what

[4] Marek Hłasko, *The Graveyard*, trans Norbert Guterman, intro James Sallis (London, Melville House Books, 2013). It was published under the title *Cmentarze* by a Paris based Polish emigré journal *Kultura*.

[5] In the original: Περὶ γενέσεως καὶ φθορᾶς, translated in Latin as *De Generatione et Corruptione*.

is clearly artificial, the perverse feels more counter-natural, in this context, than corruption. This may be why perversion will always be attacked whereas corruption is often found acceptable. This is also, however, why corruption is a disruptive force. Perversion will be isolated as somehow unnatural, whereas corruption can infiltrate everything because it feels natural.

Consider the third example: the remarkable cultural artefact of the US American suburban grass turf. If Hłasko's novel is a perfect example of the corruption of law and justice under communist totalitarianism, and Onuzo's novel is a paradigmatic example of corruption in a so-called failed state, the US American suburban turf looks innocent in comparison.[6] Yet it could and can only exist in relation to the poison industry that looked for a new market in the USA after World War Two and found a profitable target: the neat suburban grass turf lawn as an icon of style and order. Under the veil of law, considerable swathes of land were polluted and many of the living beings on it killed. Here ecological corruption was at work, firstly, because people were only concerned with their own private interests, not with the existence and welfare of the whole environment. Secondly, corrupting the environment was somehow considered to be the natural or self-evident thing to do. Thirdly, hardly anyone escaped its force because the use of poison had infiltrated a society.

The two logics in this chapter threatened by corruption are the logic of completion and of antinomy. As for the first: any system of law expects its subjects to comply. Yet compliance in itself is not enough. Compliance with the law can serve justice, or can be fortuitous or profitable. When for instance, a corporation voluntarily reports to the European Union on cartel formation or price-fixing agreements, that corporation will walk free whereas others who do not disclose this – if their crimes are proven – will have to pay up.[7] For the law, compliance is fortuitous, and for the informant it is profitable. Still, compliance with the law can also be wrong or corrupt, as the example of Hłasko's novel shows. In totalitarian systems, dictatorial ones, or exploitative ones, ruling powers expect people to comply, even if the system of law is a sham. This does not mean such a system of law is strong. Since it lacks affirmation, it will lose legitimacy, which will probably lead to it using more violence. Non-compliance, make no mistake, will weaken a system of law. In fact, this is what Gandhi called for as a strategy to free India from British colonial rule.[8] This case illustrates how justice may demand that people principally refuse to comply or obey. Forced by their ethical principles, people may feel obliged to resist and to disturb the system of law in place. All those who worked in fully functioning legal systems such as South Africa under Apartheid, Argentina under the

[6] Jonathan Cane, studying the South-African grass lawn called it falsely innocent; see Jonathan Cane, *Civilising Grass: The Art of the Lawn on the South-African Highveld* (Johannesburg, Wits University Press, 2019).

[7] Alan Riley, 'Cartel Whistleblowing: Toward an American Model?' (2002) 9 *Maastricht Journal of European and Comparative Law* 67.

[8] On Gandhi and the heritage of his strategies of noncompliance, see David Cortright, *Gandhi and Beyond: Nonviolence for a New Political Age* (London, Routledge, 2016).

generals with their dirty war, China under its so-called communist regime, had (and have) the choice to either obey the law and to comply, or to resist and deviate, and pay the price for doing so.

If compliance has ambiguous implications, then, it is worthwhile noting that there is another aspect to the verb 'to comply'. In origin it means to fulfil, to accomplish, from the Latin *complere*. This origin is traceable in the verb 'to complement', or the noun 'compliment', or the adverb 'complete'. The entire set suggests that compliance with the law can be much more than simple obedience. It concerns something that fulfils the law, that complements it, that makes it complete, and that may even imply some sort of compliment. In critical legal studies, and especially since post-structuralism, much emphasis has been laid on the fact that the law has a subjecting power, serves power, and uses violence to that order (see chapter seven). Fairly little attention has been given to a positive relation of subjects with law. If a law is felt to be right, any subject's compliance with it will be a matter of completion. Law itself cannot be fulfilled; it is only fulfilled by its subjects' completion. This also affects subjects' perceptions of fulfillment. A proper law will fulfill them too, as a matter of well-being. If a law is felt to be wrong, or the system of law is felt to be serving unjust powers, subjects will start to feel unwell.

The logical opposite to the logic of completion, is that of antinomy. The term combines *anti* with *nomos*: a law against. Yet it is not simply a law aimed against something. It concerns a law that is incompatible with another already existing law, which implies that both have their own claim to being law. Antinomy became most famous through the religious disputes that were at the heart of Protestantism, specifically Lutheranism. The two key figures were Johannes Agricola (1494–1566) and Martin Luther (1483–1546) – the first wrestled with the binding force of an already existing law and the last, ultimately, promoted it.[9] Especially the ideas of Agricola, developed since the 1520s, proved to be annoying. Perhaps this was because his reasoning was so radically logical. To Agricola the Old Testament's Mosaic law should still be upheld by non-Christians, but not by Christians because the Old Testament had been replaced by the New. The wrathful Law of God had been superseded by the forgiving Gospel of Jesus. In this context Agricola could claim, still in accordance with Luther so far, that the sole justification lies in faith – captured by the famous phrase *sola fide*. Consequently, law should come after faith. With the arrival of the New Testament, moreover, sinning was no longer an offence but an impurity that would be dealt with by God's pity, not his violent wrath. Agricola's conclusion was that the already existing law of Moses need not

[9] I am basing myself here on Mark A Lamport (ed), *Encyclopedia of Martin Luther and the Reformation*, vol 2 (New York, Rowman & Litllefield, 2017) 7–8; Timothy Wengert, *Law and Gospel: Philip Melanchthon's Debate With John Agricola of Eisleben over Poenitentia* (Grand Rapids, Baker Book House, 1997); Michael S Whiting, *Luther in English: The Influence of His Theology of Law and Gospel on Early English Evangelicals* (Eugene OR, Pickwick Publishers, 2010).

be followed. It allegedly brought some of his followers to publicly shout 'to the gallows with Moses and the Law'.[10] The by now enraged Luther came up with the invention of the term antinomianism, as a rhetorically effective, derogatory term (one that, ironically, would be quite applicable to Luther himself). In Luther's view Law and Gospel could not be incompatible. The one had to lead to the other. The Gospel would surely hold precedence, but it was not a counter-law to the already existing one.

The subtle religious intricacies are not the issue here. The discussion between Agricola and Luther is insightful as for the relation between any system of law and realm of justice. In Luther's view, civil law, the law of the Gospel, and moral law should guide Christians. In all three cases law worked on subjects externally and demanded them to complete law in a threefold way. They had to comply in fear of punishment, they had to comply by comparing themselves to the perfect law and notice their imperfection, and they had comply by taking law as moral principle for their lives. The system of law can be described shorthand, here, as the sphere of judgement. The realm of justice follows different kinds of law, however, in all three aspects. Firstly, justice is not applied from the outside, but finds a source in a force from within (much like Agricola's faith). Secondly, justice does not need to subject people by making them live in fear of punishment but instead proposes that they realise their lives according to their desires. Consequently, thirdly, the realm of justice can be defined in terms of a double desire: desire for justice, and desire as justice.[11] All in all, the realm of justice is not a sphere of judgement but of decision.[12] This demands another kind of law, one that is opposed to, and incompatible with an already existing one.

If we take the antinomian position seriously, we come to the limit of affirmation, as a consequence, and reach the radical potential of disturbance, as the case of Agricola shows. The antinomian character of the realm of justice is also at work through Hłasko's novel, which has the 48-year-old Franciszek Kowalski as protagonist. He fought in the resistance during World War Two, he is a respected citizen and member of the communist party. At some point he drinks a bit too much and sings a song in public. He is looked at with derision by some workmen and in response starts to shout some mild insults. Then two young police officers appear and in a rather short dialogue things get completely out of hand. In the end Franciszek shouts at them that they can all shove it up their ass and says a few things more about the party that go untranscribed. He is arrested. Because of his

[10] Lamport, *Encyclopedia of Martin Luther and the Reformation* (2017) 8.

[11] For the distinction between the desire for justice and desire as justice, see Frans-Willem Korsten and Tessa de Zeeuw, 'Ethics of Becoming as a Frame for Ethics: Theatricality and Balance in Greenaway's *The Cook, the Thief, his Wife and her Lover*' (2016) 10 *Polemos: Journal of Law, Literature and Culture* 249.

[12] I am referring to Gilles Deleuze, here, with his suggestion to replace 'the power of judgement with the force of decision' in the chapter 'Nietzsche and Saint Paul' *Essays Critical and Clinical* (Minnesota, University of Minnesota Press, 1997) 49.

refusal to solve things in a corrupt way, it becomes an official party affair. He is thrown out of the party as a result. In the middle of the novel, his son, a promising student, starts to pack his things. His father cannot believe he is leaving and then the following dialogue ensues. The sons says:

> 'I'll come back after you have cleared yourself.'
>
> 'What am I to do?'
>
> 'Stand up and fight. Maybe you'll find somebody, some comrades, who'll believe you and be able to settle things for you. I've got to believe the party.'
>
> 'And not me? I am your father: in spite of everything I am your father, whether you like it or not ... Can't you believe me?'
>
> Mikołaj was already in his overcoat. He walked to the window; the light of the street lamp glinted his hair.
>
> 'Believe – you? You alone? No.' He turned round violently. 'What do you know about the world. About how vile it is? You're still living in the past, in the underground – don't you realize what is going on today? Don't you really understand anything?' Once again he stared in the street. 'If they tore the fronts of the houses, we'd see pigsties. I can't afford to believe any individual. I can only believe the party. If I didn't have the party to look up to, I'd become the vilest of the vile. I couldn't live otherwise. And you want me to believe you, you of all people – a shouter and a liar?'
>
> 'I am your father!' Franciszek cried.
>
> Mikołaj smiled gloomily. 'You are Franciszek Kowalski, expelled from the party for duplicity. The rest is beside the point, an accident. If the party takes you back, I'll apologize to you.'[13]

It would be easy to side with the father and consider the son to be a deluded young man, brainwashed by an ideology. Yet the son is saying the father is deluded and has the wrong view on reality, and in this the son is basing himself on the law in place. The antinomian logic implies that from the realm of justice another law is posited against this already existing law. In this case the law of the land and the times are determined by, and intrinsically connected to, the party. In this logic the individual does not count, nor does the accidental. From the other side, in his refusal to be corrupt, in his desire to be believed as an honest individual, or as a father, Franciszek embodies another law that is incompatible with the already existing one. Precisely because the novel proposed this, it had a hard time getting published. In the eyes of ruling powers, it was as antinomian as its protagonist.

Meanwhile the disruptive third has been hinted at again. It concerns Franciszek's refusal to be corrupt or to settle things behind the scenes. It is suggested by the son when he advises his father to seek some comrades that can help him out of this, 'to settle things'. Indeed, if the system of law has become corrupt itself, the individual's survival becomes dependent on corruption.

[13] Hłasko, *The Graveyard* (2013) 81.

II. 'It's Not Me': A Culture of Corruption

In 2008 the South-Africa-based artist, curator and director William Kentridge made a multi-screen piece called *I am not me, the horse is not mine.*[14] The title of the piece refers to a Russian proverb – 'Я не я, и лошадь не моя' (*ya ne ya i loshad' ne moya*). The proverb is used when, in an awkward situation, one wants to deny having had anything to do with what happened.[15] Whereas the proverb is said to originate in circles of poor Russian farmers, it is reused by Kentridge in the context of a work of art that explicitly reflects on the Leninist or Stalinist battle for the liberation and emancipation of the subject of history; the proletariat. Yet once this battle became a totalitarian Soviet state it was in many situations 'wise' to pretend not to know anything; to deny the very possibility of having been there, of having anything to do with whatever had happened that could somehow be considered undesirable or offensive to totalitarian eyes.

Kentridge partly uses a story by Nikolai Gogol, written in 1835–36, entitled 'The Nose' (Russian *Нос*, pronounced 'nos'). Gogol tells the story of a nose that starts to live its own life. It is, literally, 'an organ without a body' as Slavoj Žižek would call it in his reversing of the Deleuzian concept of a body-without-organs.[16] The latter connotes the falling apart of a formerly assembled body into a bodily mass, as the mere potential of a body. The former connotes the force of individual organs that seem to be connected to a body but are actually forceful on their own. In his study on the subject, Žižek gives the example of the camera in films by Alfred Hitchcock that wanders as if an eye has drifted away from the body it belongs to. Likewise, the nose in Gogol's story wanders away to start a life of its own. Firstly, it is found in a piece of bread by the protagonist's barber who wants to throw the nose in the river. In the act he is caught by a policeman, whom he then attempts to bribe, as if nothing had happened. This is when the nose manages to flee. Its new life is described by Gogol in relation to the suffocating hierarchy of feudal Russian society: its former owner meets his nose parading in the uniform of a high-ranking official.

Kentridge combines Gogol's story with a more contemporary historical text as a source of inspiration: the Russian avant-garde composer Shostakovich, who was one of the main Soviet-inspired and approved artists – at least for a while. He composed an opera entitled *The Nose* in 1928. When performed in 1930 it met with general misunderstanding or rejection and, after 16 performances, it was almost forgotten. It was no coincidence, however, that Shostakovich himself was in trouble a few years later and barely escaped imprisonment or death under Stalin in 1936. Though *The Nose* was perhaps intended as a satire about the times

[14] For an impression, see www.youtube.com/watch?v=4Py86U9gS6k, Tate Modern, December 2012; for a reflection by the artist, see www.youtube.com/watch?v=Radzm-Yo4BA.

[15] See en.wikiquote.org/wiki/Russian_proverbs. On another website with Russian proverbs, the English translation is: 'The cat did it': masterrussian.com/proverbs/russian_proverbs_15.htm.

[16] Slavoj Žižek, *Organs Without Bodies: Deleuze and Consequences* (New York, Routledge, 2004).

of Tzar Alexander I, Shostakovich had made a piece that could equally well be read as a satire about the absurdities of Stalin's reign. This becomes manifest when Kentridge also uses a transcript of the historical show-trial against Nikolai Bukharin, a former close ally of Stalin's.

Accused of revisionism, in 1937, Bukharin's show trial would result in his execution on 15 March 1938. The transcript of the trial reads like an absurd play, worthy of authors such as Alfred Jarry and his *Ubu Roi*.[17] Let me take just one paradigmatic passage from the first session of the show trial, on 5 March 1938. The president is the judge and the man named Vyshinsky is the state prosecutor. Bukharin is the accused, or defendant:

> *THE PRESIDENT*: Accused Bukharin, you have again not understood me. You are not making your last plea now. You were asked to testify to your anti-Soviet, counter-revolutionary activities, but you are giving us a lecture. In your last plea you may say whatever you like. I am explaining this to you for the third time.
>
> *Bukharin:* Then permit me very briefly …
>
> *VYSHINSKY*: Tell me, accused Bukharin, how all this took shape in practice in your anti-Soviet activities.
>
> *Bukharin:* Then permit me to enumerate certain points of program. And then I will immediately pass on to relate my practical counter-revolutionary activities. May I, Citizen the President?
>
> *THE PRESIDENT*: Only more briefly, if you please. You will have an opportunity to make a speech as your own Counsel for Defence.
>
> *Bukharin:* This is not my defence, it is my self-accusation. I have not said a single word in my defence. If my program stand were to be formulated practically, it would be, in the economic sphere, state capitalism, the prosperous muzhik individual,[18] the curtailment of the collective farms, foreign concessions, surrender of the monopoly of foreign trade, and, as a result-the restoration of capitalism in the country.

It is a both absurd and horrifying transcript, in which the ones brought before the court are already declared guilty, have been tortured, or put under extreme pressure, as a result of which they define themselves as guilty beforehand. It is also this transcript that provides the pivot to the screens of Kentridge's installation. They all deal with the abyss of absurdity that opens up when any trustworthy logic of both law and justice is being disrupted.

The show-trial of Bukharin is just one telling example of how, under totalitarian rule and in the (quasi-)legal domain, complicity, corruption, resistance and collaboration often conflate into an almost indistinguishable, slippery field of association. All kinds of acts performed by both ordinary and highly positioned people, can become easily defined as falling under one of these headings and so be found guilty as enemies of the revolution, of the state, of the party, of the people.

[17] For the transcript: Nikolai Bukharin Archive, www.marxists.org/archive/bukharin/works/1938/trial/index.htm.

[18] *Muzhik*, мужи́к [mʊˈʐɨk] or *moujik* means 'peasant'.

In this light, the phrase 'I am not me, the horse is not mine' can be seen as a form of apathy (see chapter two). In this, law and justice do not matter anymore. Yet the phrase may also signal the last straw that allows one to at least survive. As such, the phrase, when used in a situation such as Bukharin's, is an act that paradoxically avoids the issue of what it is one has done. It avoids the issue of acknowledging the side one is on, because all sides are controlled by a totalitarian power. At the same time, it also implies the choice of a self who desires to live but whose status as a subject is clearly at risk, and who thus uses the phrase to avoid being framed as complicit.

The issues of framing and being framed are dominant themes in the work of Marek Hłasko. After a brief beginning as one of communist Poland's best and brightest authors in the 1950s, he went on to become an annoying presence from 1956 onwards. In the first instance, all Polish publishers refused the manuscript of *The Graveyard*, informing Hłasko that the Poland he described 'did not exist'. Ironically, the very phrase explicitly resonates with phrases and situations in the novel. At some point, for instance, the protagonist meets a friend on the street who is having a fight with his dog, because the animal – called Red – won't move. An audience has gathered, public life is not running normally, so a policeman enters the stage:

> 'What's going on here?' a brisk voice cried suddenly. A young policeman forced his way through the crowd. 'What's this?' He turned to the nearest spectator and looked him sternly in the eyes. 'Is there something you don't like? Now tell the truth: you don't like the regime?'
>
> 'Mr. Authority,' said the other. 'I'm leaving. I've already left. I've never been here.'[19]

The man who chooses to address the officer with 'Mr Authority' is offering the Polish version of 'I am not me, the horse is not mine'. He knows that he will no longer be able to define his acts independently as soon as he meets Mr Authority in the wrong way. The latter can accuse him of anything, or frame his everyday acts negatively in the light of what the party stands for. In fact, this is what has happened to the protagonist, who in a drunken state forgot to accept the ultimate power of another Mr Authority and as a consequence found himself in an unstoppable downfall, with a show trial of sorts that had his peers at the centre of it. This trial framed him as someone who, in a drunken state, had betrayed the system by saying what he 'really' thought. In doing this, he had unmasked himself as an enemy of the people.

Hłasko's novel was controversial because it showed how the communist system was corrupt, how it functioned under a rule of law that had little independent force, and how the exercise of power was based on collective complicity. The protagonist has ended up in jail for saying things he could not remember and for showing disrespect to police officers. Since he has always been a respected party member,

[19] Hłasko (n 4) 97.

he supposes that things will be corrected in no time once he gets out of jail. Yet, once in jail he finds himself not only in another situation, but also becomes aware that his status as a subject may have changed. One man says to him:

> 'If you don't remember what happened, you're surely in for it. Someone must have informed on you. Don't you remember?
>
> Franciszek looked at him sharply: 'What are you talking about?'
>
> The stranger smiled: 'Someone must have informed on you,' he repeated. 'Maybe you listen to Free Europe. You'd be in a bad way if it turned out that you listen to those broadcasts and then tell other people what you have heard.'[20]

Then the man calls in another guy, who supposedly listened to Free Europe, to testify how bad it can be. Yet the latter refutes:

> 'I never listened to Free Europe. I was locked up for listening to Radio Madrid. My wife turned it on full blast, and the woman next door informed on us. It goes to show, you can never trust a woman.'[21]

The passage serves to show how under totalitarian rule the private and the public have come to fuse. The rest of what the other prisoners bring in is enough to make Franciszek react indignantly:

> 'Stop bothering me,' he said. 'You offend me as a man and as a party member. I am honest, and the fact that I am here with you is just an unfortunate mistake. Please don't talk to me like that, or I'll tell the officer on duty of what I think of you.'
>
> His neighbor looked at him attentively. 'What do you want of me?' he asked, shrugging his shoulders. 'I haven't said anything.'[22]

This brings us back once more to the 'I am not me, the horse is not mine'. As the honest man that Franciszek claims to be, and will prove to be, he heads towards a befriended party official to ask for help. Yet this official suggests that things can best be handled behind the scenes; he has his own agenda. Franciszek refuses this suggestion, forgetting that when an entire system is corrupt all actors are concerned only with their own survival, not his. The endless chain of people who will not be held accountable in person for a wider system that they uphold, will want to prove their own purity by ritually expelling a so-called impure.

Now all this might seem a problem of the system at the time. Were the system to dissolve, this should lead to a non-corrupt system, then. If only this was the case. Scholars studying the transition from the Eastern Bloc countries from communism to capitalism by means of the so-called free market economies in the 1990s, came to the conclusion that corruption had become an integral part of how society worked, and continued to be so also under its new economic and financial logic

[20] ibid 25.
[21] ibid 25.
[22] ibid 26.

within the so-called free market.[23] In other words: systemic corruption had come to define a culture of living. Corruption was no longer the result of a system, but had turned into a mode of living. In such cultures the independent rule of law is a hindrance. It is no surprise, then, that the judiciary is under attack in almost all of the former Eastern Bloc countries. To counter this from the side of the realm of justice, would mean to take an antinomian position. Yet the latter's logic is functional only in relation to those who aim to comply with the law in the sense of completing it. There needs to be a rule of law first that subjects adhere to. Subjects have to care for law, or apathy takes over. In between the care for law and apathy, there is a culture of corruption in which people do care, but only for their individual private survival. The antinomian position becomes one, then, that proposes the rule of law in the absence of a legitimate law. It proposes a law opposite to a cultural law that has come to consider corruption as a matter of fact, accepting that how things go, is how they have always gone, and how they will always go. Antinomy refutes this idea.

III. Functional Corruption and the Proper

Those who argued in the 1960s and 1970s that so-called functional corruption was a stabilising force in ill-functioning regimes, were almost always writing from the USA and analysing Soviet Russia. Implicitly they promoted societies in which greater inequalities were considered to be more efficient. Their concern was not, moreover, how a corrupt society could ever become non-corrupt, but rather the promotion of their own cultural laws. Though in the end they were proven wrong about corruption's ability to stabilise regimes,[24] there was a resurgence of this positive view on corruption recently, with regard to Nigeria.[25] The Government's anti-corruption measurements were met with a Twitter-propelled, broadly supported 'Bring Back Our Corruption' movement. Under president Muhammad Buhari, who was elected because he was opposed to corruption,

[23] Wayne Sandholz and Rein Taagepera, 'Corruption, Culture, and Communism' (2005) 15 *International Review of Sociology* 109.

[24] For an overview of the 'functional corruption' proponents, see Charles A Schwartz, 'Corruption and Political Development in the USSR' (1979) 11 *Comparative Politics* 425. One of the big names considering corruption's positive side was Samuel Huntington, who would later become famous with *The Clash of Civilizations* (in 1992 and 1996 respectively). At the time his major study was *Political Order in Changing Societies* (New Haven, Yale University Press, 1968) in an analysis not based on data but on ideas. For the data, see Pierre-Guillaume Meon and Khalid Sekkat, 'Does corruption grease or sand the wheels of growth?' (2005) 122 *Public Choice* 69. They come to the conclusion that corruption only serves private interests, not public or communal ones, and does not propel economic growth either.

[25] Grant Walton, 'Bring Back Our Corruption and Samuel Huntington' *Devpolicy Blog* (August 2018), available at devpolicy.org/bring-back-our-corruption-and-samuel-huntington-20180827.

a policy was developed in 2015 under the heading of the Treasury Single Account. It required:

> [A]ll Federal Ministries, Departments and Agencies (MDAs) to start paying all government revenues, incomes and other receipts into a unified pool of single account with the Central Bank of Nigeria (CBN), [as] a bold and highly commendable move directed at one of the strongholds of corruption in the polity.[26]

The immediate result was that three billion American dollars were refound; surely a success.[27] Soon after, the Bring Back Our Corruption movement started. Political scientists Allison Felix Timepere and Tubotenyefa Zibima found this movement to be much more than simply a cynical one. In fact they considered it 'a genuine protest against the adverse impacts the anti-corruption campaign has had on the flow of proceeds from corruption from politicians to citizens'.[28] In their study, they interviewed many of those participating in the protest. One journalist stated: 'You have to understand that in a dysfunctional country … corruption has its advantage'.[29] Right. This proves the point that corruption may be understandable or functional. It does not, however, refute the point that corruption will ultimately be disruptive. Nor does it imply that a dysfunctional state can become functional through corruption.

Timepere and Zibima argue that corruption is the understandable effect of dysfunctional wealth distribution and functions to redistribute this. In an overview of the debates since the 1960s, they state:

> [A] blind spot of anti-corruption scholarship and activism may be the now almost mandatory tendency to focus on the adverse outcomes of corruption, and the inclination to characterise corruption as functional only when it drives economic growth … although public sector corruption produces adverse socioeconomic consequences, proceeds from public corruption distributed through patronage schemes may perform considerable informal welfare function to most poor and neglected masses in states where formal welfare measures are weak.[30]

Being critical of those who only looked at corruption in terms of its contribution or hindrance to economic growth, Timepere and Zibima see another function for corruption. When it is embedded in 'patronage schemes' it can, they suggest, serve to correct the missing, inadequate, or unjust political distribution of wealth,

[26] Chinedu U Okerekeoti and Emmanuel I Okoye, 'Treasure Single Account (TSA) in Nigeria: A Theoretical Perspective' Conference paper (2017) The 2017 International Conference on African Entrepreneurship and Innovation for Sustainable Development (AEISD) ch 38, 559.

[27] Allison Felix Timepere and Tubotenyefa Zibima, 'Bring Back Our Corruption in Nigeria: Nigeria's anti-corruption campaign faces opposition: from the citizens who voted for the government to fight corruption' (26 August 2018) *Australian Outlook*, available at www.internationalaffairs.org.au/australianoutlook/bring-back-our-corruption-in-nigeria.

[28] ibid.

[29] Allison Felix Timepere and Tubotenyefa Zibima, 'Bring Back Our Corruption: Nigeria's Post-2015 Anti-corruption Campaign and Popular Resistance' (2018) 16 *A Journal Publication of the Nigerian Political Science Association* 29.

[30] Timepere and Zibima, 'Bring Back Our Corruption' (2018) 22.

and enables a controlled form of distribution by private parties in the absence of public ones. Clearly, the Nigerian case hints at the importance of factoring in cultural historicity and specificity when the distinction between private and public is at stake. Yet even given this, corruption is still aimed simply at survival in the context of unequal and unjust power distributions. Why would this disrupt both the system of law and the realm of justice? The question is addressed in Nigerian author Chibundu Onuzo's novel, *Welcome to Lagos* (2017).[31]

Welcome to Lagos is a novel in three sections, with 69 chapters and an epilogue. The middle section (chapters 15–38) – 'Monday Morning in Lagos' – has quotes at the beginning of each chapter that are taken from the *Nigerian Journal*. The quotes look and read like forms of found footage, cut-outs, or quotes taken from real newspapers or journals. Yet one of them reveals that they are fictionalised. Chapter 22 opens with a quote that is supposedly taken from an advertisement, promising 10 million Naira (the Nigerian currency) for information on 'Chief Remi Sandayo, former minister of Education'.[32] This is one of the novel's major protagonists, and a paradigm of what was defined above as 'functional corruption'. At some point Sandayo is warned he is out of favour with the President, which means he will be replaced or removed. He decides to remove himself and run with the money. In the first instance he wants to flee to a neighbouring country, but is slowed down by the traffic, and so decides to take refuge in one of his Lagos mansions that has been standing empty for years. This, however, is by now inhabited by a group of squatters all trying to make a living in their own improvised manners. So the Minister stumbles into an already inhabited mansion and is caught by these inhabitants. Ten million dollars in funding have disappeared with him and are now in the hands of a bunch of characters who do not need to keep the Minister imprisoned because he has nowhere else to escape to. That leaves them with the question what to do with the money. The hostage-holders come up with the idea of handing it out to schools. They start buying all sorts of educational material on the Lagos markets, and the Minister at some point begins to help them. Going out on the street and mixing with the masses, he is still figuring out how he can free himself. One option is to come clean.

The editor of the *Nigerian Journal* is invited to interview Sandayo. In this interview Sandayo indeed comes clean, not just about himself, but the entire ruling elite. When the article is published, the offices of the *Nigerian Journal* are burnt down and Ahmed, the editor, has to go in hiding. To get out of this mess, Ahmed comes up with the idea to break the story internationally. Through his acquaintances in London, they organise an interview with the BBC, the British Broadcasting Corporation. The interview is preceded by Sandayo asking the journalist questions with regard to his own national history, like the theft of the commons by so-called lords, the UK's colonial exploitation, or the fact that in the City of London flows of

[31] Chibundu Onuzo, *Welcome to Lagos* (London, Faber & Faber, 2017).

[32] The Naira, the Nigerian currency, at the time of writing (May 2020), was running at an exchange rate of 0.0024 euro or 0.0026 USD.

stolen money from African countries are whitewashed. Then it's the interviewer's turn. He asks whether Sandayo did or did not take the money. The latter responds:

> 'I took it.'
>
> 'You admit you stole the money.'
>
> 'I took it but not for myself. I was tired of seeing projects we designed at the top never trickle down to the bottom. So I decided to become my own personal Ministry of Education, like I was in the days of the YPC. There are over ten schools that my team and I have fully equipped.'
>
> 'Your team?'
>
> 'Yes. I and a team of committed Nigerians who love this country and believe that she must be great again. In a few weeks we have achieved all I have been trying to in one year in the ministry.'[33]

The names of the schools are revealed, so that the BBC team can check. There is a short moment of international glory. But then the system starts to crack down again, and the heads of the schools are all arrested. Things take a turn for the worse, and the Minister decides to run again, taking what is left of the money. He then starts to feel remorse, and decides to come back.

He returns at the precise moment when the police are raiding the apartment where everyone had been hiding. Everyone is arrested, and the following exchange between Sandayo and the commanding officer takes place:

> 'Wait. I have something to say. Step back. I have an offer for you. How much did they say I stole? Answer me. How much are you to recover? Ten million dollars isn't it? There is at least nine million dollars here. Nine million dollars right here but nobody knows that except the people in this room.'
>
> 'You can't buy your way out of this. I have radioed the Police Commissioner to say that you've been captured.'
>
> 'Not me. Let them go and we'll say you only found seven million. I'll swear to it in court. That's two million dollars to share. More money than you will ever earn in your lifetime. Any of you.'[34]

It will take a few more exchanges of arguments, but the end of the story is that the police officers take the offer. Sandayo is arrested and put in jail where he gets preferential treatment. After 27 days, on a day when an earthquake in Indonesia makes the headlines, he is released. He is taken home in a car provided by the Norwegian embassy. He falls asleep on the backseat. When he wakes up, he finds himself in a place he does not recognise. He is found a day later. Beheaded.

The novel has been welcomed positively. Yet by and large critics have overlooked the theme of corruption. The English newspaper *The Guardian* describes the novel as an 'entertaining and funny picture of Lagos life and Nigerian politics',

[33] Onuzo, *Welcome to Lagos* (2017) 271–72.
[34] ibid 309.

a quote that makes it to the cover of the novel's 2017 paperback edition.[35] Some consider the novel a 'fast-paced comedy' with an 'unlikely' plot that suffers from 'excessive twists'.[36] Or they state that 'verisimilitude is sacrificed in Onuzo's novel – the Chief's situation, rooming with squatters in his own house, is highly unlikely in Lagos'.[37] So it seems. Almost all reviews emphasise either that the novel is funny or that it is a tragicomic farce.[38] Obviously, the novel is not a realistic or straightforward description of corruption in Nigerian politics and everyday life. Yet precisely through its farcical quality it hints at the problem of corruption. If farce is the hilarious mimicking of the real, then all corruption, in which the real can no longer be taken seriously, can lead to farce or even is at its root. In a sense the novel is saying that in the Nigerian context a true description of corruption is impossible because it implies a stance from the outside. When people find themselves in what Esther Edelmann defines as 'an inverted reality', the very status of reality has become the opposite of what it properly should be.[39] If corruption rules, so the novel appears to state, everything becomes farce and people find themselves in an impasse.

Formally speaking, the issue with corruption is that it has become hard to decide what the proper version of something is. To be sure, the question of what is proper cannot be answered outside of historical, economic, cultural contexts; the telling phrase: 'that what is *considered* to be proper', gestures to the impossibility of defining the proper. Still, the paradox is that one can only discard the term 'proper' by saying that it has no proper meaning, which immediately reinstates the term 'proper'. In recent decades the most common means of avoiding the issue of defining the proper was the postmodern idea of irony. With irony, the possibility of a proper position is not discarded, but permanently put on hold and located beyond the realm of the expressible or re-presentable. Whilst sensing that there must be such a thing as the proper, one knows at the same time one will never be able to reach it. Or, one senses its presence, but touching that presence lies outside of what is achievable. As a result, saying that one appears as a proper self, may be considered as a form of irony. Saying one knows that one is a liar, or a fake, or the enemy of oneself may become ironic as well. It is the ironic dynamic between positions that points to a truth outside of what is expressible.

I consider the ironic way out of the problem of defining proper-ness as a possible, defendable and sensible one. Yet, there are reasons why it is wise to keep the term 'proper' alive in a non-ironic way, both in the system of law and in the realm of justice. My third and last example proves the point.

[35] The review from which the snippet is taken, is not that positive, see Helon Habila, 'Welcome to Lagos by Chibundu Onuzo review – high hopes, big city' (18 January 2018) *The Guardian*.

[36] Lovia Gyarkye, 'Going AWOL in Africa's Largest City' (2 August 2018) *New York Times*.

[37] Timothy Ogene, 'Welcome to Lagos' (25 January 2017) *Hong Kong Review of Books*.

[38] Tory Lyne-Pirkis, 'Book review – Welcome to Lagos' (4 February 2017) *Irish Examiner*.

[39] Esther Edelmann, *Marginal Baroque and Inverted Worlds*, PhD thesis in process.

IV. Corruption in an Ecological Context: Needs for an Antinomian Response

Most readers will be familiar with the grass turf lawns that characterise almost all suburbs, at least the relatively wealthy ones, in the United States. One may recall the setting of Steven Spielberg's *ET* (1982) and Sam Mendes' *American Beauty* (1999), or that of the series *Stranger Things* (Netflix, 2016–19). Ecologically speaking, it is important to note that the grass that is used for these lawns did not exist naturally in the eco-system of the USA, nor has it easily adapted to the American climate. In fact, it requires enormous amounts of attention, begs for water, and demands continuous protection from all kinds of weeds. This is why herbicides, fungicides and pesticides, in the average American household, are mainly used on the lawn. I will not bother the reader with the diversity of herbicides, fungicides, biocides or pesticides that are on the market, but will only indicate how much garden poison, according to the USEPA (the United States Environmental Protection Agency) was used on a yearly basis between 2005 and 2012. Herbicides for home garden use hovered between 28 and 31 million lbs. Perhaps more telling is the number of households using the poison: 52 million for herbicides and 16 million for fungicides.[40] The numbers concern, moreover, the poisons 'applied by homeowners to homes and gardens, including lawns and single-and multiple-unit housing'. They do not include 'pesticides for home and garden applications by professional applicators'. Including the latter would significantly increase these numbers.

The question as to why people would want to use poison on this scale was central to a series of articles and a monograph by Paul Robbins and Julie Sharp.[41] They noted that well into the twentieth century all sorts of weeds were not considered to be a disturbance to lawns in the USA. Many people grew vegetables in their garden. After World War Two, this all changed. To trace the motivations and effects of this change, they interviewed inhabitants of suburbs in Ohio in 2003, asking them how they took care of their lawn. Most interviewees knew that the use of the chemicals could lead to serious diseases like leukaemia.[42] For instance,

[40] *EPA*, 'Pesticides Industry Sales and Usage: 2008–2012 Market Estimates', available at www.epa.gov/sites/production/files/2017-01/documents/pesticides-industry-sales-usage-2016_0.pdf.

[41] Paul Robbins and Julie Sharp, 'Turfgrass Subjects: The Political Economy of Urban Monoculture' in Nik Heynen, Maria Kaika, Erik Swyngedouw (eds), *In the Nature of Cities: Urban Political Ecology and the Politics of Urban Metabolism* (London, Routledge, 2006). This article worked out what they had found earlier, see: Paul Robbins and Julie Sharp, 'The Lawn-Chemical Economy and its Discontents' (2003) 35 *Antipode* 955. Later Paul Robbins published *Lawn People: How Grasses, Weeds, and Chemicals Make Us Who We Are* (Philadelphia, Temple University Press, 2007).

[42] June 2020, German chemical giant Bayern, which had bought US American Monsantos, reached a compromise with thousands of actors accusing Monsantos of consciously having caused non-Hodgkin's lymphoma through its product Roundup, a so-called weed-killer. The cases were settled for a sum total of 10 billion dollar; see Patricia Cohen, 'Roundup Maker to Pay $10 Billion to Settle Cancer Suits' (24 June 2020) *The New York Times*, available at www.nytimes.com/2020/06/24/business/roundup-settlement-lawsuits.html.

when 'Tom' had sprayed the lawn with his monthly dose of poison, he would put up signs that warned the youth from the neighbourhood to stay away since the grass was poisonous. His text could not be read by dogs and cats, of course, and they would bring this poison indoors on the soles of their paws, onto the carpets on which toddlers crawled. Be that as it may, the individual responsibility to at least warn people is inadequate given the amounts of poison that were, and are, being used in order to achieve and maintain the idyll of the impeccably green grass turf lawn. The question that Robbins and Sharp felt obliged to ask was: What brought people to do this?

They first looked for manipulation by the poison industry. Apparently, it had executed a number of incredibly successful advertising campaigns. And indeed, since the 1980s something has changed considerably. First, the poison would be on the shelves of garden centres and the like. It would be the passive object waiting to be chosen by a customer who was either looking for this particular poison, or who would think: 'Ah yes, I need that poison'. Thanks to the mediatisation of modern society since the 1980s, companies are now able to get into each individual room asking: 'Are you sure you do not need this poison?' This would not be a problem if personalised advertisements concerned a small segment of the industry's market. However, due to the enormous expansion of the poison industry during the World War Two, this question is being asked by a set of significantly sized companies that, after and since the war, were aggressively looking for new markets. And, as the state of suburban lawns in the USA attest, they successfully created them.

That left Robbins and Sharp with the riddle: 'How do people become convinced that certain ways of being and doing are normal, especially ways that contradict their better judgement?'[43] They looked for the answer in how the organisation of private and public space convinces its users of the fact that this is the way it should be, or convinces them that there is no alternative. They noted firstly that whoever tends to his garden is doing so in relation to his neighbours, be it direct neighbours, or the neighbours on the other side of the country, who nevertheless feel like direct neighbours via manifold forms of representation. Kaja Silverman's distinction between look, screen and gaze is of relevance here. Silverman used 'screen' to indicate the sum total of representations that a certain symbolical order provides and that defines individual and collective forms of subjectivity by means of mimicry.[44] If a spotless grass turf lawn has become iconic in the domain of the screen, many subjects are incorporated in that screen. The force of this symbolical screen was evidenced by several examples in Ohio, where negligence with regard to one's lawn led to neighbourly accusations that one was a communist. Small signs of imperfection led to feelings of guilt and shame. People could be accused,

[43] Robbins and Sharp, 'Turfgrass subjects' (2006) 119.

[44] Kaja Silverman, 'Fassbinder and Lacan: A Reconsideration of Gaze, Look and Image' in Norman Bryson, Michael Ann Holly, and Keith Moxey (eds), *Visual Culture: Images and Interpretations* (Hanover, Wesleyan University Press, 1994).

legally, for not taking adequate care of their lawn. They might go away for a weekend and come back to find their lawn neatly mown, in accordance with the other ones.[45]

If the question is who or what is behind this all, Robbins and Sharps in the end suggest that it is the grass turf lawn itself. This may seem absurd, yet this is their elaboration:

> When the lawn needs cutting, when its constituent species are rivalled by wild mints or fungi, when it becomes dry, its signals are apparent to the individual, whose response is an act of subjection, not only to the lawn, but to the ideology of the community, and the global economy of turf maintenance.[46]

Following Timothy Mitchell, Robbins and Sharp contend that the lawn 'speaks', as if it is a subject. And, indeed, the lawn *is* an actor with agency that, obviously, does not speak in a literal sense but a figurative one. Gardens could be filled with of debris, or with squares of granite tiles, or with freely growing endogenous weeds, trees and shrubs. When a garden is comprised of exogenous lawns of grass turf, however, the latter speaks and is demanding. This is testified by several parodies of the pop song 'I fought the law (and the law won)'; a hit for the Bobby Fuller Four in 1964, and again for The Clash in 1977. One only needs an extra 'n' to turn this into 'I fought the lawn – and the lawn won'. This twist has been made by a number of people, whose parodies have taken the form of, amongst others, T-shirts, cartoons and video-clips.[47]

Still, I find the suggestion by Robbins and Sharp – emphasised by the subtitle of Robbins' study *Lawn People: How Grasses, Weeds, and Chemicals Make Us Who We Are* – inadequate. A more recent study on similar grass lawns in South Africa by Jonathan Cane suggests a more complex relation. It is entitled *Civilising Grass: The Art of the Lawn on the South-African Highveld* (2019). This title is tellingly ambiguous because the phrase 'civilising grass' can have two different subjects. It is either the grass that civilises its owners or the owners civilising the grass. And there is an additional layer. Owners will hire others, often those without lawn or land, to do the civilising work, thus repeating a colonial pattern, as Cane shows. The dynamic is an example of what Gilles Deleuze in his study on the baroque, *Le pli* or *The Fold*, defines as a correlation.[48] In such a relation two bodies are related by means of an ellipsis, which is to say that two centres are only connected in relation to a third entity circling around the two so-called centres. So, when the centres are, on the one hand, the grass turf lawn, and on the other hand, the human subject, the question is what the third that circles around them, sweeping away others in its path, and keeping the two spellbound, is. The entity encircling the

[45] Robbins and Sharp (n 41) 120.

[46] ibid 121.

[47] Under this heading one can also find an example of another 'Tom' who gave up the fight with, for or against the lawn; see *Tall Clover Farm*, tallcloverfarm.com/13456/less-lawn-more-meadow.

[48] Gilles Deleuze, *The Fold*, trans Tom Conley (Minneapolis, University of Minnesota Press, 1992).

two could be communal well-being, flourishing wildlife (of any size), or a garden aesthetic in a retro-colonial fashion. For the latter, poison is required in both the USA and South Africa. This does not mean people want this, really. They may use poison, as Robbins and Sharpe noticed, against their better judgement (also see the 'family obliviousness' dealt with in chapter seven).

That it has, in such circumstances, become hard to speak of any proper position, is an important indicator of corruption. Ecologists Frederick Herbert Bormann, Diana Balmori and Gordon T Geballe suggested as much when they published *Redesigning the American Lawn: A Search for Environmental Harmony* in 2001. They noted that citizens of the USA tend to care for their lawns with a passion that is rarely seen elsewhere; and Jonathan Cane showed that South African citizens might come a good second. The speckless grass turf lawn is another example that, despite the reassuring phrase of the study's subtitle ('environmental harmony'), shows how the realm of justice is marked by differences and disparities. Yet what does disparate mean when there is not a definable proper position at stake?

Currently, the system of law in the USA supports the persistence or growth of poison usage, as ecologist Nathan Donley noted.[49] He found that the USA is out of sync, in this case, from other major players: 'Of the pesticides used in USA agriculture in 2016, 322 million pounds were of pesticides banned in the EU, 26 million pounds were of pesticides banned in Brazil and 40 million pounds were of pesticides banned in China'. The reason is that the USA, under the Federal Food, Drug, and Cosmetic Act (FFDCA), backs up the use of poison legally in a way that is different from other states:

> Unlike the safety threshold afforded by the EU, the pesticide industry only has to demonstrate that its products 'will not generally cause unreasonable adverse effects on the environment,' which is partially defined as 'any unreasonable risk to man or the environment, taking into account the economic, social, and environmental costs and benefits of the use of any pesticide …'. The FFDCA was amended in 1996 to strengthen the safety threshold in setting food residue tolerances to a 'reasonable certainty of no harm' for pesticide exposure to humans through food, water and home uses. However, harm to plants, animals, the broader environment, and harm to humans from occupational exposures remains solely a cost-benefit analysis.

The battle or struggle to change this has become complex partly because of the impressive manipulation of information from the side of corporations and other producers. Another complexity is what sociologist Zygmunt Bauman described as an emptying out of the area between political and private spheres: the *agora* or public space.[50] Whilst private parties withdrew themselves, by and large, from public decision-making, they intensified their lobbying activities behind the

[49] Nathan Donley, 'The USA lags behind other agricultural nations in banning harmful pesticides' (2019) 12 *Environmental Health* article nr 44.

[50] See Zygmunt Bauman *In Search of Politics* (Stanford, Stanford University Press, 1999) 97–99; but also *Liquid Modernity* (Cambridge, Polity Press, 2000) or *The Individualized Society* (Cambridge, Polity Press, 2001).

scenes or in courts. In what Jodi Dean calls 'communicative capitalism', taking a position has become a form of producing something – namely information. In 'communicative capitalism' private parties in control of communication are able to use information not only as a commercial product but also as a means of influencing and expanding their customer market. Even if it is only a matter of thumbs up or thumbs down, information enlarges the potential of who this information is sold to. It allows them to influence people on a massive scale, although all are individually addressed.

If in current circumstances large numbers of people do not know what to properly think of things, to realise who or what they are, properly, what they properly feel, what 'well' might properly mean, what value is, properly, what proper living is, what the body proper is, what addiction is, what sensing is, or why they would have to care about anything that is beyond their private circle, this is a culture of corruption 2.0, or 4.0. Art as an interface can only do so much in this context. One important example would be a number of works performed by American artist Fritz Haeg under the title 'Edible Estates'. The project started on Independence Day in 2005, with the planting of the first of a series of gardens in Saline, Kansas, the geographic centre of the United States. Domestic front lawns are replaced with edible landscapes which are then documented in photos, videos, stories, printed materials and exhibitions.[51] This historical irony is telling. Robbins and Sharp noted that edible estates were more or less standard before World War Two. Now, turning the lawn into an edible estate has had to become – or can only exist as – an art project. Haeg expanded the project to involve gardens globally. His aim was to raise awareness of people's poisonous dealing with their direct environment, but also to show how one could potentially use the soil around houses differently. One of the basic steps needed to change the garden was 'Do a **soil test** to see what sorts of amendments might be needed or if there are traces of lawn chemicals' (emphasis in text). A concluding publication on the project was entitled *Edible Estates: Attack on the Front Lawn*.[52] Despite its fierce title, however, the attack has had little impact so far. The reason may be that art's interface is not very effective, as yet, to translate desires from the realm of justice into matters of law.

Corruption probably won't go away by raising awareness, and as the simple example of the suburban grass turf aimed to show, corruption is no longer something that concerns human beings alone. Corruption has become a matter of life-worlds; life-worlds that are falling apart and passing away because they are not dealt with properly. If this is to be countered by the forging of new connections between a system of law and a realm of justice, then there is a new dynamic waiting and a new host of problems to be solved. In human societies, people do not have much difficulty in sensing and defining corruption, but the previous examples show how difficult it is to move from this to actually getting out of or changing a

[51] On the works, see 'Edible Estates' *Fritz Haeg*, available at www.fritzhaeg.com/garden/initiatives/edibleestates/about.html.

[52] Diana Murphy (ed), *Edible Estates: Attack on the Front Lawn* (New York, Metropolis Books, 2010).

corrupt situation. Yet the corruption of environments, with corrupt and corrupting actors involved, is less commonly sensed and rarely defined, as the case of the lawn proved. The antinomian logic of justice has a double function, here. Legally speaking, old laws that ruled human societies will be confronted by new, ecologically inspired laws; laws that are incompatible with old ones. Ecologically speaking this may mean that the old human-centred system of law has to give in to a new kind of law – say, a post-human one. In both cases, it looks like the momentum of affirmation between realm and system will be suspended in times to come and the momentum of disturbance is growing and expanding. The system of law can either legally defend people's desires to use poison in order to produce spotless lawns, or it can prohibit poison in defence of the wider environment. Systems of law can stick to placing human beings at the centre of the rule of law or work towards a new balance of powers in which the human position is just one among several. In all cases some parties will lose, others will gain. To many, the struggles involved and the outcomes are going to be, and will remain, annoying.

The next chapter will delve into law's coercive potential. As may be clear from the above, law can split parties while binding them in that all have to live by its verdicts. Law's violence is both splitting and cohesive, then. The same double quality holds for its counterpart: the logic of empathy from the side of justice.

7

Logic of Violence vs Logic of Empathy

Justice and Law in Chiasmus through George Eliot's Daniel Deronda

> 'Instrumentarian power … has no appetite for our grief, pain, or terror, although it eagerly welcomes the behavioral surplus that leaches from our anguish. It is profoundly and infinitely indifferent to our meanings and motives. Trained on measurable action, it only cares that whatever we do is *accessible* to its ever-evolving operations of rendition, calculation, modification, monetization, and control.'
>
> Shoshana Zuboff, *The Age of Surveillance Capitalism*[1]

I. The Political in Justice: Interests and Just Law

This chapter is about what one could call the 'grey area' between law's logic of violence and justice's logic of empathy. Before venturing into this area, let me first take seriously what people mean when they talk about any area being 'grey' – which never appears to be considered very positive. The grey is the awkward, often besmirched, situation in which people apparently could not choose between the clarity of the black or white, a clarity often defined morally. Yet the very opposition of black and white has become more besmirched itself, due to its implicit hierarchy in the context of all colonial, postcolonial and decolonial dynamics. In this context, the grey might be worthy of reconsideration, as an independent entity in itself. Or we might want to reconsider the fact that system of law and realm of justice do not relate as black and white, but meet rather on a colourful field of differences. If the two follow counter-logics this does not imply that the logics at stake are opposites. In origin, 'counter', going back to Latin *contra*, is a matter of comparison, not of opposition. The 'most different' is something other than the opposite. As we will see, the two options (logic of violence, logic of empathy) are

[1] Shoshana Zuboff, *The Age of Surveillance Capitalism, The Fight for a Human Future at the New Frontier of Power* (London, Profile Books, 2019) 360.

most different, also in how they relate to two incompatible definitions of politics. Yet, these two logics and their definitions often mix.

Politics implies law since politics is a form of the execution of power regulated by implicit and explicit rules that bind parties. At the same time, law is an instrument of politics since law needs ruling powers in order to be proclaimed, installed and become effective. The paradox, then, is that law, if it claims any legitimacy, both serves and controls the very powers that proclaimed it.[2] It is this element of control that also demands from law the use of controlled violence, by means of regulation. As for justice, despite the fantasy of some that universal justice is possible, there is an intrinsic political element in justice, due to its being based on conflicting interests or the differences in what people feel to be just. When Robert Cover considered meaningful law and the genesis of law to depend on a splitting of worlds, he described this as a matter of normative mitosis (see chapter two).[3] Such mitosis slumbers in the potential of difference embodied in the multitude. Different people experience things differently as just or as unjust, and as a consequence they propose different worlds. Yet this is also why there is an intrinsic element of justice to politics. Brutal or totalitarian power are not politics, precisely because they deny difference. Hannah Arendt, who considered power to be distinct from the violence intrinsic to brutal or totalitarian rule, rightfully argued that the use of violence is impotent politics.[4] Politics should be able to deal with multiplicity and the controversy that accompanies it without it leading to violence and a splitting of worlds. The paradox, then, is that justice implies multiplicity whereas a just form of politics, in its understanding controversy, implies unity. The element of understanding demands from justice, or a just politics, the use of empathy.

The two related kinds of logic at stake in this chapter, which affirm and disturb one another, are the logic of violence and the logic of empathy. They will be explored on the basis of a novel, *Daniel Deronda*, published in 1876. It is without doubt the most controversial text written by British author Mary Anne Evans (1819–80) under her pseudonym George Eliot. Published four years prior to her death, it was Eliot's final literary statement; one that continues to create controversy to this day, possibly even more so than at the time it was written.[5] Eliot concerned herself with the misery and strife of Eastern European Jewish

[2] That this is threatened globally, in many instances, is the subject of ch 8. About the dynamic of both serving and controlling, see also ch 3.

[3] Robert Cover, 'Nomos and Narrative' in Martha Minow, Michael Ryan and Austin Sarat (eds), *Narrative, Violence, and the Law, The Essays of Robert Cover* (Ann Arbor, The University of Michigan Press, 1995) 128.

[4] Hannah Arendt developed her thoughts on the issue in *The Human Condition* (Chicago, University of Chicago Press, 1998), and in *On Violence* (Orlando, Harcourt, 1970). See also Andrew Schaap, Danielle Celermajer and Vrasidas Karalis (eds), *Power, Judgment and Political Evil: In Conversation with Hannah Arendt* (Farnham, Ashgate, 2010).

[5] Paul Owen, 'Daniel Deronda: a Victorian novel that's still controversial' (10 February 2009) *The Guardian*, available at www.theguardian.com/books/booksblog/2009/feb/10/zionism-deronda-george-eliot.

communities in particular, that had to survive in circumstances considerably more unbearable than the ones to be found in the United Kingdom, where the situation was unpleasant but comparatively mild. The novel slowly unravels this issue. It is not until well over halfway through that the protagonist becomes part of the political movement aimed at forming a Jewish nation. The protagonist, Daniel Deronda, slowly discovers his Jewishness and becomes actively engaged with the cause of a Jewish state.[6]

Considering its subject, *Daniel Deronda* was not simply controversial. It was an annoying novel, in both its own temporal setting and our contemporary one. On the one hand, the novel is in several ways a study into politically inspired empathy and the dynamic between law and justice. On the other hand, it is also concerned with implicit or explicit legal violence, an aspect that is often glossed over by scholars dealing with the novel. Many read the text in terms of what literary historian Aleksandar Stevic termed 'convenient cosmopolitanism'.[7] As for the violence concerned, Ruth Wisse argued that the novel is as much about the Jewish issue as it is about the suppression of women, an equally controversial topic in Eliot's time. Wisse considers these two issues as intrinsically linked:

> Both fighting ingrained prejudice. Both demanding greater freedom yet uncertain about the ultimate aim of self-liberation. Would women and Jews try to free themselves from their essential nature in a way that will doom them to misery; or could they emancipate themselves and win their independence in a way that would release their best potential? ([*sic*]; my transcription of the web-lecture, FWK)[8]

The emancipation struggles of women and nineteenth-century European Jews were in essence issues of violence and of empathy. Both parties wanted to exist politically in non-violent circumstances. In this context, they were not only looking for a legal order that would protect them with force, they were also fleeing or fighting against a legal order that either dealt with them violently or was oblivious to their fate. Both parties exemplified disparate versions of what different people found to be just and the emancipation of both implied the more or less violent disturbance of existing orders; this is why both were regarded an annoyance for large parts of European audiences.

[6] Eliot's novel appears to pre-empt Zionism by 20 years, with Theodor Herzl's explicit defining of Zionism only published in *The Jewish State* in 1896. The latter's plea, however, did not arise from a vacuum; the aspirations for a Jewish state were growing through the pogroms in Russia and Eastern Europe, and were developed further in German-speaking Central Europe. Although Eliot would not have been familiar with *Self-emancipation* by the Russian Leon Pinsker, published in 1882, she may well have come across Moses Hess's *Rome and Jerusalem: the last national question* from 1862. On this see Isaiah Berlin, 'The Life and Opinions of Moses Hess' in Henry Hardy (ed), *Against the Current: Essays in the History of Ideas* (New York, Random House, 2013). The novel's initial German setting and the protagonists' returning to this country is perhaps no coincidence.

[7] Alexander Stevic, 'Convenient Cosmopolitanism: *Daniel Deronda*, Nationalism and the Critics' (2017) 45 *Victorian Literature and Culture* 593.

[8] Ruth Wisse, 'Ruth Wisse teaches *Daniel Deronda*: George Eliot's Novel of Jewish Nationalism' online course on *Tikvah*, available at tikvahfund.org/course/daniel-deronda.

Political conflicts of interest were radicalised by the German legal philosopher Carl Schmitt (1888–1985), who became influential towards the end of the twentieth century, though not in the field of law, but of politics. Schmitt's *The Concept of the Political* (1932) was adopted as a theoretical underpinning by those who sought to propagate an aggressive Western response to radical Islam; and Schmitt was useful here since he defined politics by the distinction between friends and foes.[9] Yet to make the distinction as drastically as he did, Schmitt had to draw law out of the equation, as a regulating force that binds opposed and differing parties in a political force field.[10] Schmitt had to ignore, that is, the intrinsic relation between politics and law. Moreover, wherever one looks for the origin and development of political practices and theories, a definition of politics in terms of irreconcilable foes is precisely non-political. Politics is the regulated art of negotiating differences, whether this is a democratic form of politics or any other one. This art needs to avoid defining others as foes, as parties one cannot negotiate with. In fact, once parties start defining one another as foes, politics fails and conflicts erupt, or there is a parting of the ways that implies parties no longer need to act politically towards one another.

Surprisingly, few questioned why a legal scholar was a major source for our thinking about politics, especially given that he had made a caricature of politics by negating the legal regulation that is characteristic of it. More seriously, scholars failed to note how Schmitt's definition of politics was actually a definition of how law is used politically. Because, if we consider the friend–foe opposition in terms of how the law should act in the service of politics, it makes perfect sense. Principally, the rule of law is irreconcilable with corruption; hence, corruption is the foe. A society in which people are allowed to live their lives in safety is irreconcilable with violence and harassment; so violent actors or harassers are foes.

Politics as a regulated form of execution of power that can bind different parties was a major theme in a text that established a watershed in the history of political theory, and that defines the regulating political actor in society as 'the defender of the peace' – in Latin: *Defensor pacis*.[11] The author was Marsilius of Padua (1275–1342), who considered how people living together in cities or states are defined by marked differences of interest, ones that need to be regulated and reconciled by a political actor. Here, he developed an extensive argument against a dominant actor who acted non-politically: the Roman Catholic Church with the Pope at its head. According to Marsilius, the church conditioned the world of politics not in terms of a public space of difference but in terms of a closed house (an *oikos*) ruled by a father, a Pope, who was a mimicry of God the Father.

[9] Carl Schmitt, *The Concept of the Political*, trans and intro George Schwab (Chicago, University of Chicago Press, 1996).

[10] I thank Richard Weisberg for sharpening my thoughts on this issue and for suggesting the phrase 'to draw law out of the equation'.

[11] Marsilius of Padua, *The Defender of the Peace*, ed and trans Annabel Brett (Cambridge, Cambridge University Press, 2005).

This Pope claimed *plenitude potestatis*: ultimate coercive power. Yet the only legitimate use of coercive power for Marsilius was in the hands of politicians in the service of the peace of the body politic.[12] To him the church was non-political in dividing the world and its peoples morally in terms of right or wrong, which may explain the many crusades waged, externally against so-called unbelievers, internally against heretics. From the current perspective the popular reduction of the term 'crusade' to the crusades aimed at the appropriation of the Holy Land may have served to propel the image of a centuries-old opposition between the West and Islam. Yet the majority of thousands of crusades was actually aimed at internal parties in European society.[13]

Granted that law's task is to maintain order against enemies of the peace, the paradox is that it must work by means of a logic of violence; a violence that is the necessary instrument of coercion. Such is the consequence of the friend–foe opposition in a legal context. This does not mean that law equates to violence. It is also determined by empathy in that it guarantees a safe space for anyone accused, for instance. Neither does law's violence imply that it cannot be reasonable; it should be, and can be (see chapters one and eight). Yet when push comes to shove, the law is tasked to safeguard society against its enemies and to this order it will deprive society's foes of their liberty, possibly even of their lives. It is law that executes, not politics. Politics will only resort to law as soon as its modes of communication are threatened. Law is asked to stop this threat and cannot be utilised to continue a discourse unless one of the participants is brought to behave, as Schmitt's text can point out so well if it is understood differently. If law speaks, it does not come to its decision in dialogue; dialogue is a matter of mediation, which is aimed at compromise and as such is a socialisation of law that leaves out its aspect of coercion and violence.

With regard to the violent, coercive aspect of law, the distinction between law and justice is key, as was recognised by Marsilius:

> [L]aw may be considered in two ways: in one way, simply in itself, so that it does no more than give an indication of what is just or unjust; advantageous or harmful; and as such it is called the science or doctrine of right. In a second way it can be considered inasmuch a command has been given in respect of its observation, which coerces by means of penalty or reward meted out in this world, or inasmuch as it is handed down by way of such a command. And considered in this way it is most properly called, and most properly is, law.[14]

Marsilius is referring to a distinction made by Aristotle in *Ethics 8*, which holds that the source of coercion is located in the domains of law. The body wielding

[12] On this see Joseph Canning, 'The Role of Power in the Political Thought of Marsilius of Padua' (1999) 20 *History of Political Thought* 21.

[13] Jonathan Phillips, *Holy Warriors: A Modern History of the Crusades* (New York, Random House, 2010).

[14] Marsilius of Padua, *The Defender of the Peace* (2005) 1.10.4, 53. See Canning, 'The Role of Power in Political Thought' (1999) 29.

power is political because it is not the master of a house (an *oikos*), but instead serves a public body or the multitude, as Marsilius terms it. This multitude embodies the ultimate legislator, since authorities

> can do nothing more than this, particularly anything involving difficulty, without the consent of the subject multitude or the legislator; and that the multitude or legislator should not be provoked by injustice, because the force and authority of the principate consists in the express will of this same multitude.[15]

This concise passage implies that political rule should be just before being legal. Then it should be just in its enactment of the law. This why its laws should be just. And all this together legitimates coercion. In short: politics is only politics if it is marked by what is just.

That said, Marsilius was confronted with a problem he did not end up addressing, and which still troubles many today. His analysis was in line with that of Hannah Arendt, who defined the 'disturbing miracle' at the heart of (democratic) politics in terms of an intrinsic tension: 'the public sphere is as consistently based on the law of equality, as the private sphere is based on the law of universal difference and differentiation'.[16] If the multitude is characterised by difference and political authority is the power that allows people to live together in difference, this can only be done on the basis of a law that holds for all and binds all. The political struggle, probably propelled by experienced injustices, consists in defining this 'all'. Inspired by Eliot's novel, I will consider the link between politics (more specifically, democratic politics) and justice in relation to this multitudinous and diverse 'body'. By this I mean an entity that consists of diverse, different beings who desire to live together politically, and who desire to have justice be done on the basis of their different interests and feelings of what is just. It concerns an entity that needs to be protected by law against those who do not care doing justice to its diversity or are oblivious to it. With the latter we meet the destructive third that can disrupt law's logic of violence and justice's logic of empathy: obliviousness. Before we move to this disruptive third, let me first consider what the annoying element in the meeting of the two logics through art's interface is.

II. Two Modes of Wilfulness and the Chiasmus of Law and Justice

Eliot's novel deals with two protagonists, Daniel Deronda and Gwendolen Harleth. The latter is a young woman with aristocratic roots, whose family experiences a

[15] Marsilius of Padua (n 11) 3.3, 557, ed Brett. The passage was translated by Canning (n 12) as follows: 'the multitude or legislator should not be provoked by injury, because in its expressed will consists the virtue and authority of rulership' (24). Here, it is unfortunate that the translator uses 'injury' where the original has *iniuria*. As Annabel Brett rightly translates, the multitude should not be provoked by injustice.

[16] Hannah Arendt, *The Origin of Totalitarianism* (Orlando, Harcourt, 1976) 301.

financial crisis. This leads her to a difficult choice: relegate her position in the social hierarchy or maintain her position by marrying a wealthy man. Bound by the social conventions at the time, she opts for the latter. When she begins to despise the man she has wed, it is a lucky stroke of destiny that he is thrown overboard whilst adjusting a sail on a boat trip in the Mediterranean Sea. We learn of the incident through Gwendolen, who was on the boat with her husband. We cannot be sure, then, if she was perhaps a tad too slow in throwing him a lifeline. We do know that she finally dives in after him, but to no avail and luckily – for her – at that exact moment another boat is nearby and fishermen promptly come to rescue her. Daniel happens to be present when the fishermen return, and takes Gwendolen to a hotel. This is how the scene unfolds, with Gwendolen speaking first:

> 'I will tell you everything now. Do you think a woman who cried, and prayed, and struggled to be saved from herself, could be a murderess?'
>
> 'Great God,' said Deronda, in a deep, shaken voice, 'don't torture me needlessly. You have not murdered him. You threw yourself into the water with the impulse to save him. Tell me the rest afterwards. This death was an accident that you could not have hindered.'
>
> 'Don't be impatient with me.' The tremor, the childlike beseeching in these words compelled Deronda to turn his head and look at her face. The poor quivering lips went on. 'You said – you used to say – you felt more for those who had done something wicked and were miserable; you said they might get better – they might be scourged into something better. If you had not spoken in that way, everything would have been worse …'[17]

Daniel's reaction to the possibility that his dear friend could be a murderess is rather prompt. Most studies and critiques agree with him, even though Gwendolen does not hide the fact she had been wanting her husband to die since she ended up in this marriage, and makes an appeal to Daniel to have compassion with those who have done something wicked. Apparently, both within the diegesis of the story and in its reception, her openness renders the possibility of her actually killing her husband unlikely.

Shortly thereafter, Gwendolen implores Daniel not to desert her. He immediately reassures her he never will, although

> all the while he felt as if he was putting his name on a blank paper which might be filled up terribly. Their attitude, his averted face with its expression of a suffering which he was solemnly resolved to undergo, might have told half the truth of the situation to a beholder who had suddenly entered.[18]

Evidently, Daniel is aware of the possibility that Gwendolen may have done something terrible. He is also conscious of his own commitment to her

[17] Quotes refer to the 1995 edition: George Eliot, *Daniel Deronda* (Harmondsworth, Penguin, 1995) 690.
[18] ibid 690–91.

as-of-yet-uncertain innocence. What this 'half the truth' is, remains obscured for now. First, the reader spends five pages learning of the depth of Gwendolen's resentment that developed over the course of her strategic marriage, how long she has suffered in it, how often she willed her husband dead. Then, abruptly, there is Gwendolyn's description of what happened. This arrives unexpectedly and is so brief that our reading experience might almost be as quick as that of a man falling – or being pushed – overboard:

> [A]nd the evil longings, the evil prayers came again and blotted everything else dim, till in the midst of them – I don't know how it was – he was turning the sail – there was a gust – I know nothing – I only know that I saw my wish outside me.[19]

The entire scene is one of dissociation. The murderous thoughts that mist Gwendolen's mind are not of her agency; they overcome her. She suddenly loses her memory ('I don't know how it was') although she does know precisely what he was doing: turning that sail. Then comes the only passive construction in the entire passage ('there was a gust'), followed by a phrase that does not suggest a loss of memory as much as a lack of *knowledge* ('I know nothing'). What she does know ('I only know') is again a principle of dissociation: what she has done has happened outside of her, or rather, her inner wishes have bizarrely come to pass outside her.

With a character, or real person, that thinks murderous thoughts about someone cold and heartless, empathy easily transitions into sympathy. The death of this cold-hearted man, thrown overboard by an unexpected swing of a sail, hence almost becomes a matter of poetic justice. Yet someone who contemplates at length the death of her husband, wishes such upon him, throws him overboard and can allegedly not recall any moment of the event, requires an alternative judgement. Tellingly enough, critics of the novel have not taken this possibility seriously, as though Gwendolen is incapable of murder.[20] Still, to bring in politics here: how much empathy is understandable if we consider this to be a paradigmatic case of one woman protesting against, or targeting centuries of oppression, and killing not just an individual husband but an icon of that oppression? Hers would be a wilful action, then, aimed against a form of systemic violence; or aimed at a system that had been oblivious with regard to not just her unhappiness and bondage alone, but to a collective one. Such wilful action would then somehow feel just; to some, that is, certainly not to all. It would at least be aimed at a new beginning that implied

[19] ibid 696.

[20] Few critics mention the possibility that Gwendolyn is a murderer, and if they do, they discard the idea as unlikely. See for instance Chase Pielak, who states: 'Nevertheless, Gwendolen's animality has guaranteed her innocence. She is but a creature, a non-subject, incapable of the saving response that Grandcourt finally demands' in Chase Pielak, 'Hunting Gwendolen: Animetaphor in *Daniel Deronda*' (2012) 40 *Victorian Literature and Culture* 99, 108. For an overview, see Kathleen McCormack, 'Yachting with Grandcourt: Gwendolen's Mutiny in *Daniel Deronda*' (2015) 43 *Victorian Literature and Culture* 83. Most explicit is Alexander Welsh who concludes: 'The whole line of suspense in the novel has more to do with psychological guilt than with the kind that would land the heroine in an Italian jail' in Alexander Welsh, *George Eliot and Blackmail* (Cambridge MA, Harvard University Press, 1985) 285.

the breaking of a rule. Patchen Markell noted that in Arendt's work the Greek terms *archê* and *archein* 'meant not only "rule" and "to rule" but also "beginning" and "to begin"'.[21] Whereas law cannot step outside of itself, politics and justice can – and at points should.

Wilfulness has always been viewed as a problem in the history of law. As Sara Ahmed contends in her study *Willful Subjects*: a 'willful action is one that is intentional, one that is done "with bad purpose" and in full knowledge of the law'.[22] For this reason, Ahmed argues in the course of her reading of Eliot's novel that we must be cautious when we want to bend the notion of wilfulness towards a positive light. Still, this is what she does in stating: 'Willfulness could be understood as a necessary horizon for politics'.[23] This would be a horizon on which the light of an opening appears after years of darkness in a closed system in which people had found themselves caught. Ahmed moves from a negative form of wilfulness in the domain of law to a positive one in the domain of politics. The shift is connected to the character of Gwendolen Harleth, as an example of 'the figure who wills wrongly or wills too much', and Ahmed presents her analysis of Eliot's novel in the context of an injustice that has persisted for centuries, if not millennia.

In this context, readers may experience general feelings of understanding towards Gwendolen, but the novel moreover provokes readers to dare to choose what they have understanding for, and whom or what they dare to enter into empathy with, even if this involves empathising with the killing of an oppressor. Malicious intent is not the same for each individual and not all bad intentions deserve equal amounts of empathy. Moreover, a judicial system that is blind to centuries of oppression, has been oblivious with regard to terminating the persistence of such oppression. Such a system has wilfully empathised with the side of the perpetrators for centuries and so has its own problem of maliciousness. Politically speaking, opposition against such maliciousness would be a positive kind of wilfulness because it would open up the realm of the justice for those who had been locked up in a closed system.

In order to do justice to Gwendolen's wilfulness, Ahmed first considers in which respects wilfulness is a matter of a conscious choice based on goodwill, or on volition.[24] She then sketches how Kant viewed goodwill as a moral capacity only when it is able to prevail free from specific interests or aspirations. For somebody who has been subjected to an unjust order, however, that is an almost impossible request, or an unethical stance towards thinking about goodwill:

> The very achievement of a good will would be a kind of death sentence; she would 'agree' with the very place assigned to her by a moral as well as social order. If moral

[21] Patchen Markell, 'The Rule of the People: Arendt, *Archê*, and Democracy' (2006) 100 *American Political Science Review* 2.

[22] Sara Ahmed, *Willful subjects* (Durham, Duke University Press, 2014) 174. Ahmed uses the American spelling, with the double 'll'.

[23] Ahmed, *Willful subjects* (2014) 165.

[24] ibid 59–60.

> norms are also gendered norms then to challenge them is to risk being assigned as wrong rather than right no matter what happens. Political and sexual liberation might require a willingness to be wrong by being affected wrongly by the right things.[25]

The problem is clear: if a particular order is unjust and asymmetrical, but sells itself as morally solid, wilfulness is the ethically justified path to take. It also lays the ground for a new legal order, since the 'no' to an unjust order is not an ultimate 'no' and, accordingly, not a case of ill intent.

By means of Gwendolen, the steps Ahmed takes are rendered all the more systemic by comparing female emancipation to those subjected to colonial rule, following Frantz Fanon in *Wretched of the Earth*.[26] Here, positive wilfulness is developed into a will to change: 'To will this change is at the same time not to be willing to bear or reproduce the present; the project of willing thus begins with, but exceeds, negation: to oppose the old directives is to will what follows'.[27] It is no coincidence that in his book Fanon proposed a violent response as necessary to overthrow colonial oppression. The crucial point, here, is that he does not do so on the basis of certain interests, or to claim a bigger piece of the pie. He engages with the muddy interstice where unlawful violence is engaged for a more just order. The central issue is to end injustice, in order to open up the possibility of a more just politics. Consequently, we require positive forms of wilfulness in the political domain. That is to say: politically speaking and in terms of justice, empathy is required to understand the inclinations of the other, but at the same time one has to obstinately stick to one's desires and interests and keep open the future in the hope that it will make a better life possible. It is this obstinacy that is behind the violence proposed.

Ahmed's engagement with the role of willfulness in the area in between law, justice and politics leads me to propose a chiasmic relation between two modes of wilfulness, as the opposite of obliviousness (on which more below). Chiasmus is the figure that both separates and binds, as in John F Kennedy's 'Let us never negotiate out of fear, but let us never fear to negotiate'. The 'but' and the reverse order of terms (negotiate/fear – fear/negotiate), separate the two options. Yet they are simultaneously intertwined in that the maxim concerns a repetition of the same terms. So, if the two modes of willfulness are in chiasmus, they are separate and relate in a criss-crossing manner to the realm of justice or domain of politics on the one hand, and the system of law on the other:

> In the domain of politics positive wilfulness marks the endeavour to achieve one's goal for the sake of, and care for justice, while negative wilfulness marks the bad intent to tear the body politic apart for the sake of power;
>
> in a legal system negative wilfulness marks the bad intent to support an unjust system, while positive wilfulness marks the endeavour and care to obstinately use law's force for the sake of justice.

[25] ibid 87.
[26] Frantz Fanon, *Wretched of the Earth*, trans R Philcox (New York, Grove Press, 1963).
[27] Ahmed (n 22) 141.

The phrase 'law's force' connotes its persistent ability to defend an order, whether just or not.[28] This force/power implies violence, be it violence of a different kind than Fanon's. In its use of violence, law has to act reasonably, in the knowledge that its function is to protect the body politic. Law concerns regulated violence, then. Here, law should not operate instrumentally. In fact, it is in need of empathy, if only to fully safeguard the space granted to anyone accused or neglected. Still, empathy has to lead to a principal division that contains both a legal and a political aspect, or an aspect of justice. Let me deal with the legal one first, in dealing with the third element that threatens both law and justice.

III. Obliviousness and the Grey Area between Law and Justice

Obliviousness introduces the third that threatens the dynamic between the two logics at stake. I choose obliviousness above negligence here because while negligence is punishable by law it also has been a characteristic of the operation of the system of law for centuries and continues to be so, for instance with regard to the fate of animals.[29] Law's negligence translates into a legal distribution of responsibilities, as legal scholar Scott Veitch argued, and this distribution implies forms of legal irresponsibility (see chapter five).[30] Obliviousness is also distinct from apathy (dealt with in chapter two). Whereas apathy overcomes beings, obliviousness incorporates an element of wilfulness. One can be fully aware of animals suffering in bio-industries, for instance, and be oblivious to their suffering, so that one can enjoy one's daily portion(s) of meat. If one is oblivious, empathy does not serve some form of common good but only one's own particular interests. Any systemic violence involved is then not taken fully into account because it does not seem to directly pertain to one's particular situation. This explains why so many were faced with obliviousness in Eliot's nineteenth-century context of England and Eastern Europe. Killing Jews or raping women needed not be defined as a crime, since most Jews and many women were not considered relevant (political) subjects. Obliviousness concerns the wilful ignorance or denial of differences of interest and what people or other beings feel to be just, then.[31] It may involve implicit or explicit violence but makes people defy responsibility for violence, yielding to a

[28] See Richard Weisberg, *In Praise of Intransigence: The Perils of Flexibility* (Oxford, Oxford University Press, 2014).

[29] This was the main argument in Berrie Vugts, *The Case against Animal Rights: A Literary Intervention* (PhD diss, Leiden University, 2014).

[30] Scott Veitch, *Law and Irresponsibility: On the Legitimation of Human Suffering* (Abingdon, Routledge-Cavendish, 2007).

[31] Moral feelings are not restricted to human beings as mentioned in ch 2, see Frans de Waal, *Our Inner Ape: A Leading Primatologist Explains Why We Are Who We Are*, or *The Age of Empathy: Nature's Lessons for a Kinder Society*.

form of carelessness by means of the selective use of empathy. When Slavoj Žižek talked about the distinction between systemic violence and subjective violence, the former – in its being nigh invisible and omnipresent – is only possible because of obliviousness.[32]

Just like apathy, or any of the other disruptive thirds mentioned in this study, such as corruption or hallucination, obliviousness can be produced and has a function. A study by psychologist Paul C Rosenblatt, for instance, introduced the phrase 'family obliviousness'.[33] With this Rosenblatt indicated families where most members of a family know that what has happened or is still happening, is wrong, but prefer to be oblivious to it. This also hints at the paradox involved with Rosenblatt's definition of obliviousness: it combines knowing with not knowing. One example he gives concerns the fact that the poison used to 'save' the suburban lawn from so-called weeds is dangerous for toddlers. Families using such poison may silently proceed with using it for years while knowing that is the case, up until their own grandchild comes to visit. This brings in a second characteristic of the paradox inherent to obliviousness: it is contingent to situations. Within families or organisations, or societies, people may share obliviousness whereas outside of such spheres, they may not.[34] If in an organisation sexual abuse is committed by a high-ranking figure, this can go on for years, with almost everyone knowing what is happening, and talking about it late in the evening with friends. Yet, within the organisation they act oblivious to it, while knowing it is wrong. This shows how obliviousness is indeed disruptive for both a system of law and a realm of justice. Crimes are taking place without being reported, people or other beings are being hurt or abused without anyone intervening, while we 'know'.

In order to counter or avoid obliviousness, calls for increased or broadened forms of empathy in the legal domain can be traced, firstly, to the 1970s, as part of the reaction against a positivist or instrumentalist approach to law.[35] To enlarge empathy, James Boyd White and Jeanne Gaakeer called for a narrative approach.[36] Defining the issue of empathy more broadly, Greta Olson called for an affective approach to law.[37] Secondly, the call for more empathy in the legal system found its

[32] Slavoj Žižek, *Violence* (London, Polity Books, 2009).

[33] Paul C Rosenblatt, *Shared Obliviousness in Family Systems* (Albany NY, State University of New York Press, 2009) 141.

[34] One example of obliviousness in organisations is Alesha Doan and Shannon Portillo, *Organizational Obliviousness: Entrenched Resistance to Gender Integration in the Military* (Cambridge, Cambridge University Press 2019).

[35] Amy Coplan and Peter Goldie (eds), *Empathy: Philosophical and Psychological Perspectives* (Oxford, Oxford University Press, 2011).

[36] cf ch 1, James Boyd White, *The Legal Imagination* (1973); *When Words Lose Their Meaning* (1984); *Justice as Translation* (1990); *Acts of Hope* (1994); and AMP (Jeanne) Gaakeer, *Hope Springs Eternal. An Introduction to the Work of James Boyd White* (Amsterdam, Amsterdam University Press, 1988); *Judging from Experience. Law, Praxis, Humanities* (Edinburgh, Edinburgh University Press, 2019). Claudia Bouteligier marks a new generation which presents itself in this line of thinking, see Claudia Bouteligier and Timo Slootweg (eds), *Empathie en recht* (Apeldoorn, Garant/Maklu, 2018).

[37] Greta Olson, 'The Turn to Passion: Has Law and Literature become Law and Affect?' (2016) 28 *Law and Literature* 335–53.

sources in all those groups that promoted or fought for the interests of oppressed or subjected beings, both within and beyond the context of the law.[38] Thirdly, there were many who advocated a more cosmopolitan or multicultural position, in which the legal order, if it wants to do justice to understanding all parties involved, needs to be based on the largest possible common denominator of empathy.[39]

Additionally, we find those who warned against using empathy as a tool to greater understanding or broader sensibility. Most recently, psychologist Paul Bloom published *Against Empathy: The Case for Rational Compassion*.[40] To him empathy was a dangerous route to take because people tend to side with those they know or are familiar with as a result of which they come to be oblivious to the fate of others. In a legal context, Carolyn Pedwell published *Affective Relations: The Transnational Politics of Empathy*. In an interview she noted:[41]

> [E]mpathy today seems to be everywhere – and is everywhere presumed to be 'good'. … Yet precisely because empathy … is so widely and unquestioningly viewed as positive, critical analysis of its limits and problems in the context of transnational power relations tends to be avoided or deferred.

Pedwell's study argues that, from a legal perspective, there is always a concrete imbalance in the distributive dynamic in empathy. Firstly, in every legal situation, the relationship is not reciprocal and dialogical, but instead is hierarchically defined. Secondly, law is always related to power and order. Whether this is the order of the contemporary or of the future, law must enforce order and this directs and distributes forms of empathy. Thirdly, the role of empathy in a transnational or internally fragmented field is complex because contentions evolve between opposing but equally valid political interests and so it is sometimes impossible to find a balance or distributed judgment. Arguments that make a judgment possible can radically vary, based as they are on interests and their associated empathies. For instance, if *Daniel Deronda* is still controversial or annoying today it is because the strife for a Jewish state was successful in the end, with Palestinians suffering great injustice as a consequence.

The principal limits of any empathic approach to law were at stake when lawyer Robert Cover dryly noted that we do not talk criminals into prison.[42] Because language does play an important role in any legal process, convicted persons may

[38] Dean Spade and Craig Willse, 'Sex, Gender, and War in an Age of Multicultural Imperialism' (2014) 1 *QED: A Journal in GLBTQ Worldmaking* 5.

[39] For an overview, see Greta Olson, 'Mapping the Pluralist Character of Cultural Approaches to Law' (2017) 18 *German Law Journal* 233.

[40] Paul Bloom, *Against Empathy: The Case for Rational Compassion* (New York, Vintage, 2016).

[41] Carolyn Pedwell, *Affective Relations: The Transnational Politics of Empathy* (London, Palgrave Macmillan, 2014); for the interview, see Gwendolyn Beetham, 'The Academic Feminist Goes Global: A Conversation with Carolyn Pedwell' (2012) *Feministing*, available at feministing.com/2012/05/22/the-academic-feminist-goes-global-a-conversation-with-carolyn-pedwell.

[42] Robert Cover, 'Violence and the Word' (1986) 95 *Yale Law School* 1601. My argument was inspired by Jason A Beckett's reading of Cover's work: 'The Violence of Wording: Robert Cover on Legal Interpretation' (2011) 8 *NoFo* 3.

walk, ostensibly courteously, to their imprisonment. Yet if they don't, they will be dragged there. As soon as they resist, the law reveals its indomitability and violent force. According to Cover:

> The perpetrator and victim of organized violence will undergo achingly disparate significant experiences. For the perpetrator, the pain and fear are remote, unreal, and largely unshared. They are, therefore, almost never made a part of the interpretive artefact, such as the judicial opinion. On the other hand, for those who impose the violence the justification is important, real and carefully cultivated. Conversely, for the victim, the justification for the violence recedes in reality and significance in proportion to the overwhelming reality of the pain and fear that is suffered. Between the idea and the reality of common meaning falls the shadow of the violence of law, itself.[43]

Cover is not only discussing the different forms of reasonability that are at work in relation to various parties in legal procedures and enforcement here. He is also leveling a principal argument against a seeming commonality. Legally, such commonality does not exist, neither in concept (the *idea*) nor in practice (the *reality*; emphases mine). Law divides parties through a violent scission.

In contrast, an empathetic approach in the *political* context implies the ability to sense and understand the at times radically different interests of others. With respect to this, all those critically assessing the violent underpinning and preservation of the legal order or the state – from Carl Schmitt in his dialogue with Walter Benjamin to Giorgio Agamben, to Terry Eagleton, to Jacques Derrida, to Judith Butler, to Slavoj Žižek, to Roberto Esposito or Simon Critchley[44] – have tended to avoid the basic question: what factors, beside enforcement or coercion, make the body politic hold together despite the fact that it is a body of differing interests and struggles? The question is pivotal for any attempt to define the body politic positively, in terms of the sense that people want to preserve a body politic regardless of mutual conflicts of interest. In this context, the last decades have seen much attention been paid to the issue of how the body politic rests on theologically or quasi-metaphysically constructed fundaments, or in which the body politic is defined by its power to install the state of exception, as was Schmitt's or Agamben's option.

[43] Cover, 'Violence and the Word' (1986) 1601.

[44] The starting point is Walter Benjamin, 'Zur Kritik zur Gewalt' in Herbert Marcuse (ed), *Zur Kritik zur Gewalt und andere Aufsätze* (Berlin, Suhrkamp, 1965), originally published in 1921. For the others, see Giorgio Agamben, 'On the Limits of Violence' (2009) 39 *Diacritics* 103, a republication of a paper published in 1970; Terry Eagleton, *Benjamin or Towards a Revolutionary Criticism* (London, Verso, 1981); Jacques Derrida, 'Force of Law: The "Mystical Foundation of Authority"' in G Anidjar (ed), *Acts of Religion* (New York, Routledge, 2002), originally published in French in 1994; Judith Butler, 'Critique, Coercion, and Sacred Life in Benjamin's "Critique of Violence"' in Hent de Vries and Lawrence J Sullivan (eds), *Political Theologies: Public Religion in a Post-Secular World* (New York, Fordham University Press, 2006); Slavoj Žižek, *Violence* (London, Polity Books, 2009); Simon Critchley, 'Violent Thoughts About Slavoj Žižek' in Nathan Eckstrand and Christopher Yates (eds), *Philosophy and the Return of Violence: Studies from this Widening Gyre* (New York, The Continuum International Publishing Group, 2011); Roberto Esposito, *Immunitas: The Protection and Negation of Life* (London, Polity, 2011). All these publications have, in turn, led to yet other volumes.

Yet if one chooses to understand politics for its radically open character, for its embodying the realm of the potential, this connotes the realm of justice. Politics is considered firstly, in this context, as the struggle in practice for a more just and peaceful society; secondly, as the expectation of possible participation of all subjects, especially those who did not have a voice – this is a point raised by Jacques Rancière.[45] To this order, politics is considered in terms of conscious regulation, be it a regulation that needs to remain open. With respect to this, Alan Keenan, in his dealing with democracy, pointed to an annoying paradox. Democracy's tendency to include all and its presupposition that it rests on its own foundations, implies a radical openness. Yet to achieve this it needs regulation and closure. Thus, democracy becomes a site of 'perpetual contestation' and an ideal 'at odds with itself' (13), characterised by 'inevitable trespass, failure, frustration, disappointments, and incompletion that characterize all democratic action and all democratic (and non-democratic) actors' (22).[46]

If law's task is to preserve order, it may be clear that law builds on what has been decided in the past, that it is the guarantee for things being preserved as they are and secured for tomorrow, unless laws would change today. Politically speaking, this is a matter of policing, but not of the political per se. Politically speaking, no one knows what will happen tomorrow, and this is the freedom of politics. Such a stance is diametrically opposed to the definition of politics given by Schmitt, not only in his defining the root of the political as the distinction between friend and foe, but also in his considering the state as the only political subject. To reduce politics to one political subject, the state, is not a matter of politics but one of power. The political is the willingness to live together in a regulated body that consists of conflicting interests. Such conflicting interests cannot be reconciled and consequently propel struggle, as argued by Chantal Mouffe.[47] This is also why they carry the potential of unpredictable outcomes. As soon as conflicting interests lead to violence, the political is placed out of order. Or, to repeat this in the terms of Hannah Arendt: the use of violence is political impotence.

Consequently, the logic of law's necessarily divisive logic of violence finds an argumentative counterpart, in a logic of empathy on the political plane, as a plane of justice. Politicians are concerned with the negotiation of differences. For them it is pivotal to understand the motivations of those who have different interests. Whereas sympathy is a word that connotes friendship, empathy connotes the larger or broader ability to feel what others go through, even if they may be very different, have opposing interests, or behave badly. In this context it is noteworthy that after a given verdict, the judge and the condemned do not tend to

[45] Jacques Rancière, *Disagreement: Politics and Philosophy*, trans Julie Rose (Minnesota, University of Minnesota Press, 1999).

[46] Alan Keenan, *Democracy in Question: Democratic Openness in a Time of Political Closure* (Stanford, Stanford University Press, 2003). Also see Markell, 'The Rule of the People' (2006) 3.

[47] Chantal Mouffe, *The Democratic Paradox* (London, Verso, 2000).

embrace or slap one another on the shoulder. They cannot, in fact, because the context of order prescribes them as foes and follows the logic of enmity. Yet politicians can embrace and slap one another on the shoulder despite lengthy periods of disagreements, accusations, negotiations, lies, crises and the struggle for a final or temporary solution. The reason is that politicians, despite differences, need to understand their counterparts. If they want to solve matters politically, they need a logic of empathy.

Note that the connection to the realm of justice is not straightforward, here. It would be too obvious to define the realm of justice only on the basis of empathy. The aforementioned Robert Cover with his 'normative mitosis' noticed that paideic communities may refuse compromise (see chapter two). No mistake, one can safely say that the realm of justice is intensely defined by empathy. But to many the execution of a violent opponent – say a torturer or mass killer – may be felt to be just. If ever the two logics of the system of law and the realm of justice meet in a grey area, it is here. On the one hand, the violent logic of law prevents a use of violence that is felt to be just. On the other hand, one could ask whether law's violence can ever be defined as just. Additionally, one can even ask whether law's working against all forms of violence is felt to be just in all cases. The legal and political position taken together with regard to issues of justice was the topic of Judith Butler's most recent book in which she argues that nonviolence is an ethical position that is located at the centre of the domain of politics. However, such a position need not simply be based on empathy.[48]

This is the grey area explored in Eliot's novel, in its dealing with a character that annoys and seems to resist empathy: Gwendolen Harleth is considered to be stubborn, resistant, inflexible, contrary, unwavering, pig-headed, hard-headed, obstinate and malicious. With regards to the latter, Ahmed points to the description of Gwendolen's hands whilst her husband is drowning. These remain tense and still as her husband is thrown overboard ('I kept my hands tight'), and once she looks for, finds, and holds onto a rope, she still keeps her throwing hand still ('I held my hand …'). Into these unmoving hands, Ahmed reads a decisive power.[49] Although she does not consider Gwendolen to be a murderer, she retains the possibility of a politically motivated wilfulness transitioning into a maliciousness that should be ethically defined as wrong.[50] Still, Ahmed also considers the necessity of acting wilfully in a positive sense, against persisting injustice. As such, the distinction between positive and negative wilfulness discussed earlier is relevant. This being said, Ahmed's argument implicitly poses the problem of the dynamic of empathy and violence in its distribution over the legal order and the realm of justice. The latter is marked politically, due to differences of interest or of what people feel to be just.

[48] Judith Butler, *The Force of Nonviolence: The Ethical in the Political* (London, Verso, 2020).
[49] Ahmed (n 21) 176–77.
[50] ibid 59–60.

IV. Divisive Empathy, Cohesive Violence

The common, perhaps even universal 'goodness' of empathy, was a major theme in the work of legal philosopher Martha Nussbaum in her studies that span almost four decades.[51] From *Love's Knowledge* (1990) and *Cultivating Humanity* (1997), to *The New Religious Intolerance* (2013) and *Anger and Forgiveness* (2016) Nussbaum argues for the use of 'inner eyes', using a 'curious and sympathetic imagination' which will allow readers to empathically recognise the strange and the stranger as someone sharing a general humanity. In drawing on Aristotle, Nussbaum time and again underlines the human ability to envision the position of another. She argues against emotional or formal 'distance' in this light, as when she considers that literary texts should not be read in a detached mode:

> But it is next to impossible to see what it could mean to read a drama of Sophocles, or a novel of Dickens or George Eliot, in the detached way. It is impossible to care about the characters and their well-being in the way the text invites, without having some very definite political and moral interests awakened in oneself – interests, for example, in the just treatment of workers and in the reform of education. Both Dickens and Eliot frequently address the reader, alluding to such common interests.[52]

An opposition is set up, here, between a formal approach that is 'detached' and a sensitive reading that demonstrates an involvement with what happens to the characters. By setting up this opposition of approaches, Nussbaum suggests that empathetic readings are not specific but 'common'. According to one critic, Rohan Maitzen, this is 'morally inert', because the *general* empathy Nussbaum discusses lacks actualisation in a legal or political practice.[53] Lauren Berlant, in another context, defined such an option as an 'ongoing ethics of privilege',[54] just as Pedell warned for empathy being more likely 'to remain the purview of those who are already socially privileged'.[55] All this can be seen in light of the mimetic impulse: to only empathise with those one recognises as 'one's own', as Paul Bloom argued. Likewise, Suzanne Keen asked in *Empathy and the Novel* what the causal relation between reading and altruism could be. She emphasised, like Bloom, how open and flexible, but also how biased the process of identification can become.[56]

Still, I would like to politicise Nussbaum's proposal by detaching it from the frame of universality and placing it at the heart of the body politic, considering that empathy is not something that one gives (the problem of tolerance) but that is

[51] For the titles of Nussbaum's works see ch 1.

[52] Nussbaum, *Cultivating Humanity: A Classical Defense of Reform in Liberal Education* (Cambridge, MA, Harvard University Press, 1997) 104.

[53] Rohan Maitzen, 'Martha Nussbaum and the Moral Life of *Middlemarch*' (2006) 30 *Philosophy and Literature* 190.

[54] Lauren Berlant, *Compassion: The Culture and Politics of an Emotion* (New York, Routledge, 2004) 1.

[55] Pedwell, *Affective Relations* (2014) xii.

[56] Suzanne Keen, *Empathy and the Novel* (New York, Oxford University Press, 2007).

needed in order to enter into a relationship. There is a discrepancy in Nussbaum's quote given above between common interests on the one hand, and 'very definite political and moral interests' on the other. If anything characterises the latter, it is precisely their difference, their not being in common. In politicising Nussbaum's understanding of empathy, I highlight that empathy is always a matter of choice, and this choice is unavoidably divisive. Such empathy is incompatible with the universal, since the choice to understand one party entails that understanding another must be curtailed.[57] Or, more principally, as Anna Lindhé puts it:

> [I]f literature creates an understanding of the Other, as submitted by Nussbaum and others, it simultaneously creates an Other – or the Other's Other – towards whom less favorable feelings may be directed, a paradox that complicates the supposed ethical effects of literature and may even short-circuit its ethical efficacy.[58]

The struggle with the paradox described here is evidenced in a volume entitled *For Love of Country*, in which Nussbaum responds to a number of critics. Especially in response to Elaine Scarry, Nussbaum states:[59]

> If we left our world citizenship to the vagaries of our own daily reflections, we would act less well than if we were to institutionalize our best ideas. I agree with Elaine Scarry, therefore, that the imagination needs laws – especially constitutional arrangements – that do as much as possible to institutionalize the equal worth of persons. But these laws must take their impetus from the imagination … We must, therefore, cultivate world citizenship in our hearts and minds as well as our codes of law.[60]

Firstly, commonality is at the heart of 'our world citizenship' yet the issue of who the implied 'we' is, remains unspecified. Moreover, 'citizen' is a conscious choice of term, one that, unlike 'cosmopolitan', has a political basis. We are dealing with an additional but connected paradox here, which Hannah Arendt delineated in the context of human rights, namely that rights are universal but can only be realised on the basis of nation-state specificity.[61] 'We' become citizens because a particular state legally acknowledges us as such. So what happens to those who are not acknowledged on such basis? Consecutively, Nussbaum states that any legal order

[57] In the comparable field of pedagogy, Leigh Patel, in dealing with issues of inclusivity, argued that dialogues for empathy 'can all too easily become parking lots for emotionality and white fragility, recentering whiteness and irrationally requiring people of color to bear witness to these emotions'. See Leigh Patel, 'The Irrationality of Antiracist Empathy' (2016) 106 *English Journal* 81, 83.

[58] Anna Lindhé, 'The Paradox of Narrative Empathy and the Form of the Novel, or What George Eliot Knew' (2016) 48 *Studies in the Novel* 19, 20–21.

[59] Martha Nussbaum, 'Reply' in Joshua Cohen (ed), *For Love of Country*: Debating the Limits of Patriotism (Boston, Beacon Press, 2006). Elaine Scarry is author of *The Body in Pain: The Making and Unmaking of the World* (Oxford, Oxford University Press, 1985); *Rule of Law, Misrule of Men* (Cambridge MA, MIT Press, 2010); *Thinking in an Emergency* (New York, WW Norton & Company, 2011).

[60] Nussbaum, 'Reply' (2006) 138.

[61] Hannah Arendt, *The Origins of Totalitarianism*, ch 9. The obligation to protect the 'universal' and 'inalienable' rights of all human beings, depends on the modern institution of the state, which is defined by national and territorial sovereignty; see also ch 3.

should guarantee 'the equal worth of *persons*' (my emphasis). Alongside 'citizen', this is another charged choice of terms: 'person'. Its legal status is highlighted by adding the term 'constitutional'. So, equal worth can only be attributed to legally recognised and constitutionally respected subjects: persons.

The issue at stake is thus both legal and political. Each political system embodies a divide internally and externally. Internally, parties hold differing or opposing interests but are one by way of a legal order that works on the basis of granting equality for all. Externally, states are particular, but because all of them grant legal citizenship individually, we can conceive of a unitary global citizenship. Meanwhile, with regard to both forms of one-ness, a pivotal point is emphatically avoided: that of law's enforcement, or violence. In order 'to institutionalize the equal worth of persons' this equal worth needs to be safeguarded against those who do not care about such equality. Likewise, universal global citizenship needs to be protected against those who want to shred it to pieces.

The fact that every legal order can only exist by means of violence is a shared idea that nevertheless remains awkward and controversial. In particular, post-structuralist thinkers, in their attack of the state, were much concerned. In Jacques Derrida's 'Force de loi' – Force of Law – we are reminded: 'there is no such thing as law (*droit*) that does not imply in itself, in the analytic structure of its concept, the possibility of being "enforced", applied by force'.[62] Derrida's partners in dialogue in this text are Immanuel Kant, Michel de Montaigne, Blaise Pascal, Emanuel Levinas and especially Walter Benjamin, with his inevitable sidekick, Carl Schmitt. Kant stated that there cannot be law without force and Montaigne described the foundation of law as mystical, which inspired the subtitle of Derrida's reflections: the 'Mystical Foundation of Authority'. Pascal offers Derrida a stepping stone for his argument with the chiasmic phrase: 'Justice without force is impotent. Force without justice is tyrannical'.[63] Benjamin offers another stepping stone with his distinction between pure or divine violence on the one hand and the founding and preserving violence of law on the other. The latter two led Benjamin to contend that the relation between law and violence is principally 'rotten'.[64] This may be so. It leaves the problem of how one can safeguard any space of justice against those who want to exploit if for their own purposes unresolved, and this is a problem that Derrida does not address (or attempts to resolve) at all. His major concern is law's grounding or foundation, and its basis in violence.

Especially Derrida's reading of Pascal's reflection on justice is not exactly a close reading.[65] In Pascal's reflection three different but related notions all

[62] Derrida, 'Force of Law' (2002) 6.

[63] Blaise Pascal, *Pensées, Oeuvres Complètes* vol II, (ed) Michel le Guern (Paris, Gallimard, 1998) nr 94.

[64] Walter Benjamin, 'Critique of Violence' in Marcus Bullock and Michael W Jennings (eds), *Walter Benjamin: Selected Writings* Vol 1 (Cambridge MA, The Belknap Press of Harvard University Press, 2004) 242.

[65] In the original: 'Il est juste que ce qui est juste soit suivi; il est nécessaire que ce qui est le plus fort soit suivi. La justice sans la force est impuissante; la force sans la justice est tyrannique. La justice sans

need to be followed: *le juste* ('that what is just'), *le plus fort* ('that what has most force/power') and *la justice*. The latter either means what people consider to be just or the judiciary system: the system of law. This is implied when Pascal notes that if the law is not powerful, criminals would gain power, and any justice would be lost. Yet, he also notes that when one tries to combine justice with power, justice is always a matter of dispute. Here the realm of justice is at stake, with all the differences of that realm involved. In this case, what is just can have its own force, but it would be wrong to enforce matters of dispute by means of power, for then power may come to contradict justice. Derrida uses the passage to weigh the notions of law (French *loi*), right (French *droit*), justice (French *la justice*), and the just (French *le juste*) against one another while assessing their relation with the meanings of French *force* as force, power and violence. This playing with terms leads Derrida to the establishment of one major distinction: he defines deconstruction as undecidability, or the avoidance of a decisive cut, as a result of which a cut can be made between violent law and non-violent justice.

It is of relevance, though, that Pascal mentions neither law nor right, nor violence. For a mind as sharp as Pascal's, had he been talking about law from the beginning, he would have used *loi*. Instead he uses *juste*, of which the apparent meaning is the 'just'. Pascal is also not simply talking about coercive power. He uses 'le plus fort' and 'la force', which can mean either force or power. Transposed to the realm of justice or to the system of law, the term connotes strength or vibrancy and enforcement or coercion, respectively. For instance, principles of justice can have a force, or appeal, without their being enforced, as a matter of power. I read Pascal's concluding sentence, consequently, in the light of all the double meanings involved. 'Et ainsi ne pouvant faire que ce qui est juste fût fort, on a fait que ce qui est fort fût juste' has two translations or interpretations that do not so much contradict one another but comment on one another. One is 'When people were not able to make that what is just have force, they made it that what has force would be just'. This can be interpreted as follows. Principles of justice cannot be *given* any force; they have their own force of conviction, of inspiration, of appeal on the basis of which people decide that this must be just. Consider, for instance, that I would suggest that all sparrows in Europe should be exterminated and that I would define this as a call for justice since these animals eat our grain. Few of my readers would find this just. As a result, the call would not have much force or appeal. If one wants to turn it into an idea that is followed nevertheless, one might need to use power, which brings in the second reading: 'When people were not able to make that what is just have power, they made it that what has power must be just'. This is the more cynical reading, which can be interpreted as follows. Since it impossible to translate all the differences in what people feel to be just into power, one has to accept that those in power act justly. This was, in fact, the case when Mao Zedong called for the extermination of all sparrows in China during the years 1958–60, in what was called the Smash Sparrows Campaign. Because Mao said it, it had to be just, so this is what people started to do, causing such ecological imbalance that it led to the Great Chinese Famine. It made Mao redirect his call, in 1960, to smash bedbugs instead.

In Pascal's reflection law's coercion or violence is an issue, then, when criminals of any kind (*des méchants*) are to be dealt with forcefully and powerfully, since they threaten justice. Subjection is at stake when people simply accept that what ruling powers say must be the right thing to do. As the example of Mao indicates, this is not a matter of politics but of brute power. Force of conviction, or of appeal, is at stake with regard to what is felt to be just, which will always be a matter of dispute. Such disputes connote the realm of politics and make it unjust to enforce disputed issues of justice. The multiple translations of Pascal's terms lead me to the formulation of a chiasmic relationship between politics and law, with violence and justice as an in-between and marking a difference between force and power: 'Politics is no longer just or loses legitimate power as soon as it transitions into violence; the avoidance of violence makes actual law forceless and threatens the capacity of politics to serve the just'. Put differently, a legal order that revolves around empathetic comprehension but that cannot act with force, in the sense of coercion and violence, is worthless. Such a legal system cannot guarantee the cohesion that is necessary to keep the political domain of justified differences intact. With respect to this, a legal order must be positively wilful, in the sense of being stubborn and obstinate in its service to a politics that serves the just. Make no mistake, a legal order may violently serve unjust politics; in fact, there is ample historical evidence of this. This, however, is precisely the implication of the chiasmus. Such a legal system then becomes part of a politics that transitions into violent power and loses legitimacy. If Judith Butler posits nonviolence as the ethical heart of politics, she is right.[66] The consequence of this position is that we have to locate violence at the heart of law. The two do not exist separately, they are both separated and bound in chiasmus.

In the next chapter we will consider a major element that keeps law's violence in check, namely reasonability, and we will consider what happens if reasonability is threatened systemically in times of hallucination. Such hallucination threatens as much the realm of justice, moreover, in its following a logic of dreams.

force est contredite parce qu'il y a toujours des méchants. La force sans la justice est accusée. Il faut donc mettre ensemble la justice et la force, et pour cela faire que ce qui est juste soit fort ou que ce qui est fort soit juste. La justice est sujette à dispute. La force est très reconnaissable et sans dispute. Ainsi on n'a pu donner la force à la justice, parce que la force a contredit la justice, et a dit qu'elle était injuste, et a dit que c'était elle qui était juste. Et ainsi ne pouvant faire que ce qui est juste fût fort, on a fait que ce qui est fort fût juste.' Pascal, *Pensées* (1998) 110.

[66] Butler, *The Force of Non-Violence* (2020).

8

Logic of Reason vs Logic of Dream

Epistemic Authority, Habeas Corpus, *Hallucination – Nicholas Refn's* Only God Forgives

'Reason is always a region carved out of the irrational – it is not sheltered from the irrational at all, but traversed by it and only defined by a particular kind of relationship among irrational factors. Underneath all reason lies delirium and drift. Everything about capitalism is rational, except capital and capitalism. A stock market is a perfectly rational mechanism, you can understand it, learn how it works; capitalists know how to use it; and yet what a delirium, it's nuts …'

Gilles Deleuze, 'On Capitalism and Desire'[1]

'The building's labyrinthine architecture is, in a way, a replica of the US immigration system. And, as in any labyrinth, some find their way out and some don't. Those who don't might remain here forever, invisible specters who go up and down elevators and wander the hallways, imprisoned in circular nightmares.'

Valeria Luiselli, *Tell Me How It Ends*[2]

I. Reason, Dream and Disruptive Hallucination

The movie *Only God Forgives* (2013) by Danish director Nicolas Winding Refn is set in Bangkok, Thailand. The protagonist or antagonist – depending on whose side one takes – is a police officer called Chang (played by Vithaya Pansringarm). He has to deal with two American brothers, Billy and Julian (played by Tom Burke and Ryan Gosling). The two run a drug network behind the front of a boxing club. After one fight the older brother Billy pays his winning candidate and then says: 'Time to meet the devil'.[3] He starts to roam the streets in search of a 14-year-old girl.

[1] Gilles Deleuze, 'On Capitalism and Desire' in *Desert Islands and Other Texts 1953–1974* (Cambridge MA, Semiotext(e), 2004) 262.

[2] Valeria Luiselli, *Tell Me How It Ends, An Essay in Forty Questions* (London, 4th Estate, 2017) 35–36.

[3] The sequence I discuss here runs from 6:30 to 12:46, *Only God Forgives* (2013, The Weinstein Company/Cinéart).

Since he cannot find one, he has to satisfy his lust with a 16-year-old one. This is not shown. Instead, we see Chang for the first time. He walks towards the viewer in an almost deserted, rainy street, heading for what has become a place of crime. Next we see the bloody dead body of the young woman lying on the floor and Billy standing, waiting. There is almost no interrogation, Chang just looks and sees. He brings in the father of the girl who is handed a wooden table leg. Next, we see the mutilated dead body of Billy. This makes it seem a matter of revenge. Yet the father's act is directed by Chang. If Billy's execution is far from a legal procedure, it is not completely extra-legal either, then.

Chang's authority shows itself in his being a very controlled, rational and, one could say, composed figure, who acts according to a particular logic. For instance, after the father Choi Yan Lee (played by Kowit Wattankul) has killed Billy, he is called before Chang. A dialogue in Thai ensues, that in translation runs as follows:

> Chang: Why did you kill him?
>
> Choi Yan Lee: Because he murdered my daughter!
>
> Chang: You knew what your daughter was doing. Why didn't you stop her?
>
> Choi Yan Lee: How else was I to make ends meet? I have four daughters and no sons. What else was I supposed to do? Don't you understand? My daughter's just been murdered!
>
> Chang: This isn't about your dead daughter. It's about your three living daughters. This is to make sure you never forget them.

Chang then draws his razor-sharp machete and chops off one of the father's hands. In light of moments like this, critic Ada Tseng read the character of Chang as follows: 'he has the spiritual power inside of him that gives him this authority – almost like a judge – to decide who's right and who's wrong'.[4] The least one can say is that 'spiritual power' does not have any of its usual harmonious or irenic connotations, then. And a judge who also chops off hands does somewhat more than decide who or what was right and wrong. Still, Chang is not acting arbitrarily or angrily, nor does he have supreme power. He acts in the service of justice, it seems. To that order he can take lives, engage in fist fights, torture people, or chop off body parts. According to reviews, many found the movie disturbing, or annoying,[5] though almost none found it annoying that justice is served here by a judicial officer who does not need a judiciary, independent investigation or court. Rather, what many viewers found either fascinating or confusing was that several

[4] Ada Tseng, *Only God Forgives*, Thai Connection, available at adatseng.com/2013/07/23/ryan-gosling-and-thailand.

[5] The movie got mixed responses from upon its screening at the Cannes festival and subsequently. At the festival 'the film didn't go over so well with the critics upon its first screening at Cannes, garnering audible boos and a mild spatter of applause'; see www.indiewire.com/2013/05/nicolas-winding-refn-on-the-tepid-cannes-reaction-to-only-god-forgives-and-why-his-second-time-at-the-festival-was-like-going-to-the-office-37970.

of the scenes are hard to assess in terms of their logic.[6] They do not fit into a more or less logical chain of real actions and events, nor can they be defined as dream scenes. The film rather presents a 'neon-saturated' world that is partly real, partly hallucinatory. Some of the hallucinations can be traced to a character, but most also acquire a more general, overarching status. In either form, they imbue the rest of the movie with a hallucinatory quality. One of the critics defined it, consequently, as a 'kind of hallucinogenic Thai Western'.[7]

At the same time, Chang's violence is familiar in the context of the brutal violence that surrounds any drug cartel conflict globally, in which mutilated bodies, or chopped-off limbs are everyday business. Moreover, in the context of the setting of Bangkok, Chang can be read as an echo of the Thai Prime Minister Thaksin Shinawatra, a former police lieutenant-colonel, who not only was capable of combining his function in the police with setting up businesses, but as leader of the country also organised a war on drugs between 2003 and 2006.[8] At the time this war had popular support in Thailand and was waged entirely through extrajudicial means. Later, official investigations found out that of the 2,500 people who were killed in the beginning of this war, 1,400 had nothing to do with drugs.[9] Unfortunately such a conclusion leaves the impression that the others were killed with reason. Yet the status of this 'reason' remains unfounded. People were killed without due process, without knowing what they were accused of, and without being brought before a court.

As the Shinawatra Government demonstrated, whenever reason and reasonability are not the anchor points of a system of law, people will be threatened by both legal and extra-legal police forces, judicial arbitrariness, perversion, irregularities or anything that is the opposite of trustworthiness. In the historical struggles for lawfulness that were aimed at limiting raw, arbitrary or perverse powers, reason and reasonability were key. To be sure, legal systems have often served powers even if these powers were or became unjust, and would do so with reason, by using reason. This has been a recurring topic in the study of law. It was at the core of so-called critical legal studies (see chapter one). The fundamental questions raised time and again was what law's appeal to reason meant, what it meant that legal

[6] Scott Macleod, 'Masterpiece or Misfire: Nicolas Winding Refn's *Only God Forgives*' *Kill Your Darlings* (20 August 2013), available at www.killyourdarlings.com.au/2013/08/masterpiece-or-misfire-nicolas-winding-refns-only-god-forgives-2.

[7] Steve Dollar, 'Nicolas Winding Refn Talks About "Only God Forgives"' (15 July 2013) *The Wall Street Journal*, available at www.wsj.com/articles/SB10001424127887323394504578608153721060998. Likewise, critic Peter Bradshaw called it 'a kind of hallucinated tragi-exploitation shocker' *The Guardian* (1 August 2013), available at www.theguardian.com/film/2013/aug/01/only-god-forgives-review.

[8] Takshin Shinawatra became one of Thailand's most controversial politicians of the last decades. The number of cases brought against him is considerable. He fled to self-imposed exile in Dubai. According to Forbes his 'real time net worth' as of 17 July 2020 is 1.9 billion USD; www.forbes.com/profile/thaksin-shinawatra.

[9] Janjiri Sombatpoonsiri and Aries Arugay, 'Duterte's war on drugs: bitter lessons from Thailand's failed campaign' *The Conversation*, available at theconversation.com/dutertes-war-on-drugs-bitter-lessons-from-thailands-failed-campaign-66096.

actors claimed to be reasonable or rational, and whether the very claim law makes to reason did not depend on the suppression of law's own madness or the wilful suppression of its own emotional or irrational qualities.[10]

In response, some defenders of law's reasonability accused critical legal scholars of denying 'the rational determinacy of legal reason'.[11] The issues are pivotal because they determine what will ground law's power to protect an order on a just basis. It may be inevitable that if a system of law is to protect an order with good reason, it has to veil its own idiocy or control its madness. Still, even if there is idiocy and madness in law, any reader may ask herself whether she would prefer to be brought to court for serious accusations in, say, Russia, the Netherlands, China, the United States of America, Congo, Ecuador, Australia, Germany or Egypt. Most, I suppose, would want to opt for a country where a rule of law is in place and legal actors act according to the demands of reason and reasonability. And whatever the evolutionary, cultural, social, political or symbolical characteristics, and by consequence the affectively charged characteristics of law's reasonability are, there is an intrinsic relation between reason and law if only because any system of law, with its judiciary, requires rules and forms of reasoning. This chapter's consideration of the logic of reason as characteristic for a system of law is thus, in a sense, tautological.

To some there is also an intrinsic link between reason and justice. For instance, philosopher of law Robin West states that the 'usual standard for reason in the law is *justice*, and the usual standard for justice is the universal (and individual) welfare of all members of society, taking all into account and disregarding no one'.[12] West is taking a specific position, here, in which law is framed by justice. And when justice is to be the frame of law's reasonability, it needs a reasonable standard itself, which is defined here as a matter of radical inclusivity. West's use of 'universal' in the realm of justice implies that no one should be privileged, and no one should be neglected. This standard is not determined, obviously, by what is actually the case, but what should be the case. Consequently, one could find West's standard for law's

[10] See, for instance, Austin Sarat, Lawrence Douglas, and Martha Merrill Umphrey (eds), *Law's Madness* (Ann Arbor, University of Michigan Press, 2006). The volume's aim was not to say that law is mad but to use madness as a trope 'to signal a disturbing, disrupting, indeterminate, yet constitutive relation – the relation between that which is imagined as law and that which is withheld or masked as something other than law in order to produce that imagining' (1). Previous to this Peter Goodrich addressed this relation in *Law and the Unconscious: A Legendre Reader* and in Peter Goodrich and David Gray Carlson (eds), *Law and the Postmodern Mind: Essays on Psychoanalysis and Jurisprudence* (Ann Arbor, University of Michigan Press, 2009). Anne Daily noted that the relation between law and irrationality as it was explored in relation to law has never sufficiently landed in the study of law; see Anne Daily, 'Striving for Rationality' (2000) 86 *Virginia Law Review* 349. For an excellent overview of the relation between law's rationality and the role of emotions in the legal domain in the last decades, see Patricia Mindus, 'The Wrath of Reason and the Grace of Sentiment' in MNS Sellers (ed), *Law, Reason, and Emotion* (Cambridge, Cambridge University Press, 2017).

[11] Allan C Hutchinson and Patrick J Monahan, 'Law, Politics, and the Critical Legal Scholars: The Unfolding Drama of American Legal Thought' (Januray 1984) 36 *Stanford Law Review* 199.

[12] Robin West, 'Law's Emotions' in MNS Sellers, *Law, Reason, and Emotion* (Cambridge, Cambridge University Press, 2017) 13.

reasonability to be not only unrealistic but also historically flawed. It might also be found to be too conceptually vague. One could question what welfare means, for instance, or why justice would have to apply to 'members of society' only; and what the 'all' would consequently imply. More principally, with the standard for law's reasonability formulated thus, the realm of justice is severely limited since it now has to be reasonable in and of itself. Yet the realm of justice, filled as it is with affects and emotions, need not be reasonable at all, nor need it be restricted to the limits and orders of a given society.

Instead of framing law through justice, this chapter proposes once more that art functions as an interface that creates a common ground by connecting law's logic of reason with an opposite logic operative in the realm of justice, that I propose to be the logic of dreams. In chapter one, we met one expert on this connection: the biblical figure of Joseph, who was a paradigmatic example for the other great dream-logician, Sigmund Freud.[13] Joseph, when asked to explain the dreams of the Pharaoh, argued that the latter's dreams carried an intelligible message. The dreams of the Pharaoh did not pose a problem of law. They did pose a problem of justice. Again, these were his dreams:

> He was standing by the Nile, when out of the river there came up seven cows, sleek and fat, and they grazed among the reeds. After them, seven other cows, ugly and gaunt, came up out of the Nile and stood beside those on the riverbank. And the cows that were ugly and gaunt ate up the seven sleek, fat cows. Then Pharaoh woke up.
>
> He fell asleep again and had a second dream: Seven heads of grain, healthy and good, were growing on a single stalk. After them, seven other heads of grain sprouted–thin and scorched by the east wind. The thin heads of grain swallowed up the seven healthy, full heads. Then Pharaoh woke up; it had been a dream.
>
> (*Genesis* 41:1–7, New International Version)

The last sentence – 'it had been a dream' – suggests that even if the dreams made sense, they need not matter that much. They were just dreams. Yet the dreams confuse and disturb the Pharaoh precisely because they present a sort of reality that somehow feels both wrong, and related to the reality of everyday life. Evidently, the dreams were not argumentative forms of discursive organisation that, convincingly or not, led to a conclusion. As with most dreams, they were not even a matter of language, but predominantly visual. Still, the dreams had argumentative force, and their message was apparently compelling. This was not because they were absurd, but because they made sense. They dealt with a matter of justice in the sense that they addressed problems of balance, distribution and consumption. Gauntness ate fatness; thinness swallowed healthiness. Why?

The question was answered by Joseph who was capable of translating the issue of justice to a matter of law as a result of which he could come to perform what his name means: he who 'adds' or 'increases'. He translated the dreams by predicting

[13] Sigmund Freud, *The Interpretation of Dreams* (New York, Macmillan, 1900) esp ch 2.

that seven years of abundance would be followed by seven years of scarcity. If in the first period enough food was stored, the people would all survive the years of scarcity. The complex domain of justice as it showed itself in dreams was systematised by Joseph, and brought to operate on one plane by means of reason and law, in the sense that people would now have to obey to a rule of distribution. In fact, the translator or master of interpretation himself was appointed governor in charge of the fair distribution (*Genesis* 41:36–37). This serves to show that if the logic of dreams from within the realm of justice needs to be translated to a logic of reason in a system of law, this is not simply a matter of translation. As the figure of Joseph makes clear, the translation of the logic of dreams into the logic of reason relies on epistemic authority. Things, that is, come to make sense through the expertise of the sense-maker and the trust they are granted.

Only God Forgives deals with this element of expertise and trust in an ambiguous way. Chang is a figure with authority and he clearly knows a lot. Yet what is his epistemic authority based on, and can it – or he – be trusted?

II. Epistemic Authority and Deviant Investigators in Times of Multiple Insurgencies

Chang in no way resembles the classic rational detective or investigation officer, let alone a judge acting according to institutionally defined demands of justice. There is much more to being a judge than simply having the ability to decide who is right and who is wrong. Chang intuitively appears to know who has done what, and how. As the dialogue above made clear, he perhaps only wants to know why. On the basis of his intuitively acquired knowledge and the (in)adequacy of answers as to the why, he reaches a verdict that someone else or he himself executes. He is a 'disturbingly stoic and spectral-like antagonist' as one reviewer described him.[14] As such, he acts not only as an impeccable and ruthless police officer, but also as a torturer, judge, and executioner – as well as a karaoke aficionado. He is not the familiar index or synecdoche for the authority of the sovereign state or the supreme power that guarantees order and justice as a matter of reason, despite being a servant of societal order.

In the context of popular culture, the character of Chang both does and does not fit in with the increasingly familiar type of investigation. From nineteenth-century detective fiction through to the crime series of the 1980s, investigating agents are by and large marked by their ability to reason, even if they are avid users of drugs, as Sherlock Holmes was (or Sigmund Freud). Yet since then a new type of legal investigators has gained popularity in the cultural imagination. The type concerns people suffering from bipolarity, vigilantes, psychopaths,

[14] Scott Macleod, 'Masterpiece or Misfire' (2013).

loners and rangers.[15] The ranger, for one, when defined as 'a. one of a body of organized armed men who range over a region especially to enforce the law' or 'b. a soldier specially trained in close-range fighting and in raiding tactics' (Webster) is especially relevant for the figure of Chang. He ranges over his region to enforce the law and to that order is an expert in close-range fighting. Yet we never see Chang investigating. He seems to *have* knowledge of what has happened and his fight against a world out of balance is based on his being part and parcel of a world that is of a higher order; his is indeed a spiritual authority as Ada Tseng suggested. As a spiritual authority, he works either outside of the system of law, since that system itself is not relevant or corrupt, or he works inside the corrupt legal system, knowing how to use its extra-legal outside in order to purify society. He does so on the basis of a specific sort of epistemic authority: a spiritual one. His spiritual powers, however lofty, manifest themselves in practice in his executing of people in passing, on a busy street, during the night, or in isolated locations.

Literary scholar Inge 't Hart defined this new type of investigators as follows. According to her, one telling example, the series *Hannibal* (NBC, 2013–15)

> [U]ndermines the foundation of humanist order and subjectivity by: (1) corrupting the classic, rational and empirical perspective of the detective, in pathologizing the detective figure and emphasizing his intuitive powers of imagination; (2) hyper-aestheticising the visualization of transgressive death; (3) stripping away the possibility to maintain a rational distance from increasingly explicit visualizations of violence; (4) compromising the integrity of plot linearity and narrative dynamics; and (5) highlighting the not just morally ambiguous but diffuse and broken institutional system/environment this detective figure operates in, but often cannot *act* in.[16]

On the basis of these characteristics number (1) is applicable in part to the character of Chang, for he is not pathological but does work on the basis of intuitive knowledge. Aspects (2) and (3) are applicable; (4) and (5) are again only in part applicable. He may safeguard plot linearity though that linearity is fluid due to its blurring into hallucinations. As for the institutional environment, its status is unclear; he does not have an office. His figure is clearly culturally and ethnographically specific in that he is very capable of acting like a *shaman*, or what in Thai terminology is called a *phram* or *mo phi*. He acts, that is, as an exorcising agent or a mediator between the forces of the dead and the living, with the ultimate aim of restoring balance.

In his mysterious capacity to know all, he does not provoke the question of what establishes epistemic authority or what kind of epistemic authority is at stake, but rather blurs the issue of how this kind of authority is manifest. He is a walking

[15] One can think here of series such as *Hannibal* (NBC, 2013–15), *Luther* (BBC, 2010–13), *True Detective* (HBO, 2014–17), *The Fall* (BBC/RTÉ, 2013–16), *The Bridge* (FX, 2013–15) and *The Tunnel* (Canal+, 2013–14), but also series like *Sherlock* (BBC 2010–14) or *Homeland* (Netflix 2011–19).

[16] Inge 't Hart, 'Criminality And The Limits Of Human Subjectivity In The Flesh: A Fundamental Shift In The Television Detective Genre' (unpublished paper, 2014).

emblem of what Forensic Architecture called 'dark epistemology' (see chapter four, and below). Here, apart from his referencing a familiar type in popular culture or art, Chang also references the type of an average judicial officer in what Saskia Sassen defined as 'global cities' – cities that consist in, and thrive through, all sorts of global connections which defy not only the borders and limits of sovereign nation states but also the lines between the legal and extra-legal.[17] In too many places, many officers have ample space to use their rights and the law at will, and particularly do so in socially deprived areas or in their dealings with not fully established citizens, or so-called criminals. Chang fits the pattern in his taking justice in own hands. He is not corrupt, though, whereas many of his colleagues in reality will abuse this situation, as historian Nils Gilman described:

> There's nice tourism, and then sex tourism, such as in Thailand and Switzerland. The vast pharmacology industry is matched by a vast traffic in illegal drugs. The underside of waste disposal is the criminal dumping in the developing world of toxic wastes from the developed world. Military activities worldwide are fed by a huge gray market in weapons. Internet communications are undermined by floods of malware doubling every year. Among the commodities shipped around the world are exotic hardwoods, endangered species, blood diamonds, and stolen art worth billions in ransom. Illegitimate health care includes the provision of human organs from poor people – you can get a new kidney with no waiting for $150,000 in places like Brazil, the Philippines, Istanbul, and South Africa. Far overwhelming legal immigration are torrents of illegal immigrants who pay large sums to get across borders. And money laundering accounts for 4–12% of world GDP – $1.5 to 5 trillion dollars a year.
>
> These are not marginal, 'informal' activities. These are enormous, complex businesses straight out of the Harvard Business Review. The drug business in Mexico, for example, employs 400,000 people. A thousand-dollar kilo of cocaine grows in value by 1400-percent when it crosses into the US – nice profit margin there.
>
> The whole phenomenon is driven by state regulators acting on ethical taboos. When we outlaw or tax certain goods and services, we reduce supply while demand increases, and that provides an irresistible opportunity for risk-taking entrepreneurs.[18]

If this is a rather bleak picture, it helps to read *Only God Forgives* as a symptom of current circumstances in a global force field where the network structure of many industries – the drugs and sex industries are only two examples, though powerful ones – transcends the international system of nation states, the sovereignty of which is defined by some as 'waning'.[19] The consequences make themselves felt in the flesh, bodily; the film is explicit about this.

In 2019 the United Nations Office on Drugs and Crime (UNODC) published its yearly report on global drugs production, trafficking, uses and effects.[20]

[17] Saskia Sassen, *The Global City*, revd edn (Princeton, Princeton University Press, 2001).

[18] Nils Gilman, 'Deviant Globalization' *The Long Now*, seminar, available at longnow.org/seminars/02010/may/03/deviant-globalization.

[19] Wendy Brown, *Walled States, Waning Sovereignty* (Cambridge MA, MIT Press, 2017).

[20] World Drug Report 2019 (United Nations publication, Sales No E.18.XI.9), available at wdr.unodc.org/wdr2019/en/exsum.html.

It sketched a worrying picture, with reporting that 'globally, in 2017, there were 585,000 deaths and 42 million years of "healthy" life lost as a result of the use of drugs'. The figures are confirmed by others:

> In 2017, two countries hit a milestone. In Mexico, there were 29,168 murders, the highest number on record. Across the border in the United States, nearly 70,000 people died from drug overdoses, over three times as many as were dying annually less than two decades ago. More Americans now die every year from overdoses than died in the entire Vietnam, Afghanistan, and Iraq wars.[21]

Since 2006, an estimated 150,000 people lost their lives due to drug-related violence in Mexico alone.[22] Equally worrying is the fact that people simply disappeared: '61,637 people have disappeared since 1964, the vast majority since 2006, when then-president Felipe Calderón began cracking down on drug cartels'.[23] Law is not even close to addressing this problem. Globally, neither national or international police organisations and political bodies have successfully halted this violence, despite a handful of spectacular successes that are often loudly celebrated but fail to outweigh the enormous losses of life and sanity that go unreported. It is this incapacity of law that propels these fantasies of problem-solving characters, both in fiction and in reality, as when political rulers are elected on the basis of their claims of knowing how to resolve this issue. The current president of the Philippines, Rodrigo 'Rody' Duterte, is just one example of a global manifestation of authoritarian leaders who have a weak link with the demands of the rule of law and an even weaker link with standards of justice.[24] Still they often claim to know what is just and will not hesitate to use violence in order to maintain or restore order.

[21] Brianne Rennix and Nathan J Robinson, 'Death and the Drug War' (June 2018) *Culture Affairs*. The article used information provided by *The New York Times*: Josh Katz, 'Drug Deaths in America Are Rising Faster Than Ever' (5 June 2017), available at www.nytimes.com/interactive/2017/06/05/upshot/opioid-epidemic-drug-overdose-deaths-are-rising-faster-than-ever.html. The USA has by far the largest amount of deaths through drugs of all wealthy nation states: 'drug overdose death rates in the United States are 3.5 times higher on average when compared to 17 other high-income countries' see: 'American Drug Overdose Death Rates the Highest Among Wealthy Nations' *Science Daily* (21 February 2019), available at www.sciencedaily.com/releases/2019/02/190221083419.htm. As for the pervasiveness of drug industries, legal and illegal, one can follow the yearly reports by the United Nations Office on Drugs and Crime, for instance the one from 2018, that says: 'Non-medical use of prescription drugs has reached epidemic proportions in parts of the world'; *Drugs and Age: Drugs and Associated Issues Among Young People and Older People* (2018) 1, available at www.unodc.org/wdr2018/prelaunch/WDR18_Booklet_4_YOUTH.pdf.

[22] June S Beittel, 'Mexico: Organized Crime and Drug Trafficking' (3 July 2018) *Congressional Research Service*, available at fas.org/sgp/crs/row/R41576.pdf.

[23] Paulina Villegas, 'A New Toll in Mexico's Drug War: More Than 61,000 Vanished' *The New York Times* (6 January 2020), available at www.nytimes.com/2020/01/06/world/americas/mexico-drug-war-death-toll.html.

[24] On this see the Public Broadcasting Service *Frontline* documentary *On the President's Orders*, available at www.youtube.com/watch?v=qugduxazBBg, or Alexander Mora's *The Nightcrawlers* (2019), on the journalists and photographers following what is happening in the partly legal, partly illegal battle against drug industries.

In this context, the hallucinatory quality of the film is not merely a formal issue, but connotes what Forensic Architecture called 'dark epistemology' in showing what happens when the search for truth and the attempt to find out what has happened to people and their bodies, is no longer a matter of concern, because powers wilfully thwart the very idea of truth. This loss of concern relates to a set of problems of which I will mention two. Firstly, drug industries are one part of what Gilman called a 'twin insurgency'.[25] In step with him, Robert J Bunker and Pamela Ligouri Bunker argued that two simultaneously operative insurgencies colour the domain of power in the last decades.[26] One consists of a both nationally and internationally defined set of the ultra-wealthy: a global plutocracy that includes corporations, institutions, non-official networks but also individuals, amongst which several presidents. The other consists of 'deviant globalization's winners', as Gilman coined it: powerful criminal cartels. Both parties fall back on the rule of law whenever it benefits their businesses, or protects their purchases and property, but do not respect the rule of law in principle. They use the reasonability that resides in the heart of law whenever it serves their interests; and ignore or pervert it when it does not. They do not consider the judge as someone with the authority to intervene, but as a servant that does what she is told, and if not, needs to be removed. They will buy, threaten or kill anyone operative in the system that they consider to be a nuisance.

If *Only God Forgives* runs the risk of exoticising this violence by taking Bangkok as its setting, the Netherlands may offer a less exotic counterpoint, as a country with a fully developed illegal drug industry. Currently, the so-called Marengo case is the largest criminal case ever in Dutch history, with around 30 suspects. The case rests for a considerable part on crown witnesses, like Nabil B, who testified against Redouan Taghi the supposed leader of the drugs cartel. The specific crown witness was defended by lawyer Derk Wiersum. The latter was shot to death in broad daylight on 18 September 2019. All the legal officials involved with this case whose names were known, were threatened. Currently, whether this case should thus be dealt with behind closed doors and under the supervision of anonymous judges has become a point of debate. However, this would not only disrupt the publicity that is at the heart of law, but would also threaten the epistemic authorities of courts, for how can any audience assess what is happening? This would play in the hands of those who fare well in a hallucinatory situation. With increasing numbers of complex stories and culprits, crown witnesses, anonymous judges and ghosts of dead lawyers, we might then find ourselves in a whirl of distracting sensations.

The issues sketched above unfortunately coincide with problems that have vexed the legal domain deeply. One is that the status of what is made visible, publicly, has become difficult to assess due to the massively extended scope of

[25] Nils Gilman, 'The Twin Insurgency' (June 2014) 9 *The American Interest*, available at www.the-american-interest.com/2014/06/15/the-twin-insurgency.

[26] J Bunker and Pamela Ligouri Bunker, *Global Criminal and Sovereign Free Economies and the Demise of the Western Economies: Dark Renaissance* (London, Routledge, 2014).

media technologies and other technologies. Consider established practices such as DNA matches. It is no longer very difficult to proclaim or bring forward such a match, legally and publicly, in terms of data. Yet, the question is what people see, and what they can check. Those who did check found that DNA matching is at the basis of many miscarriages of justice.[27] Just one other example: what does it mean when someone is not brought before a court to be accused of terrorist activities because they have already been killed, or whilst major evidence of terrorist activities remains outside of the public eye, partly because it is being classified, partly because the evidence is purely digital, partly because the general audience cannot assess what is being disclosed and what is not? The problem was addressed by artist and researcher Susan Schuppli, who is also connected to the London-based investigation collective Forensic Architecture:

> What sort of public assembly will be able to prevent the premature closure of a certain 'epistemology of facts', as Bruno Latour would say, that are at present cloaked under a veil of secrecy called 'national security interests' – the same order of facts that scripts the current DOD roadmap for unmanned systems?[28]

The DOD mentioned here is the US Department of Defense. It is just one particular instance of all those more-or-less official state entities that have great capacities to make, hide, thwart or manipulate digital and visual evidence.[29]

The struggles to establish or defend epistemic authority in issues such as these are not new. They connect to other, centuries-long struggles. One of these struggles arises as a dominant theme in *Only God Forgives*, namely the status or sovereignty of the individual body. Perhaps not surprisingly, the *habeas corpus* principle is not defended in Refn's movie. Nor is it attacked. More frighteningly, it doesn't seem to matter anymore. I read this as a symptom. In current circumstances, many bodies, in contrast to what the legal principle requires, need not be brought forward. Bodies have become merely flesh to be dealt with, whether legally or extra-legally. This might be a straightforward example of historical regression, for what did the struggles for the *habeas corpus* law and principle establish again?

III. *Habeas Corpus*: Historical Struggles for a Common Ground

Apart from being a specific writ in the Anglo-Saxon systems, *habeas corpus* is a matter of principle in many different systems of law. The officially accepted law of

[27] For a good overview, see David Lazer (ed), *DNA and the Criminal Justice System: The Technology of Justice* (Chicago, MIT Press, 2004).

[28] Susan Schuppli, 'Deadly Algorithms: Can Legal Codes Hold Software Accountable for Code that Kills?' (2014) 187 *Radical Philosophy* 2.

[29] For an analysis of the contemporary situation by Forensic Architecture, see Eyal Weizman, 'An Impromptu Glossary, Open Verification' in Maria Hlavajova and Wietske Maas (eds), *Propositions for Non-Fascist Living, Tentative and Urgent* (Cambridge, MA, MIT Press, Basic Series, 2019).

habeas corpus – in full: *habeas corpus ad subiiciendum* ('you shall have a/the body to be questioned') – holds that a body could be summoned by a higher authority to be brought forward from illegal detention.[30] The way in which it developed itself into a broader legal principle comes down to the following. Any suspect will have to learn within a reasonable amount of time of which crime she was accused; she is to be brought before a judge alive; she can only be imprisoned by order of a judge. Basically, it sets out that someone accused, in order to have a fair chance, should be publicly handled by a legally authorised court that acts in terms of reasonability, instead of being subjected to a supreme power that can act at will. *Habeas corpus* is one of the great steps, then, in the historical struggles for the establishment of right of the individual in terms of law's reasonability. These battles, propelled by desires for justice, have led to the realisation of laws that limit arbitrary or absolute power.

The *habeas corpus* found its first form of expression especially in the English Magna Carta of 1215. Here, the feudal lords made the King assure them that 'no freeman shall be taken or imprisoned or disseised or exiled or in any way destroyed, nor will we go upon him nor will we send upon him except upon the lawful judgment of his peers or the law of the land'. There are two epistemic aspects involved in this phrasing. 'The lawful judgment of his peers' is a formula that is also behind the institution of the judicial jury. Peers, that is, had to have the right to *know*, independently. Law did not rule supreme, or sovereignly, then, but ruled both under and counter to the sovereign, as a limiting force. A second epistemic aspect relates to this power. In order to be able to know a body, it first has to be brought forward. It needs to be physically seen, in order to be real.

The historical and legal motivation for the *habeas corpus* principle finds itself in the arbitrary use of might, which would in principle be much more than just a royal abuse of power. We find ourselves in times in which brutal and violent tournaments, for instance, were commonplace. These tournaments involved games that were both acts of play and actions with serious physical consequences (chopped-off limbs were daily business here as well).[31] There were not many rules and the major aim of the *hastiludium* or lance game was to be able to claim the armour and horse of an opponent, and through this extort a ransom to his family. Paying this ransom was the wise thing to do, because the winner had the right to take the defeated knight's life. The historical situation provoked the question, then: whose body is it? The question became the more vexing since these were times of both regional and increasingly overarching political or religious powers that all claimed to have supremacy within their own domain or sphere.[32] For instance, the famous (or infamous) King Richard I (nicknamed the Lionheart)

[30] For the history of the writ in England and the Anglo-Saxon world, see Neil Douglas McFeele, 'The Historical Development of Habeas Corpus' (1976) 30 *South Western Law Journal* 585.

[31] For the history of tournaments in Europe, especially France, see David Crouch, *Tournament* (London, Hambledon Continuum, 2006).

[32] For an overview of the complex situation, see Richard Kaeuper, *Chivalry and Violence in Medieval Europe* (Oxford, Oxford University Press, 1999).

was captured by the Austrian lord Leopold V (nicknamed the Virtuous).[33] The latter had wanted to be the equal of the two major kings leading the third crusade from 1189 to 1192: Richard and Filip II of France. Yet as a sign of his superiority, Richard had Leopold's banner thrown to the floor at some point. When returning home to England around Christmas of 1192, he had to travel through the lands of Leopold, who captured him and handed him over to his feudal lord, the Roman Emperor Henry VI. The latter, though banned by the Pope for the very fact that he kept Richard imprisoned, would move Richard around several of his castles, and demanded a ransom of 150,000 marks in silver (the equivalent of 35,000 kilograms of silver). When two-thirds of it was paid, through severe taxes that affected the entire English populace, Richard was released, but only after 200 hostages were handed over to Henry in order to ensure the rest of the ransom would be paid as well. Here as well the issue was: whose body is it?

In this context, from the twelfth century onwards, through practical demands, theoretical reflections and combined political and societal pressures, powers came to answer more and more to a rule of law that was limiting and limited. The issues at stake were the fullness of power for the entity that wielded it (*plenitudo potestatis*), the range and status of such power (*potestats absoluta* and *potestas ordinaria*) and the limits that should be put on this power, limits that were based on the exercise of reason (*pro ratione voluntas*). The most basic principle of natural law, reasonability, was called upon in this context, in the work of powerful thinkers such as Marsilius of Padua, Aquinas and, later, Grotius. When the reasonability was not sufficiently used by the sovereign, subjects would see to it through law that their rights were to be respected and not violated by arbitrary might. This explains not only a document such as the English *Magna Carta Libertatum* (1215) but also the Hungarian *Golden Bull* or Golden Edict (1222) or, later, an act formulated by Theodore Beza in 1574, *Du droit des Magistrats sur leurs sujets*, that inspired yet another document in the battle against arbitrary rule: the Dutch Act of Abjuration of 1581. With this act the Dutch states said farewell to what they called a tyrant: their king and sovereign, Philip II, who now was no longer accepted as rightful king.

It is no coincidence that the English writ of *habeas corpus* found its final formulation in 1679, in a century that can be considered as the major battleground, in a literal and figural sense, for the definition and constitution of the sovereign as a reasonable power that respects the sovereignty of its subjects. That the matter was not solved eternally with this is writ evident in the context of the contemporary so-called fight against terrorism, in which several sovereign states respect neither the principle or law of *habeas corpus*. Make no mistake, the principle of *habeas corpus* was defended in a verdict of that the Supreme Court of the USA issued on 12 June 2008. The case that had been brought before the court, *Boumediene v Bush*, was whether detainees can be held in the Cuba-based American prison of

[33] I am basing myself on John Gillingham, *Richard I* (New Haven, Yale University Press, 2002).

Guantanamo without being brought to court. The Supreme Court, as articulated by Justice Anthony Kennedy, decided by majority that this was a matter of 'fidelity to freedom's first principles. Chief among these are freedom from arbitrary and unlawful restraint and the personal liberty that is secured by adherence to the separation of powers'.[34] The court took the *habeas corpus* law to be an indisputable one, then. Yet, were the detainees brought to court, consequently? No. Theirs is the situation of a permanent nightmare. In being locked up in their isolated and in itself extra-legal place, in their not being brought to court, they have only one option: to dream that justice will be done. Many subjects today do not learn what they are exactly accused of; they are imprisoned without a judge proclaiming a legal verdict; many can no longer be brought to court because they are already dead. Bodies, both real and legal ones, are not brought forward, partly because they have come to matter less.

If from the side of justice a dream logic is at work, this does not mean justice is restricted to the domain of dreams. This cannot be the case because dreams relate to reality and contain the kernel of an alternative order. In the entire development of psychoanalysis the imaginable expressed in and through dreams was not unreal. On the contrary, dreams reworked what is defined and defended as real in a given order and may either confirm or start to destabilise this. And psychoanalysis was just one modern and Western way of dealing with the relation between dreams and reality. In all cultures throughout history, dreams have been considered to be meaningful in relation to reality or to a multiplicity of realities. As said: dreams are the gateways to alternative realities. Moreover, all those who live in disaccord with an existing order, whether legally supported or not, may dream of things that are dangerous to express but embody an alternative nevertheless. And the world is brimming with legal cases that were never dealt with as a result of which their possible realisation took refuge in the domain of dreams where at least the potential of such a realisation could be kept alive. Finally, dreams are subjective. What feels to be just and reasonable to the one may be deeply unreasonable to the other.[35] In this light, tellingly, the Bible makes explicit that only Egyptians got food, and not the others who were equally starving. Not all desires of justice were fulfilled, then, or only the desires of a selective group were. Still, the suggestion of universality, of an 'all', in Joseph's story, remains.

Only God Forgives, in its representing the force of hallucination, effectively blocks both the logic of dreams and the logic of reason and shows the impossibility

[34] *Boumediene v Bush*; Supreme Court of the United States, 553 US 128 S Ct 2229, 171 L (ed) 2d 41 (2008). The case is dealt with in Arthur H Garrison, *Supreme Court Jurisprudence in Times of National Crisis, Terrorism, and War: A Historical Perspective* (Lanham, Lexington Books, 2011). The case is also mentioned in Steven J Barela (ed), *Legitimacy and Drones: Investigating the Legality, Morality and Efficacy of UCAVs* (London, Routledge, 2016), a study on killings that take place in an ambiguous legal/ extra-legal domain.

[35] The tension involved made Ko Hasegawa explore whether one should not be speaking of 'interactive reason' in the domain of law instead of reason per se; Ko Hasegawa, 'Interactive Reason in Law' in MNS Sellers (ed), *Law, Reason, and Emotion* (Cambridge, Cambridge University Press, 2017).

of a common ground for either law or justice. When Eyal Weizman defined the core principles of Forensic Architecture's research, one of these was the 'unlikely common':

> The struggle for a common ground is an essential meta-political condition: a precondition for any practice to take place. This common might seem analogous to a natural resource such as air of a freshwater, and as such one must protect it when it is polluted by the toxins of dark epistemology. Yet unlike water and air, it is neither pre-existing nor natural, but a social reality that needs to be constantly remade, reinforced and fought over. It must not be fenced off but kept with its margins open to new information and ever-new perspectives, evidence, interpretation, and disagreement.[36]

Different aspects are mentioned here that either connote, are part of, follow from, or are propelled by a dream logic. This starts with the 'unlikely' in 'unlikely commons'. Then there is the associative connection between this common ground and natural conditions through the metaphor of air and water. Finally, there is the principal openness to new information and 'ever-new perspectives'. I am far from suggesting, here, that Forensic Architecture works according to a dream logic. It does not. Its investigations can and have been held up to any scholarly standard and in that sense they very much follow a logic of reasoning. It is in their radical commonality, in their desire and capacity to sense the many layers of being, in their attempt to find an alternative to polluted socio-political environments that is not predefined, that a dream logic is at stake.

As Weizman suggests, law and justice can only productively interact when there is a common ground on the basis of which art's interface can come to work. In times of hallucination this common ground evaporates. Such hallucination is neither a natural given nor an unfortunate coincidence. There are forces that thrive on a hallucinogenic reality precisely because they want to avoid commonality or common grounds.

IV. Familiar Orders and Current Unchecked Powers

It is relatively easy to read *Only God Forgives* according to the dream logic of a familiar symbolical order that, in Freudian terms, was defined as an Oedipal one. One sequence close to the end of the movie, when the brutal, terrifying and terrorising mother Crystal is executed by Chang seems to show as much.[37] Briefly after the execution, her son Julian enters the room where his mother is lying, dead. Then his hand disappears in her womb through the wound produced by Chang; a scene that cuts to a scene in which both of Julian's hands are cut off, again by Chang. The entire sequence has been read in terms of an Oedipal logic, although

[36] Weizman, 'An Impromptu Glossary' (2019) 158–59.
[37] I am considering the sequence here that runs from 1.18:58 to 1.23.08.

the allusion to this logic in *Only God Forgives* is so explicit that it might also be a sign of caution, instead of a rhetorical tope simply to be followed. It is simply followed when critic Charles Reece states in his review:

> In Bangkok, Julian (Ryan Gosling), a man-child, is all seething impotency under matriarchal oppression …, yearning to be punished by patriarchal law (Chang, aka the Angel of Vengeance …). Julian is without a father figure, since he murdered him at Crystal's insistence some time prior to the current story. Her maternal control is a smothering totality that's produced this one son who can't make any decision without mother's approval and his older brother, Billy, who proves his virile independence by brutalizing and killing adolescent prostitutes.[38]

Reece developed a full Oedipal reading of the film in the context of recent forms of feminist criticism, which all grapple with the persistent force of patriarchal hierarchies.[39] Yet what Reece and others appear to be missing is that sequences such as this reflect how the Oedipal complex is active as a dreamlike element from a distinct, and probably former order. The Oedipus complex is rather parodied in this movie, than that it is a structuring principle. Or it is shifted from being the Freudian anchor point of a symbolical order to being just another visual element in a collection of visual wanderings that blur the line between reality, dream and hallucination. The blurring of this line is why so many viewers found the movie weird.

Obviously, Julian's hands disappearing in his mother's body, into her womb, can be explained in a familiar psychoanalytical way. Yet the hands disappearing into her body also, literally, show the disappearance of a distinction between outer and inner. Analogously his hands being cut off do not simply symbolise castration by an unforgiving Father. As said, other hands (or heads) have been cut off before, not only in this film but on a far larger scale in reality. Instead of reading the movie symbolically, then, I read it literally and symptomatically, considering its scenes for their showing of how the integrity of the body no longer functions in the frame of what we have come to know as the *habeas corpus*, due to a situation that has acquired an *in toto* a hallucinatory quality.

Such a hallucination is both straightforwardly and indexically indicated by the drug industry, and the many corrupting and criminal activities connected to it. It is also hinted at by the neon-saturated imagery of prostitution, and becomes explicit in scenes of which we do not know the subjective origin. This happens for

[38] Charles Reece, 'His Mother's Voice: Only God Forgives' Feminism' Amoeba (blog), available at www.amoeba.com/blog/2013/09/writings-from-the-holy-texan/his-mother-s-voice-only-god-forgives-feminism.html. Reece relates his argument to Kaja Silverman's study, *The Acoustic Mirror: The Female Voice in Psychoanalysis and Cinema* (Bloomington, Indiana University Press, 1988), in which she quotes Michel Chion: 'In the beginning, in the uterine night, was the voice, that of the Mother' 74. Reece considers this to be an apt epigraph for *Only God Forgives*.

[39] In this context another reviewer notes: 'Either Nicholas Winding Refn is a Freudian scholar who has made a didactic film illustrating the nuances of the Oedipus complex, or psychic reality really does have an Oedipal structure. I vote for the latter' Frosty Chud, 'A Clinical Study on Perversion'; see *IMDB*, www.imdb.com/title/tt1602613/reviews-8.

instance in the scenes building up to Billy's murdering of the young woman at the beginning, which show a sequence of hand shots. When Billy is on his way, there is a cut to Julian's hands, who first has them opened and then turns them into fists. From there we turn to Billy beating one girl at the bar where he is refused a prostitute, and then, unseen by us, beating a girl to death, whom we will only see after Chang has arrived, with his fists preemptively closed. The father who allowed or forced his daughter into prostitution, will finally lose a hand. The way in which these hands and fists, attached and chopped off, interchange, cannot be brought back to a singular symbolical order. They rather suggest a situation of hallucinatory wandering that associatively links characters instead of functioning as a fantasy one of them has. It concerns, that is, a distinct characteristic of a situation in which all characters find themselves unmoored in the haze of the interface.

This collective state of hallucination was analysed by Gilles Deleuze and Félix Guattari. With what they defined as schizoanalysis they purposefully refused the familiar Freudian version of psychoanalysis and its dominant Oedipal model. In the view of Deleuze and Guattari, the contemporary problem had become how subjects could be freed from authorities, forces and powers of oppression that vexed them and made them live in a schizoid, industrialised, capitalist, hallucinatory world. In relation to such a world, schizoanalysis, in the 1960s and 1970s, was distinctly anti-authoritarian. Dreams would not lead us straight to the unconscious, but rather showed how to escape it and create an alternative order. Yet, as I have argued, hallucination is a force that disrupts this routing. Currently, the work of Deleuze and Guattari would have to be reconsidered or rethought, now that new non-state powers have come to regulate much of people's lives, and a renewed popular desire for authoritarian figures is traceable both in popular culture and in scholarly approaches.[40] There is, globally, considerable popular support for authoritarian politicians that embody excessive sovereignty, and this in a context of new non-governmental actors continuing to gain vast and only partly checked powers.

When the sovereignty of the nation state is threatened or, indeed, waning, a common response has been to counter this decline by seeking refuge in what one

[40] In the Netherlands alone studies by politicians and scholars on the need for new authoritarian father figures appeared since the 1990s. One of the first was sociologist and politician Pim Fortuyn (who was murdered by an environmentalist in 2002), with *The orphaned society* or *De verweesde samenleving* (Utrecht, Bruna, 1995). Then psychoanalyst Paul Verhaeghe added several studies, such as *Authority*, or *Autoriteit* (Amsterdam, De Bezige Bij, 2015) and articles in which he discused the necessity of authority, as in 'Voorbij Oedipus. Over de noodzakelijke functie van autoriteit' in Peter Verstraten and Sjef Houppermans (eds), *Oedipus heerst!?* (Antwerpen, Garant, 2016). Internationally Slavoj Žižek was influential with respect to this theme, ever since *The Fragile Absolute: Or Why is the Christian Legend Worth Fighting For?* (London, Verso, 2008); *The Ticklish Subject: The Absent Centre of Political Ontology* (London, Verso, 2008); and *The Sublime Object of Ideology* (London, Verso, 2008). For an overview, see Bart Vieveen, *The Emancipation of the tragic hero: Hamlet, Katadreuffe and Van Egters explore the borders of the Father-land* or *De ontvoogding van de tragische held: Hamlet, Katadreuffe en Van Egters verkennen de grenzen van het bedreigde Vader-land* (Utrecht, Garant, 2019).

could call excessive sovereignty. The excess exists in attempts to dismantle, move beyond or ignore the limits that have been set to sovereign power in the course of last eight centuries. As Saskia Sassen noted in *Territory, Authority, Rights* the changes in the nature of sovereignty taking place currently relate to a both global and local–internal dynamic that has some general features. Globally the power of the executive has been growing in most states, and meanwhile the focus of most systems of law has tended to become increasingly economical at the expense of the study and practice of constitutional law or the study and development of laws with regard to distributional matters.[41] Sassen argued, in addition, that current circumstances are not so much the result of Enlightenment and modernity but might be traced to the medieval constellation of different forms, levels, and mixtures of sovereignty that, taken together, do not fall under the rule of one supreme *political* power. In this messy situation the rule of law may become a stand-in for an absent supreme power. It may serve forms of quasi-supreme power. It may withdraw itself into its own compartmentalisation, doing its work within the confines of what practically works. Or it may be a formidable stronghold in the fight for justice.

If law is characterised by a logic of reason, one question has become how to maintain or achieve epistemic authority in a mediatised, socio-economic or socio-financial situation that has a strong hallucinatory quality. This is the argument in Shoshana Zuboff's *The Age of Surveillance Capitalism: The Fight for a Human Future at the New Frontier of Power* and McKenzie Wark's *Capitalism is Dead: Is This Something Worse?*.[42] In the analysis of both scholars, organisations such as Google, Facebook or Baidu, in their dealing with the information of subjects without being transparent of what they exactly do with it, hold a new form of considerable power that also allows them to target people without their even knowing they are being targeted. In new ways and despite their guarantees, they show little concern for the sovereignty of the individual state, person or body and much of their power is invisible or veiled. Most importantly in relation to our argument, they have redefined the very status of the real. This is a situation studied by legal scholar Mireille Hildebrandt, who holds a chair in 'Smart Environments, Data Protection and the Rule of the Law'. In a powerful study entitled *Smart Technologies and the End(s) of Law*, she explored how the shift from an information society to a data society threatens pivotal domains of life ranging from privacy to identity, from autonomy to non-discrimination but also, practically, from due process to the presumption of innocence, and concerns a situation in which 'smart technologies undermine, reconfigure and overrule the ends of the

[41] Saskia Sassen, *Territory, Authority, Rights: From Medieval to Global Assemblages* (Princeton, Princeton University Press, 2008) 148–221.

[42] Shoshana Zuboff, *The Age of Surveillance Capitalism: The Fight for a Human Future at the New Frontier of Power* (New York, PublicAffairs, 2019); McKenzie Wark, *Capitalism is Dead: Is This Something Worse*? (London, Verso, 2019).

law in a constitutional democracy, jeopardizing law as an instrument of justice, legal certainty and the public good'.[43]

Only God Forgives not only shows how the logic of dreams in the realm of justice is disrupted by technological or drug-induced hallucinations but also, more generally, how a specific socio-economic and mediatised system produces a hallucinatory reality. In this context, law may have its problems, but problems of justice are equally large. In terms of justice, the issue thus becomes how to promote or safeguard people's connection with their own dreams, individually and collectively, against forces of hallucination. The issue is also how to promote, safeguard and maintain the potential of an alternative to these structurally induced hallucinations. If the film explicitly uses the drug industry as a theme, this hints at industries, legal and illegal, which have not only made it their business to consume human beings, but also to make money out of the chemical technologies that enable them to alter, intensify, or to change the human body and mind. These effects are not shown in the film in the sense of depicting people using drugs. Instead the film took up the effect of drugs into its formal structure, by turning reality and hallucination into one long, wandering, scene. As may have become clear, I read the movie's hallucinatory quality in the light of a historical development. When biopower fused with biopolitics this was still in circumstances of sovereign rule by the state. Yet with biopower and biopolitics now being overtaken by media technologies and biotechnologies that are in the hands of different actors, often in part unchecked, we find ourselves in a different predicament: how this state of affairs can be defined in terms of familiar forms of a reasonable authority and what this implies for the dreams coming from the realm of justice is a matter of struggle.

In the current situation, the *habeas corpus* principle has not disappeared, though it is clearly threatened by different mechanisms. Some of them are hallucinatory in nature, with porous borders between not only life and death, but also between what could call one's own and what can be taken from one's own; between outer and inner; between an executive power checked by public institutions and privatised power unchecked by political and legal authorities; between a reasonable and limited rule of law and a wandering, excessive one. With the fantasy of, or desire for strong leaders now having become real again, principles of law and justice achieved in centuries-long struggles for epistemic authority are threatened. This is a warning call for those who consider the realm of justice to be predominantly ethically just. The logic of dreams has ample room for desires and fears that relate to totalitarian societies, the longing for strong leaders and the unequal distribution of power that are considered to be just by many. Art's interface is not a safe haven to flee to, in this context. It is a space from which forces in systems of law and realm of justice can be felt, and can be connected. As may have

[43] Mireille Hildebrandt, *Smart Technologies and the End(s) of Law* (Cheltenham, Elgar, 2016).

become clear, whereas many consider the realm of justice as a framing power for a system of law, this study proposed something else. If, for instance, in centuries-long battles for justice basic principles of law have been defined and made official, this makes a translation back to the realms of justice threatened by disruptive forces worthwhile. Art is not a straightforward translator. It may be confusing, annoying or disrupting. As stated above, *Only God Forgives* does not make clear what *habeas corpus* means or implies, nor does it defend it. It shows what world we come to inhabit once the principle does not matter anymore.

BIBLIOGRAPHY

Acosta, Abraham, 'Orality and Politics in Latin America, Thresholds of Illiteracy' (2013) 13 *The New Centennial Review* 203.

Agamben, Giorgio, 'On the Limits of Violence' (2009) 39 *Diacritics* 103.

—— *The Signature of All Things: On Method*, translated by Luca D'Isanto and Kevin Attell (New York, Zone Books, 2009).

Ahlers, W, 'Jacob van Deventer, nieuwe ideeën en nieuwe vragen' (2004) 23 *Caert-Thresoor* 59.

Ahmed, Sara, *Willful Subjects* (Durham, Duke University Press, 2014).

Alpers, Svetlana, *The Art of Describing, Dutch Art in the Seventeenth Century* (Chicago, University of Chicago Press, 1983).

Arendt, Hannah, *Between Past and Future* (New York, Penguin Books, 1977).

—— *On Revolution* (New York, The Viking Press, 1963).

—— *On Violence* (Orlando, Harcourt, 1970).

—— *The Human Condition* (Chicago, University of Chicago Press, 1998).

—— *The Origin of Totalitarianism* (Orlando, Harcourt, 1976).

Aristodemou, Maria, *Law and Literature, Journeys from Her to Eternity* (Oxford, Oxford University Press, 2001).

Aristophanes, *Lysistrata and Other Plays*, Penguin Classics (Boston, Addison Wesley, 2003).

Asbury, Bret D, 'Law as Palimpsest, Conceptualizing Contingency in Judicial Opinions' (2009) 121 *Alabama Law Review* 121.

Atkinson, Logan and Majury, Diana (eds), *Law, Mystery, and the Humanities, Collected Essays* (Toronto, University of Toronto Press, 2008).

Bakhtin, Mikhael, *The Dialogic Imagination, Four Essays* (Austin, Texas University Press, 1982).

Bal, Mieke, *Quoting Carravagio, Contemporary Art, Preposterous History* (Chicago, Chicago University Press, 1999).

Bandes, Susan A (ed), *The Passions of Law* (New York University Press, 2001).

Banks, John, *The Island Queens, or, The Death of Mary, Queen of Scotland A Tragedy* [1684] (Los Angeles, Augustan Reprint Society, 1995).

Barbour, Charles, 'Between Politics and Law, Hannah Arendt and the Subject of Rights' in Marco Goldoni and Christopher McCorkindale (eds), *Hannah Arendt and the Law* (Oxford, Hart Publishers, 2012) 307–19.

—— 'The Secret, the Sovereign, and the Lie, Reading Derrida's Last Seminar' (2013) 3 *Societies* 117.

Barela, Steven J (ed), *Legitimacy and Drones, Investigating the Legality, Morality and Efficacy of UCAVs* (London, Routledge, 2016).

Bartelson, Jens, 'The Concept of Sovereignty Revisited' (2006) 17 *The European Journal of International Law* 463.

Barthes, Roland, 'Diderot, Brecht, Eisenstein' in *Image/Music/Text*, translated by Stephen Heath (New York, Farrar, Strauss, and Giroux, 1977) 69–78.

Bar, Ludwig von, *A History of Continental Criminal Law* [1916] (Boston, Little, Brown, and Company, 1999).

Barad, Karen, '"Matter feels, converses, suffers, desires, yearns and remembers" – Interview with Karen Barad' in Rick Dolphijn and Iris van Tuin (eds), *New Materialism, Interviews & Cartographies* (London, Open Humanities Press – University of Michigan Library, 2012).

Bauman, Zygmunt, *In Search of Politics* (Stanford, Stanford University Press, 1999).

—— *Liquid modernity* (Cambridge, Polity Press, 2000).

—— *The Individualized Society* (Cambridge, Polity Press, 2001).

Beckett, Jason A, 'The Violence of Wording, Robert Cover on Legal Interpretation' (2011) 8 *NoFo* 3.
Beittel, June S, 'Mexico, Organized Crime and Drug Trafficking' (3 July 2018) Congressional Research Service.
Benjamin, Walter, 'Critique of Violence' in M Bullock and MW Jennings (eds), *Walter Benjamin, Selected Writings* Vol 1 (Cambridge, MA, The Belknap Press of Harvard University Press, 2004) 236–52.
—— 'What is Epic Theater?' in *Understanding Brecht*, translated by Anna Bostock, introduction by Stanley Mitchell (London, Verso, 1998) 1–22.
—— 'Zur Kritik zur Gewalt' in H Marcuse (ed), *Zur Kritik zur Gewalt und andere Aufsätze* [1921] (reprint, Berlin, Suhrkamp, 2016).
Berlant, Lauren, *Cruel Optimism* (Durham, Duke University Press, 2011).
—— *Compassion: The Culture and Politics of an Emotion* (New York, Routledge, 2004).
Berlin, Isaiah, 'The life and opinions of Moses Hess' in H Hardy (ed), *Against the Current, Essays in the History of Ideas* (New York, Random House, 2013) 276–316.
Bernstein, Michael A, *Foregone Conclusions: Against Apocalyptic History* (Berkeley, University of California Press, 1994).
Bertschy, Eva, Rolf Bossart and Mirjam Knapp (eds), *Das Kongo Tribunal* (Berlin, Verbrecher Verlag, 2017).
Bizos, George, *No One to Blame?: In Pursuit of Justice in South Africa* (Claremont, David Philip, 1998).
Bloom, Paul, *Against Empathy, The Case for Rational Compassion* (New York, Vintage, 2016).
Boal, Augusto, *Legislative Theatre, Using Performance to Make Politics* (London, Routledge, 1998).
Bönisch, Dana, 'Of "terror brides" and "jihadi poster girls", how explaining "female" terrorism can only fail' (April 2015) *Kaput, Magazin for Insolvenz & Pop*.
Boomgaard, Jeroen, Rini Hurkmans, and Judith Westerveld (eds), *Compassion, A Paradox in Art and Society* (Amsterdam, Valiz/LAP, 2017).
Bormann, Frederick Herbert, Diana Balmori and Gordon T Geballe, *Redesigning the American Lawn, A Search for Environmental Harmony* (New Haven, Yale University Press, 2001).
Bos, René ten, *Water: Een geofilososche geschiedenis* (Amsterdam, Boom, 2014).
Bourdieu, Pierre, *Outline of a Theory of Practice* (Cambridge, Cambridge University Press, 1977).
Bouteligier, Claudia and Timo Slootweg (eds), *Empathie en recht* (Apeldoorn, Garant / Maklu, 2018).
Boyd White, James, *Acts of Hope, Creating Authority in Literature, Law, and Politics* (Chicago, University of Chicago Press, 1994).
—— *Justice as Translation, An Essay in Cultural and Legal Criticism* (Chicago, University of Chicago Press, 1990).
—— *The Legal Imagination, Studies in the Nature of Legal Thought and Expression* (Boston, Little, Brown, 1973).
—— *When Words Lose Their Meaning, Constitutions and Reconstitutions of Language, Character, and Community* (Chicago, University of Chicago Press, 1984).
Braidotti, Rosi, 'Non-Fascist Ethics, Learning to Live and Die as Affirmation' in Maria Hlavajova and Wietske Maas (eds), *Propositions for Non-Fascist Living, Tentative and Urgent* (Cambridge, MA, MIT Press, Basic Series, 2019) 25–40.
Brecht, Bertolt, *Brecht on Theater, The Development of an Aesthetic* (New York, Hill and Wang, 1964).
Brooks, Peter and Paul Gewirtz (eds), *Law's Stories, Narrative and Rhetoric in the Law* (New Haven, Yale University Press, 1996).
Brown, Wendy, *Walled States, Waning Sovereignty* (Cambridge, MA, MIT Press, 2017).
Bunker, J and Pamela Ligouri Bunker, *Global Criminal and Sovereign Free Economies and the Demise of the Western Economies, Dark Renaissance* (London, Routledge, 2014).
Buruma, Y, 'Invloed van de media op de rechtspraak' (1979) 20 *Trema* 305.
Buta, Nehal, 'The mystery of the state: State concept, state theory and state making in Schmitt and Oakshot' in David Dyzenhaus and Thomas Poole (eds), *Law, Liberty and State, Oakeshott, Hayek and Schmitt on the Rule of Law* (Cambridge, Cambridge University Press, 2015) 10–37.
Butler, Judith, *Bodies that matter* (London, Taylor and Francis, 2010).

—— 'Critique, Coercion, and Sacred Life in Benjamin's "Critique of Violence"' in Hent de Vries and Lawrence J Sullivan (eds), *Political Theologies, Public Religion in a Post-Secular World* (New York, Fordham University Press, 2006) 201–20.

—— *The Force of Nonviolence, The Ethical in the Political* (London, Verso, 2020).

Cane, Jonathan, *Civilising Grass, The Art of the Lawn on the South-African Highveld*, (Johannesburg, Wits University Press, 2019).

Canetti, Elias, *Crowds and Power*, translated by Carol Stewart (New York, Farrar, Straus and Giroux, 1984).

Canning, Joseph, 'The Role of Power in the Political Thought of Marsilius of Padua' (1999) 20 *History of Political Thought* 21.

Cathomas, Florin, Matthias N Hartmann, Erich Seifritz, Christopher R Pryce and Stefan Kaiser, 'The translational study of apathy – an ecological approach (2015) 9 *Frontiers in Behavioral Neuroscience* 1.

Charpleix, Liz 'The Whanganui River as Te Awa Tupua: Place-based law in a legally pluralistic society' (2017) 184 *Geographical Journal* 19.

Chishti, Muzaffar and Faye Hipsman, 'The Child and Family Immigration Surge of Summer 2014: A Short-lived Crisis with a Lasting Impact' (2015) 68 *Journal of International Affairs* 95.

Colvin, Sarah, *Ulrike Meinhof and West German Terrorism, Language, Violence, and Identity* (New York, Camden House, 2009).

Conway, Heather and John Stannard (eds), *The Emotional Dynamics of Law and Legal Discourse* (Oxford, Hart Publishing, 2016).

Coplan, Amy and Peter Goldie (eds), *Empathy, Philosophical and psychological perspectives* (Oxford, Oxford University Press, 2011).

Cortright, David, *Gandhi and Beyond, Nonviolence for a New Political Age* (London, Routledge, 2016).

Cover, Robert, 'Nomos and Narrative' in Martha Minow, Michael Ryan and Austin Sarat (eds), *Narrative, Violence, and the Law, The Essays of Robert Cover* (Ann Arbor, The University of Michigan Press, 1995) 95–172.

—— 'Violence and the Word' (1986) 95 *Yale Law School* 1601.

Critchley, Simon, 'Violent Thoughts About Slavoj Zizek' in Nathan Eckstrand and Christopher Yates (eds), *Philosophy and the Return of Violence, Studies from this Widening Gyre* (New York, The Continuum International Publishing Group, 2011) 183–204.

Crouch, David, *Tournament* (London, Hambledon and London, 2006).

Dagognet, François, *Faces, Surfaces, Interfaces* (Paris, Librairie Philosophique J Vrin, 1982).

Daily, Anne, 'Striving for Rationality' (2000) 86 *Virginia Law Review* 349.

Dante, Joe (dir), *Gremlins*, Warner Bros, 1984.

—— *Gremlins 2, The New Batch*, Warner Bros, 1990.

Danto, Arthur C, *The Politics of Imagination* (Lawrence, University of Kansas, 1988).

Debord, Guy, *The Society of the Spectacle*, translated by Donald Nicholson-Smith (New York, Zone Books, 1994).

Deleuze, Gilles, 'J for Joy' in *Gilles Deleuze from A to Z*, interview with Claire Parnet, translated by Charles J Stivale (Cambridge, MA, MIT Press, 2011) DVD.

—— 'Nietzsche and Saint Paul' in *Essays Critical and Clinical*, translated by Daniel W Smith and Michael A Greco (Minneapolis, University of Minnesota Press, 1997) 36–52.

—— 'On Capitalism and Desire' in *Desert Islands and Other Texts 1953–1974* (Cambridge MA, Semiotext(e), 2004).

—— *The Fold*, translated by Tom Conley (Minneapolis, University of Minnesota Press, 1992).

Deleuze, Gilles and Constantin V Boundas (eds), *The Logic of Sense*, translated by Mark Lester and Charles Stivale (New York, Columbia University Press, 1993).

Deleuze, Gilles and Félix Guattari, *Anti-Oedipus, Capitalism and Schizophrenia*, foreword Michel Foucault, translated by Brian Massumi (Minneapolis, University of Minnesota Press, 1983).

—— *A Thousand Plateaus, Capitalism and Schizophrenia*, translated by Brian Massumi (London, Continuum, 2004).

Derrida, Jacques, 'Before the Law' in Derek Attridge (ed), *Acts of Literature* (London, Routledge, 1992) 181–233.
—— *Deconstruction and the Possibility of Justice* (London, Routledge, 1993).
—— 'Force of Law, The "Mystical Foundation of Authority"' in G Anidjar, *Acts of Religion* (New York, Routledge, 2002) 230–58.
—— *Sur parole, Instantanés philosophiques* (Paris, Éditions de l'Aube, 1999).
—— '"This strange institution called literature": An Interview with Jacques Derrida' in Derek Attridge (ed), *Acts of Literature* (London, Routledge, 1992) 33–75.
Doan, Alesha and Shannon Portillo, *Organizational Obliviousness, Entrenched Resistance to Gender Integration in the Military* (Cambridge, Cambridge University Press, 2019).
Dollar, Steve, 'Nicolas Winding Refn Talks About "Only God Forgives"' (15 July 2013) *The Wall Street Journal*.
Donley, Nathan, 'The USA lags behind other agricultural nations in banning harmful pesticides' (2019) 12 *Environmental Health*, article nr 44.
Douglas-Scott, Sionaidh, *Law after Modernity* (Oxford, Hart Publishing, 2013).
Dunn, Jane, *Elizabeth and Mary, Cousins, Rivals, Queens* (New York, Alfred A Knopf, 2004).
Eagleton, Terry, *Benjamin or Towards a Revolutionary Criticism* (London, Verso, 1981).
Eliot, George, *Daniel Deronda* [1876] (Harmondsworth, Penguin, 1997).
Esposito, Roberto, *Communitas, The Origin and Destiny of Community*, translated by Timothy Campbell (Stanford, CA, Stanford University Press, 2010).
—— *Immunitas, The Protection and Negation of Life* (London, Polity, 2011).
Fanon, Frantz, *Wretched of the Earth*, translated by R Philcox (New York, Grove Press, 1963).
Fenster, Thelma and Daniel Lord Smail (eds), *The Politics of Talk and Reputation in Medieval Europe* (Ithaca, NY, Cornell University Press, 2003).
Fisher, George, 'Plea Bargaining's Triumph' (2003) 109 *The Yale Law Journal* 868.
Fortuyn, Pim, *De verweesde samenleving* (Utrecht, Bruna, 1995).
Foucault, Michel, *The Archaeology of Knowledge* [1969], translated by AM Sheridan Smith (London, Routledge, 2002).
Freeman, Barbara Claire, *The Feminine Sublime, Gender and Excess in Women's Fiction*, (Berkeley, University of California Press, 1995).
Freire, Paulo, *Pedagogy of Hope, Reliving Pedagogy of the Oppressed* (London/New York, Bloomsbury Academic, 2014).
Freire, Paulo, *Education For Critical Consciousness* (London, Continuum International Publishing Group, 2005).
—— *Pedagogy of Hope, Reliving Pedagogy of the Oppressed* (London/New York, Bloomsbury Academic, 2014).
Freud, Sigmund, *The Interpretation of Dreams* (New York, Macmillan, 1900).
Fuller, Lon L, *The Morality of Law* [1964] (New Haven, Yale University Press, 1969).
Gaakeer, AMP (Jeanne), *Hope Springs Eternal, An Introduction to the Work of James Boyd White* (Amsterdam, Amsterdam University Press, 1988).
—— *Judging from Experience, Law, Praxis, Humanities* (Edinburgh, Edinburgh University Press, 2019).
Galloway, Alexander, *The Interface Effect* (Cambridge, Polity Press, 2012).
—— 'The Unworkable Interface' (2008) 39 *New Literary History* Special issue 'Re-examining Literary Theories and Practices 931.
Garrison, Arthur H., *Supreme Court Jurisprudence in Times of National Crisis, Terrorism, and War, A Historical Perspective* (Lanham, Lexington Books, 2011).
Gelderblom, Arie-Jan, 'Dichter bij een droogmakerij' in EK Grootes and SF Witstein (eds), *Visies op Vondel na 300 jaar* (The Hague, Martinus Nijhoff, 1979) 104–17.
Gillingham, John, *Richard I* (New Haven, Yale University Press, 2002).
Gilman, Nils, 'The Twin Insurgency' (2014) 9 *The American Interest* 3.
Gogol, Nikolay, 'The Nose' in *The Diary of a Madman, the Government Inspector, and Selected Stories*, translated by Ronald Wilks (London, Penguin Classics, 2006).
Goodrich, Peter, 'How Strange the Change from Major to Minor' (2017) 21 *Law Text Culture* 30.

—— *Languages of Law, From Logics of Memory to Nomadic Masks* (Cambridge, Cambridge University Press, 1990).
—— *Law in the Courts of Love, Literature and Other Minor Jurisprudences* (London, Routledge, 1996).
—— *Legal Emblems and the Art of Law, Obiter Depicta as the Vision of Governance* (Cambridge, Cambridge University Press, 2014).
—— *Oedipus Lex, Psychoanalysis, History, Law* (Berkeley and Los Angeles, University of California Press, 1995).
—— 'The Evidence of Things Not Seen' in Peter Goodrich and Valérie Hayaer (eds), *Genealogies of Legal Vision* (London, Routledge, 2015) 53–78.
Goodrich, Peter and David Gray Carlson (eds), *Law and the Postmodern Mind, Essays on Psychoanalysis and Jurisprudence* (Ann Arbor, University of Michigan Press, 2009).
Goodrich, Peter, and Christian Delage (eds), *The Scene of the Mass Crime, History, Film and International Tribunals* (London, Routledge, 2012).
Goodrich, Peter and Michel Rosenfeld (eds), *Administering Interpretation, Derrida, Agamben, and the Political Theology of Law* (New York, Fordham University Press, 2019).
Graglia, Lino A, 'Book Review: *Law and Literature, A Misunderstood Relation.* by Richard A. Posner' (1989) *Constitutional Commentary* 437.
Greer, Allan, 'Commons and Enclosure in the Colonization of North America' (2012) 117 *The American Historical Review* 365.
Greer, Germaine and Wilmot, Phil, *Lysistrata, The Sex Strike – after Aristophanes* (London, Aurora Metro Publications, 2000).
Groenhuijsen, MS, 'Openbaarheid en publiciteit in strafzaken' (1997) 27 *Delikt & Delikwent* 417–22.
Grootes, Eddy K and Sonja F Witstein (eds), *Visies op Vondel na 300 jaar* (The Hague, Martinus Nijhoff, 1979).
Grossman, Michelle, 'When They Write What We Read, Unsettling Indigenous Australian Life-writing' (2006) 39–40 *Australian Humanities Review*.
Gutjahr, Ortrud, 'Königinnenstreit, Eine Annäherung an Elfriede Jelinieks Ulrike Maria Stuart und ein Blick auf Friedrich Schillers Maria Stuart' in Ortrud Gutjahr (ed), *Ulrike Maria Stuart; von Elfriede Jelinek, Urafführung am Thalia Theater Hamburg in der Inszenierung von Nicolas Stemann* (Würzburg, Köningshausen & Neuman, 2007) 19–38.
Guy, John, *Queen of Scots, The True Life of Mary Stuart* (Boston, Houghton Mifflin, 2004).
Gyarkye, Lovia, 'Going AWOL in Africa's Largest City' *New York Times* (2 August 2018).
Habila, Helon, 'Welcome to Lagos by Chibundu Onuzo review – high hopes, big city' *The Guardian* (18 January 2018).
Hallyn, Fernand, *Gemma Frisius, arpenteur de la terre et du ciel* (Paris, Honoré Champion, 2008).
Haraway, Donna J, 'Situated Knowledges, The Science Question in Feminism and the Privilege of Partial Perspective' in *Simians, Cyborgs, and Women, the Reinvention of Nature* (New York, Routledge, 1991) 183–202.
Hardin, Garrit, 'The Tragedy of the Commons' (1968) 162 *Science* 1243.
Hart, Herbert LA, *The Concept of Law* (Oxford, Clarendon Press, 1961).
't Hart, Inge, 'Criminality And The Limits Of Human Subjectivity In The Flesh, A Fundamental Shift In The Television Detective Genre', unpublished paper (2014).
Hasegawa, Ko, 'Interactive Reason in Law' in MNS Sellers (ed), *Law, Reason, and Emotion* (Cambridge, Cambridge University Press, 2017) 184–201.
Hauser, Dorothea, 'das stück, das tanten typen voraus haben, (Zur Beziehung von Ulrike Meinhof und Gudrun Ennslin' in Ortrud Gutjahr (ed), *Ulrike Maria Stuart, von Elfriede Jelinek* (Würzburg, Königshausen & Neumann, 2007) 39–55.
Haushofer, Marlen, *Die Wand*, München, Claassen, [1963] (1998).
Hausman, David and Jayashri Srikantiah, 'Time, due process, and representation, An empirical and legal analysis of continuances in immigration court' (2016) 84 *Fordham Law Review* 1823.
Havel, Václav, 'The Power of the Powerless' in *Open Letters, Selected Writings, 1965–1900*, edited by Paul Wilson, (New York, Vintage Books, 1992).
Hildebrandt, Mireille, *Smart Technologies and the End(s) of Law* (Cheltenham, Elgar, 2016).

Hill, Leslie, *The Cambridge Introduction to Jacques Derrida* (Cambridge, Cambridge University Press, 2007).
Hing, Bill Ong, *American Presidents, Deportations and Human Rights Violations, From Carter to Trump* (Cambridge, Cambridge University Press, 2019).
Hłasko, Marek, *The Graveyard*, Translated by Norbert Guterman, introduced by James Sallis (London, Melville House Books, 2013).
Hobbes, Thomas, Richard Tuck and Michael Silverthorne (eds), *On the Citizen, De Cive* [1651] (Cambridge, Cambridge University Press, 1998).
Huizinga, Johan, *Homo ludens, a study of the play-element of culture* (Brooklyn NY, Angelico Press, 2016).
Huntington, Samuel, *Political Order in Changing Societies* (New Haven, Yale University Press, 1968).
Hutchinson, Allan C, and Patrick J Monahan, 'Law, Politics, and the Critical Legal Scholars, The Unfolding Drama of American Legal Thought' (1984) 36 *Stanford Law Review* 199.
Iveson, Richard, 'Deeply Ecological Deleuze and Guattari, Humanism's Becoming-Animal' (2013) 4 *Humanimalia, a journal of human/animal interface studies* 20.
Jelinek, Elfriede, *Der Tod und das Mädchen, Fünf Prinzessinnendramen* (München, Goldmann Verlag, 2003).
—— *Das Schweigende Mädchen / Ulrike Maria Stuart, Zwei Theaterstücke* (Hamburg, Rowohlt, 2015).
Johnson, Barbara, 'Anthropomorphism in Lyric and Law' (1998) 10 *Yale Journal of Law and the Humanities* 549.
Jones, Emma, *Emotions in the Law School, Transforming Legal Education Through the Passions* (London, Routledge, 2019).
Kant, Immanuel, Paul Guyer (ed), *Critique of the Power of Judgment, The Cambridge Edition of the Works of Immanuel Kant)*, translated by Paul Guyer and Eric Matthews (Cambridge, Cambridge University Press, 2000).
Kaeuper, Richard, *Chivalry and Violence in Medieval Europe* (Oxford, Oxford University Press, 1999).
Keen, Suzanne, *Empathy and the Novel* (New York, Oxford University Press, 2007).
Keenan, Alan, *Democracy in Question, Democratic Openness in a Time of Political Closure* (Stanford, Stanford University Press, 2003).
Kelly, Patrick William, *Sovereign Emergencies, Latin America and the Making of Global Human Rights Politics* (Cambridge, Cambridge University Press, 2018).
Kelsen, Hans, *Pure Theory of Law*, (Berkeley, University of California Press, 1967).
Kentridge, William, *I am not me, the horse is not mine*, Multiscreen piece, first performed in The South African National Gallery, Cape Town, South Africa, 2008.
Kiebuzinska, Christina, Fatima Festic (ed), 'Violence and Pornography in Elfriede Jelinek's "Princess Plays"' in *Gender and Trauma, Interdisciplinary Dialogues* (Newcastle upon Tyne, Cambridge Scholars Publishing, 2012) 115–53.
Koerner, Morgan Marcell, 'Beyond Media-Critique, Performance and Pop-Cultural Pleasures in Elfriede Jelinek and Frank Castorf's *Raststätte oder sie machens alle*' in Claude Desmarais (ed), *A Different Germany, Pop and the Negotiation of German Culture* (Newcastle (Cambridge Scholars Publishing, 2014) 121–38.
Korsten, Frans-Willem, '*Öffentlichkeit* and Law's Behind-the-Scenes, Theatrical and Dramatic Appearance in European and US American Criminal Law' (2017) 18 *German Law Journal* 172–93.
—— 'The Comedic Sublime in a Dynamic of Worlds, the Work of Frans Hals in a Dutch Baroque' (2016) 8 *Journal of Historians of Netherlandish Art*.
Korsten, Frans-Willem and Bennett Carpenter, 'Corporate personhood as inhuman, the paradigm of asbestos cases and Dracula' (2014) 84 *Quaderni* 13.
Korsten, Frans-Willem and Tessa de Zeeuw, 'Ethics of Becoming as a Frame for Ethics, Theatricality and Balance in Greenaway's *The Cook, the Thief, his Wife and her Lover*' (2016) 10 *Polemos, Journal of Law, Literature and Culture* 249.
Kuiters, AT (Loek), Maurice JJ La Haye, Gerhard JDM Müskens and Ruud JM van Kats, 'Perspectieven voor een duurzame bescherming van de hamster in Nederland' *Alterra Rapport* 2022 (Wageningen, 2010).

Lamport, Mark A (ed), *Encyclopedia of Martin Luther and the Reformation*, Vol 2 (New York, Rowman & Littlefield, 2017).

Lazer, David (ed), *DNA and the Criminal Justice System, The Technology of Justice* (Chicago, MIT Press, 2004).

Lee, Daniel, *Popular Sovereignty in Early Modern Constitutional Thought* (Oxford, Oxford University Press, 2016).

Legaspi, Michael C, 'Job's Wives in the 'Testament of Job (A Note on the Synthesis of Two Traditions' (2008) 127 *Journal of Biblical Literature* 71.

Legendre, Pierre, Peter Goodrich (ed), *Law and the Unconscious, A Legendre Reader*, translated by Peter Goodrich (Houndmills, MacMillan, 1997).

Legendre, Pierre, *Leçons I, La 901e conclusion, Étude sur le théâtre de la raison* (Paris, Fayard, 1998).

—— *Leçons X, Dogma, Instituer l'animal humain, Chemins réitérés de questionnement* (Paris, Fayard, 2017).

—— *Le Crime du Caporal Lortie, Traité sur le Père* (Paris, Champs Flammarion, 1989).

Lehman, Hans-Thies, *Postdramatic Theatre*, translated by Karen Jürs-Munby (London, Taylor and Francis, 2016).

Lesaffer, Randall CH, 'Roman law and the early historiography of international law: Ward, Wheaton, Hosack and Walker' in T Marauhn and H Steiger (eds), *Universality and Continuity in International Law* (The Hague, Eleven International Publishing, 2011) 149–84.

Levinas, Emmanuel, *Humanism of the Other*, translated by Nidra Poller, introduction by Richard A Cohen (Urbana, Illinois University Press, 2003).

—— *Time and the Other*, translated by Richard A Cohen (Pittsburgh, Duquesne University Press, 1987).

Levinson, Natasha, 'Teaching in the Midst of Belatedness, The Paradox of Natality in Hannah Arendt's Educational Thought' (2005) 47 *Educational Theory* 435.

Lindhé, Anna, 'The Paradox of Narrative Empathy and the Form of the Novel, or What George Eliot Knew' (2016) 48 *Studies in the Novel* 19–42.

Lloyd, Vincent (ed), *Race and Political Theology* (Stanford, CA, Stanford California Press, 2012) 1–22.

Long, Norman, *Development Sociology, Actor Perspectives* (London, Routledge, 2001).

Loughlin, Martin, 'The Erosion of Sovereignty' (2016) 2 *Netherlands Journal of Legal Philosophy* 257.

—— 'Why Sovereignty?' in Richard Rawlings, Peter Leyland and Alison L Young (eds), *Sovereignty and Law, Domestic, Regional and International Perspectives* (Oxford, Oxford University Press, 2013) 34–49.

Loytomaki, Stiina, *Politics of Memory, Confronting the Past* (London, Taylor and Francis, 2015).

Luiselli, Valeria, *Lost Children Archive, A Novel* (New York, Alfred A Knopf, 2019).

—— *Tell me How it Ends: An Essay in Forty Questions* (London, 4th Estate, 2017).

Luther, Martin, 'Against Hanswurst' in *Luther's works: Church and Ministry III* vol 41, edited by Eric W Gritsch (Minneapolis, Fortress Press, 1966).

Lyne-Pirkis, Tory, 'Book review – Welcome to Lagos' *Irish Examiner* (4 February 2017).

Macleod, Scott, 'Masterpiece or Misfire, Nicolas Winding Refn's *Only God Forgives*' (20 August 2013) *Kill Your Darlings*.

Maitzen, Rohan, 'Martha Nussbaum and the Moral Life of *Middlemarch*' (2006) 30 *Philosophy and literature* 190.

Malcolm X, '"Not just an American problem but a world problem", Corn Hill Methodist Church, Rochester, February 16, 1965' in *February 1965, The Final Speeches*, edited by Steve Clark (Atlanta, Pathfinder Press, 1992).

Malsch, M, and JF Nijboer, *De zichtbaarheid van het recht, openbaarheid van de strafrechtspleging* (Den Haag, Kluwer, 2005).

Manderson, Desmond, *Danse Macabre: Temporalities of Law in the Visual Arts* (Cambridge, Cambridge University Press, 2019).

—— (ed), *Law and the Visual: Representations, Technologies, Critique* (Toronto, Toronto University Press, 2018).

Markell, Pratchen, 'The Rule of the People, Arendt, *Archê*, and Democracy' (2006) 100 *American Political Science Review* 1.
Marrani, David, *Space, Time, Justice, From Archaic Rituals to Contemporary Perspectives* (Abingdon, Routledge, 2018).
Marsilius of Padua, Annabel Brett (ed), *The Defender of the Peace*, translated by Annabel Brett (Cambridge, Cambridge University Press, 2005).
Mbembe, Achille, *Out of the Dark Night* (New York, Columbia University Press, 2019).
McCormack, Kathleen, 'Yachting with Grandcourt, Gwendolen's Mutiny in *Daniel Deronda*' (2015) 43 *Victorian Literature and Culture* 83.
McCracker, Tony, *Apathy in Literature: A Discourse on Emotionless Characters and Concepts* (Hamburg, Ancher, 2014).
McFeele, Neil Douglas, 'The Historical Development of Habeas Corpus' (1976) 30 *South Western Law Journal* 585.
McLuhan, Marshall and Eric McLuhan, *Laws of Media, The New Science* (Toronto, Toronto University Press, 1988).
Meijer, Maaike, *In tekst gevat, Inleiding tot een kritiek van representatie* [1996] (Amsterdam (Amsterdam Academic Archive, 2005).
Meon, Pierre-Guillaume and Khalid Sekkat, 'Does corruption grease or sand the wheels of growth?' (2005) 122 *Public Choice* 69.
Merryman, John Henry, *Law Ethics and the Visual Arts*, 5th edn, co-authored with Albert E Elsen and Stephen K Urice (Alphen aan de Rijn, Kluwer International, 2007).
Métraux, Guy PR, 'Ancient Housing, "Oikos" and "Domus" in Greece and Rome' (1999) 58 *Journal of the Society of Architectural Historians* 392.
Mindus, Patricia, 'The Wrath of Reason and the Grace of Sentiment' in Sellers, MNS (ed), *Law, Reason, and Emotion* (Cambridge, Cambridge University Press, 2017) 202–37.
Minkkinen, Panu, *Sovereignty, Knowledge, Law* (London, Routledge, 2009).
—— *Thinking Without Desire: A First Philosophy of Law* (Oxford, Hart Publishing, 1999).
Modrsohn, Mechtold, *Natura als Göttin im Mittelalter, Ikonographische Studien zu Darstellungen der personifizierten Natur* (Berlin, De Gruyter, 1997).
Mora, Alexander (dir), *Nightcrawlers* (2019).
Mouffe, Chantal, *The Democratic Paradox* (London, Verso, 2000).
Mousourakis, George, *A Legal History of Rome* (London, Taylor and Francis, 2007).
—— *Roman Law and the Origins of the Civil Law Tradition* (Heidelberg, Springer Verlag, 2014).
Mulcahy, Linda, *Legal Architecture, Justice, Due Process and the Place of Law* (London, Routledge, 2010).
Mulgan, Richard, 'Aristotle on Legality and Corruption' in *Corruption, Expanding the Focus*, edited by Manuhuia Barcham, Barry Hindess, and Peter Larmour (Canberra, ANU Press, 2012) 25–36.
Munns, Jessica and Penny Richards (eds), *Aspiration, Representation and Memory, The Guise in Europe, 1506–1688* (London, Routledge, 2015).
Murphy, Diana (ed), *Edible Estates: Attack on the Front Lawn* (New York, Metropolis Books, 2010).
Mussawir, Edward, *Jurisdiction in Deleuze, The Expression and Representation of Law* (London, Routledge, 2011).
Negri, Antonio, *The Savage Anomaly, Power of Spinoza's Metaphysics and Politics* (Minnesota, University of Minnesota Press, 1991).
Neumann, Klaus, and Jana Thomson (eds), *Historical Justice and Memory* (Madison, University of Wisconsin Press, 2015).
Nieuwenhuis, Hans, Jan HA Lokin, Corjo Jansen and Antoine Hol (eds), *Recht en drama* (Den Haag, Boom, 2014).
Nikolai Bukharin Archive, 'The Case of Bukharin', first published as 'The Case of the Anti-Soviet Block of Rights and Trotskyites' (Rome, Red Star Press, 1973).
Nussbaum, Martha, *Anger and Forgiveness, Resentment, Generosity, Justice* (Oxford, Oxford University Press, 2016).
—— *Cultivating Humanity: A Classical Defense of Reform in Liberal Education* (Cambridge, MA, Harvard University Press, 1997).

—— *Love's Knowledge: Essays on Philosophy and Literature* (New York, Oxford University Press, 1990).
—— *Poetic Justice: The Literary Imagination and Public Life* (Boston, Beacon Press, 1995).
—— 'Reply' in J Cohen (ed), *For Love of Country: Debating the Limits of Patriotism* (Boston, Beacon Press, 2006) 131–44.
—— *The New Religious Intolerance: Overcoming the Politics of Fear in an Anxious Age* (Cambridge, Belknap Press of Harvard University, 2013).
Ogene, Timothy, 'Welcome to Lagos' *Hong Kong Review of Books* (25 January 2017).
Okerekeoti, Chinedu U and Emmanuel I, Okoye, 'Treasure Single Account (TSA) in Nigeria, A Theoretical Perspective' (2017) conference paper, The 2017 International Conference on African Entrepreneurship and Innovation for Sustainable Development (AEISD) 558–76.
Olson, Greta, 'Law is not Turgid and Literature not Soft and Fleshy, Gendering and Heteronormativity in Law and Literature Scholarship' (2012) 36 *Australian Feminist Law Journal* 65.
—— 'Mapping the Pluralist Character of Cultural Approaches to Law' (2017) 18 *German Law Journal* 233.
—— 'On Narrating and Troping the Law, The Conjoined Use of Narrative and Metaphor in Legal Discourse' in Michael Hanne and Robert Weisberg (eds), *Narrative and Metaphor in the Law* (Cambridge, Cambridge University Press, 2018) 19–36.
—— 'The Turn to Passion, Has Law and Literature become Law and Affect?' (2016) 28 *Law and Literature* 335.
Onuzo, Chibundu, *Welcome to Lagos* (London, Faber & Faber, 2017).
O'Rourky, David K, *Oikos – Domus – Household, The Many Lives of a Common Word* (Berlin, Peter Lang, 2013).
Orr MacDonald, Lesley, 'A Spirituality for Justice, The Enemy of Apathy' (2000) 8 *Feminist Theology* 13–21.
Papaioannou, Sophia, Andreas Serafim, and Beatrice da Vela (eds), *The Theatre of Justice: Aspects of Performance in Greco-Roman Oratory and Rhetoric* (Leiden, Brill, 2017).
Park, Katharine, 'Nature in Person, Renaissance Allegories and Emblems' in Lorraine Daston and Fernando Vidal (eds), *The Moral Authority of Nature* (Chicago, University of Chicago Press, 2003) 50–73.
Parker, Geoffrey, *The Grand Strategy of Philip II* (New York, Yale University Press, 2000).
Parker, James EK, *Acoustic Jurisprudence, Listening to the Trial of Simon Bikindi* (Oxford, Oxford University Press, 2015).
Partelow, Stefan, Abson, David J, Schlüter, Achim, Fernández-Giménez, Maria E, Wehrden Henrik von and Collier, Neil 'Privatizing the commons: New approaches need broader evaluative criteria for sustainability' (2019) 13 *International Journal of the Commons* 747.
Pascal, Blaise, le Guern, Michel (ed), *Pensées* (Paris, Gallimard, 2004).
Patel, Leigh, 'The Irrationality of Antiracist Empathy' (2016) 106 *English Journal* 81.
Paulson, Michael G, *The Queens' Encounter, The Mary Stuart Anachronism in Dramas by Diamante, Boursault, Schiller and Donizetti* (Berlin, Peter Lang, 1987).
Pedwell, Carolyn, *Affective Relations: The Transnational Politics of Empathy* (London, Palgrave Macmillan, 2014).
Pewny, Katharina, *Das Drama des Prekären, Über die Wiederkehr der Ethik in Theater und Performance* (Bielefeld, transcript Verlag, 2011).
Phillips, Jonathan, *Holy Warriors: A Modern History of the Crusades* (New York, Random House, 2010).
Pickles, John, *A History of Spaces, Cartographic Reason, Mapping and the Geo-Coded World* (London, Routledge, 2004).
Pielak, Chase, 'Hunting Gwendolen: Animetaphor in *Daniel Deronda*' (2012) 40 *Victorian Literature and Culture* 99.
Pomerantsev, Peter, *Nothing is True and Everything is Possible: Adventures in Modern Russia* (London, Faber & Faber, 2015).
—— *This Is Not Propaganda: Adventures in the War Against Reality* (London, Faber & Faber, 2019).
Posner, Richard, *Law and Literature: A Misunderstood Relation*, revd edn (Cambridge, MA, Harvard University Press, 1998).

Preece, Julian, *Baader-Meinhof and the Novel, Narratives of the Nation / Fantasies of the Revolution* (New York, Palgrave MacMillan, 2012) 1970–2010.
Prozorov, Sergei, *Foucault, Freedom and Sovereignty* (Abingdon, Ashgate, 2007).
Rama, Angel, *The Lettered City*, translated by John Charles Chasteen (Durham, NC, Duke University Press, 1996).
Rancière, Jacques, *Disagreement, Politics and Philosophy*, translated by Julie Rose (Minnesota, University of Minnesota Press, 1999).
Rau, Milo, *The Congo Tribunal*, Eva Bertschy, Rolf Bossart, and Mirjam Knapp (eds) (Berlin, Verbrecher Verlag, 2017).
Reichman, Amnon, 'Law, Literature, and Empathy, Between Withholding and Reserving Judgment' (2006) 56 *Journal of Legal Education* 296.
Rennix, Brianne and Nathan J Robinson, 'Death and the Drug War' (4 June 2018) *Culture Affairs*.
Resnik, Judith and Dennis Curtis, *Representing Justice, Invention, Controversy, and Rights in City-States and Democratic Courtrooms* (New Haven, Yale University Press, 2011).
Revermann, Martin (ed), *A Cultural History of Theatre in Antiquity*, Vol 1 (London, Bloomsbury, 2017).
Ricoeur, Paul, *Reflections on the Just*, translated by David Pellauer (Chicago, University of Chicago Press, 2007).
Riley, Alan, 'Cartel Whistleblowing, Toward an American Model?' (March 2002) 9 *Maastricht Journal of European and Comparative Law* 67.
Robertson, Ritchie, 'From Martyr to Vampire, The Figure of Mary Stuart in Drama from Vondel to Swinburne' in Jeffrey L High, Nicholas Martin and Norbert Oellers (eds), *Who is this Schiller Now?, Essays on His Reception and Significance* (Rochester, Camden House, 2011) 321–39.
Robbins, Paul, *Lawn People: How Grasses, Weeds, and Chemicals Make Us Who We Are* (Philadelphia, Temple University Press, 2007).
Robbins, Paul and Julie Sharp, 'The Lawn-Chemical Economy and its Discontents' (2003) 35 *Antipode* 955–79.
—— 'Turfgrass Subjects, the Political Economy of Urban Monoculture' in Nik Heynen, Maria Kaika and Erik Swyngedouw (eds), *In the Nature of Cities, Urban Political Ecology and the Politics of Urban Metabolism* (London, Routledge, 2006) 110–28.
Roever, JG, *Jan Adriaensz, Leeghwater, Het leven en werk van een zeventiende-eeuws waterbouwkundige* (Amsterdam, NV, Wed, J, Ahrend & Zoon, 1944).
Ronell, Avital, *The Test Drive* (Champaign, University of Illinois Press, 2005).
Rooijendijk, Cordula. *Waterwolven, een geschiedenis van stormvloeden, dijkenbouwers en droogmakers* (Amsterdam, Atlas, 2009).
Rose, Carol M, 'The Comedy of the Commons, Commerce, Customs, and Inherently Public Property' (1986) 53 *The University of Chicago Law Review* 711.
Rosenblatt, Paul C, *Shared Obliviousness in Family Systems* (Albany, NY, State University of New York Press, 2009).
Sandholz, Wayne and Rein Taagepera, 'Corruption, Culture, and Communism' (2005) 15 *International Review of Sociology* 109.
Saranpa, Kathy Jo, *Schiller's Wallenstein, Maria Stuart, and Die Jungfrau Von Orleans, The Critical Legacy* (Rochester, Camden House, 2002).
Sarat, Austin (ed), *History, Memory and the* Law (Ann Arbor, University of Michigan Press, 1999).
Sarat, Austin, Lawrence Douglas and Martha Merrill Umphrey (eds), *Law's Madness* (Ann Arbor, University of Michigan Press, 2006).
Sarat, Austin and Kearns, Thomas R, 'Making Peace With Violence, Robert Cover on Law and Legal Theory' in Austin Sarat (ed), *Law, Violence, and the Possibility of Justice* (Princeton, Princeton University Press, 2001) 49–84.
Sassen, Saskia, *Territory, Authority, Rights, From Medieval to Global Assemblages* (Princeton, Princeton University Press, 2008).
—— *The Global City*, revd edn (Princeton, Princeton University Press, 2001).
Scarry, Elaine, *The Body in Pain, The Making and Unmaking of the World* (Oxford, Oxford University Press, 1985).

—— *Rule of Law, Misrule of Men* (Cambridge, MA, MIT Press, 2010).

—— *Thinking in an Emergency* (New York, WW, Norton & Company, 2011).

Schaap, Andrew, Danielle Celermajer and Vrasidas Karalis, *Power, Judgment and Political Evil, In Conversation with Hannah Arendt* (Farnham, Ashgate, 2010).

Scheler, Max, *GW XIII, Schriften aus dem Nachlaß, Bd, 4, Philosophie und Geschichte* (Bonn, Bouvier-Verlag, 1990).

Schiller, Friedrich, *Maria Stuart, Ein Trauerspiel* [1800], Holzinger (ed) (Scotts Valley, CAL, CreateSpace, 2016).

Schmitt, Carl, *The Concept of the Political*, translated and introduced by George Schwab (Chicago, University of Chicago Press, 1996).

—— *Political Theology, Four Chapters on the Concept of Sovereignty*, translated by George Schwab (ed) (Chicago, University of Chicago Press, 2005).

Schuppli, Susan, 'Deadly Algorithms, Can Legal Codes Hold Software Accountable For Code That Kills?' (2014) 187 *Radical Philosophy* 2.

Schutte, Xandra, 'De Jeanne D'Arc van links' (23 June 2010) *De Groene Amsterdammer* 25.

Schwartz, Charles A, 'Corruption and Political Development in the USSR' (1979) 11 *Comparative Politics* 425.

Sellers, MNS (ed), *Law, Reason, and Emotion* (Cambridge, Cambridge University Press, 2017).

Sen, Amartya, *The Idea of Justice* (Cambridge, MA, Belknap Press, 2009).

Serres, Michel, *The Parasite*, translated by Lawrence R Schehr, introduced by Cary Wolfe, (Minneapolis, University of Minnesota Press, 2007).

Severy, Beth, *Augustus and the Family at the Birth of the Roman Empire* (London, Routledge, 2003).

Sharp, Andrew, 'Blood, Custom, and Consent, Three Kinds of Māori Groups and the Challenges They Present to Governments' (2002) 52 *The University of Toronto Law Journal* 9.

Shaw, Julia A, *Law and the Passions, Why Emotions Matter for Justice* (New York, Routledge, 2019).

Shostakovich, Dmitri, *The Nose*, Opera [1928] (Recording Valery Gergiev, Mariinsky label, 2008).

Siegert, Bernhard, *Cultural Techniques, Grids, Filters, Doors, and Other Articulations of the Real* (New York, Fordham University Press, 2015).

Silverman, Kaja, 'Fassbinder and Lacan: A Reconsideration of Gaze, Look and Image' in Norman Bryson, Michael Ann Holly and Keith Moxey (eds), *Visual Culture, Images and Interpretations* (Hanover, Wesleyan University Press, 1994) 272–301.

—— *The Acoustic Mirror, The Female Voice in Psychoanalysis and Cinema* (Bloomington, Indiana University Press, 1988).

Simone, Nina, 'Mississippi Goddam', *Nina Simone in Concert*, Philips Records, 1964.

Smit, WAP, *Van Pascha tot Noah, Deel 1, Het Pascha - Leeuwendalers* (Zwolle, WEJ, Tjeenk Willink, 1956).

Smith, Daniel W, 'Deleuze and the Question of Desire, Toward an Immanent Theory of Ethics' (2007) 2 *Parrhesia* 66–78.

Sousa Santos, Buaventura de, *The End of the Cognitive Empire, The Coming of Age of Epistemologies of the South* (Durham, Duke University Press, 2018).

Southerton, Dale (ed), *Encyclopedia of Consumer Culture*, Vol 1 (Los Angeles, Sage, 2011).

Spade, Dean and Craig Willse, 'Sex, Gender, and War in an Age of Multicultural Imperialism' (2014) 1 *QED, A Journal in GLBTQ Worldmaking* 5.

Specht, Doug and Anna Feigenbaum, 'From Cartographic Gaze to Contestatory Cartographies' in Pol Bargués-Pedreny, David Chandler and Elena Simon (eds), *Mapping and Politics in the Digital Age* (London, Routledge, 2018) 35–52.

Spies, Marijke, 'Verbeeldingen van Vrijheid, David en Mozes, Burgerhart en Bato, Brutus en Cato' (1994) 10 *De zeventiende eeuw* 141.

Spinoza, Benedict de, *Ethics*, edited and translated by Edwin Curley, introduced by Stuart Hampshire (London, Penguin Books, 1996).

Stefanovska, Malina, 'The Baroque Social Bond in the *Memoirs* of the Cardinal de Retz' in Massimo Ciavolella and Patrick Coleman (eds), *Culture and Authority in the Baroque* (Toronto, Toronto University Press, 2005) 208–28.

Stevic, Alexander, 'Convenient Cosmopolitanism, *Daniel Deronda*, Nationalism and the Critics' (2017) 45 *Victorian Literature and Culture* 593–614.

Strigl, Daniela, 'Gegen die Wand, Zu Elfriede Jelineks Lektüre von Marlen Haushofers Roman in *Der Tod und das Mädchen V* (2006) 39 *Modern Austrian Literature* 73.

Stone Peters, Julie, 'Theatrocracy Unwired, Legal Performance in the Modern Mediasphere' (2014) 26 *Law & Literature* 31.

'The Stammheim "Suicides"' *German Guerilla* (4 October 2007).

Timepere, Allison Felix and Tubotenyefa Zibima, 'Bring Back Our Corruption in Nigeria, Nigeria's anti-corruption campaign faces opposition, from the citizens who voted for the government to fight corruption' *Australian Outlook* (26 August 2018).

Tindemans, Klaas, 'De theatraliteit van het recht' *Etcetera* 15 (September 2017).

Tocqueville, Alexis de, *Democracy in America* [1840] translated by Henry Reeve (Pennsylvania, The Pennsylvania State University, 2002).

Vannieuwenhuyze, Bram and Jelle Lisson, 'De stadsplannen van Jacob van Deventer, Een schitterende bron voor de stads- en dorpsgeschiedenis' (2012) 4 *Bladwijzer, Wegwijs met Heemkunde Vlaanderen* 3.

Van Zyl Smit, Betine (ed), *A Handbook to the Reception of Greek Drama* (Chichester, Wiley Blackwell, 2016).

Veitch, Scott, *Law and Irresponsibility, On the Legitimation of Human Suffering* (Abingdon, Routledge-Cavendish, 2007).

Ven, Gerard van der (ed), *Leefbaar laagland, Geschiedenis van de waterbeheersing en landaanwinning in Nederland* (Utrecht, Matrijs, 2003).

Verhaeghe, Paul, *Autoriteit, Authority* (Amsterdam, De Bezige Bij, 2015).

—— 'Voorbij Oedipus, Over de noodzakelijke functie van autoriteit' in Peter Verstraten and Sjef Houppermans (eds), *Oedipus heerst!?* (Antwerpen, Garant, 2016) 81–94.

Vieveen, Bart, *De ontvoogding van de tragische held, Hamlet, Katadreuffe en Van Egters verkennen de grenzen van het bedreigde Vader-land, The Emancipation of the tragic hero, Hamlet, Katadreuffe and Van Egters explore the borders of the Father-land*) (Utrecht, Garant, 2019).

Villegas, Paulina, 'A New Toll in Mexico's Drug War, More Than 61,000 Vanished' *New York Times* (6 January 2020).

Vismann, Cornelia, *Files, Law and Media Technology*, translated by Geoffrey Winthrop-Young (Stanford, Stanford University Press, 2008), first published as *Akten, Medientechnik und Recht* (Frankfurt, Fischer Taschenbuch, 2000).

Vondel, Joost van den, 'Aen den Leeuw van Hollant' in Arie Jan Gelderblom (ed), *'k Wil rijmen wat ik bouw, Twee eeuwen topografische poëzie* (Amsterdam, Querido's Uitgeverij, 1994).

—— 'De Beemster' in JFM Sterck, HWE Moller, CGN de Vooys, CR de Klerk, BH Molkenboer, J Prinsen, J Lzn and L Simons, CC van de Graft, LC Michels and AA Verdenius (eds), *De werken van Vondel* IV (Amsterdam, De Maatschappij voor goede en goedkoope lectuur, 1930).

—— *Maria Stuart, of Gemartelde Majesteit* [1646] in JFM Sterck, HWE Moller, CGN de Vooys, CR de Klerk, BH Molkenboer, J Prinsen J Lzn and L Simons, CC van de Graft, LC Michels and AA Verdenius (eds), *De werken van Vondel* IV (Amsterdam, De Maatschappij voor goede en goedkoope lectuur, 1930).

Vugts, Berrie, *The Case against Animal Rights, A Literary Intervention*, PhD diss (Leiden University, 2014).

Waal, Frans de, *Our Inner Ape: A Leading Primatologist Explains Why We Are Who We Are* (New York, Penguin Group, 2005).

—— *The Age of Empathy: Nature's Lessons for a Kinder Society* (New York, Three Rivers Press, 2009).

Wagner, Anne and Richard K, Sherwin (eds), *Law Culture and Visual Arts* (Dordrecht, Springer, 2014).

Wark, McKenzie, *Capitalism is Dead, Is This Something Worse*? (London, Verso, 2019).

Watt, Gary, *Dress, Law and Naked Truth, A Cultural Study of Fashion and Form* (Oxford, Bloomsbury, 2013).

Weisberg, Richard, *In Praise of Intransigence, The Perils of Flexibility* (Oxford, Oxford University Press, 2014).

Weizman, Eyal, 'An Impromptu Glossary, Open Verification' in Maria Hlavajova and Wietske Maas (eds), *Propositions for Non-Fascist Living, Tentative and Urgent* (Cambridge, MA, MIT Press, Basic Series, 2019) 141–64.
—— *Forensic Architecture, Violence at the Threshold of Detectability* (Cambridge, MA, MIT Press, Zone Books, 2017).
Welsh, Alexander, *George Eliot and Blackmail* (Cambridge, MA, Harvard University Press, 1985).
Wengert, Timothy, *Law and Gospel, Philip Melanchthon's Debate With John Agricola of Eisleben over Poenitentia* (Grand Rapids, Baker Book House, 1997).
West, Robin, 'Law's Emotions' in MNS Sellers (ed), *Law, Reason, and Emotion* (Cambridge, Cambridge University Press, 2017) 32–54.
West Lunsford, Virginia, *Piracy and Privateering in the Golden Age Netherlands* (New York, Palgrave Macmillan, 2005).
White, Hayden, *Metahistory, The Historical Imagination in Nineteenth-Century Europe* (Baltimore, Johns Hopkins University, 1975).
White, Martin, *Renaissance Drama in Action, An Introduction to Aspects of Theatre Practice and Performance* (London, Routledge, 1998).
Whiting, Michael S, *Luther in English, The Influence of His Theology of Law and Gospel on Early English Evangelicals* (Eugene, OR, Pickwick Publishers, 2010).
Windig Refn, Nicolas (dir), *Only God Forgives* (The Weinstein Company/Cinéart, 2013).
Witteveen, Willem, *De denkbeeldige staat, voorstellingen van democratische vernieuwing* (Amsterdam, Amsterdam University Press, 2000).
—— *De geordende wereld van het recht, Een inleiding* (Amsterdam, Amsterdam University Press, 2003).
—— *De retoriek in het recht, over retorica en interpretatie, staatsrecht en democratie* (Zwolle, Tjeenk Willink, 1988).
—— *De wet als kunstwerk, Een andere filosofie van het recht* (Amsterdam, Boom, 2014).
—— *Evenwicht van machten* (Zwolle, WEJ, Tjeenk Willink, 1991).
—— *Het theater van de politiek, publieke retorica en de paspoortaffaire* (Amsterdam, Amber, 1992).
Witteveen, Willem and Wibren van der Burg (eds), *Rediscovering Fuller, Essays on Implicit Law and Institutional Design* (Amsterdam University Press, 1999).
Zeischka, Siger, *Minerva in de polder, Waterstaat en techniek in het Hoogheemraadschap van Rijnland 1500–1856* (Hilversum, Verloren, 2008).
Žižek, Slavoj, *Organs Without Bodies, Deleuze and Consequences* (New York, Routledge, 2004).
—— *The Fragile Absolute, Or Why is the Christian Legend Worth Fighting For?* (London, Verso, 2008).
—— *The Sublime Object of Ideology* (London, Verso, 2008).
—— *The Ticklish Subject, The Absent Centre of Political Ontology* (London, Verso, 2008).
—— *Violence* (London, Polity Books, 2009).
Zuboff, Shoshana, *The Age of Surveillance Capitalism, The Fight for a Human Future at the New Frontier of Power* (London, Profile Books, 2019).
Zug, Marcia, 'The Mirage of Immigration Reform, The Devastating Consequences of Obama's Immigration Policy' (2015) 63 *Kansas Law Review* 953.
Zupančič, Alenka, *The Odd One In, On Comedy* (Cambridge MA, MIT Press, 2008).
Zwet, H, van, *Lofwaerdighe dijckagies en miserabele polders, een financiële analyse van landaanwinningsprojecten in Hollands Noorderkwartier, 1597–1643* (Hilversum, Verloren, 2009).

INDEX

www.ingramcontent.com/pod-product-compliance
Ingram Content Group UK Ltd.
Pitfield, Milton Keynes, MK11 3LW, UK
UKHW020815290926
15470UKWH00003B/1166

9 781509 944347